THE NEW HUMAN REVOLUTION

VOLUME 10

DAISAKU IKEDA

ILLUSTRATIONS BY
KENICHIRO UCHIDA

World Tribune
Press

Published by World Tribune Press
606 Wilshire Boulevard
Santa Monica, California 90401

©2004 by Soka Gakkai
All rights reserved
Printed in the United States of America

Complete Set   ISBN 0-915678-32-2
Volume 10   ISBN 0-915678-42-X

Interior and cover designed by Gopa & Ted2, Inc.

10 9 8 7 6 5 4 3 2 1

Contents

Chapter 1: Bastion of the Pen   1

Chapter 2: Winds of Happiness   81

Chapter 3: A New Course   159

Chapter 4: Crown Champions   243

Index   337

Editor's Note

The citations most commonly used in this book have been abbreviated as follows:

◆ GZ refers to the *Gosho Zenshu*, the Japanese-language compilation of letters, treatises, essays and oral teachings of Nichiren Daishonin.

◆ LS refers to *The Lotus Sutra*, translated by Burton Watson (New York: Columbia University Press, 1993). The citation usually appears as (LSXX,xx), where XX refers to the chapter number and xx is the page number.

◆ WND refers to *The Writings of Nichiren Daishonin* (Tokyo: Soka Gakkai, 1999).

Bastion of the Pen

HUMAN REVOLUTION is the starting point of everything. The human being, the individual, is the foundation of all. Changing our own life will effect a change in our family, our community and the society in which we live. It will change the age, history and indeed the world. The great tide of the power of Buddhism, which makes human revolution possible, had begun to surge like a billowing wave across the vast ocean.

The year 1965, designated as the "Year of Victory" by the Soka Gakkai, began with the newspaper serialization of President Shin'ichi Yamamoto's novel, *The Human Revolution*. Members throughout Japan eagerly looked forward to the first installment of the novel, which appeared in the New Year's Day issue of the *Seikyo Shimbun*. It was President Yamamoto's first novel, and it depicted the life of second Soka Gakkai president Josei Toda from the day of his release from prison.

Members were excited to think that, thanks to President Yamamoto, the true story of Toda's life and character, his dedication to truth and justice and his firm conviction in faith, would be revealed for the first time.

The initial installment was set on July 3, 1945, just before Japan's defeat in World War II, and began with a description of "a gaunt, middle-aged man" leaving prison. The story read: "Wrapped in a light cotton robe, his tall frame seemed almost buoyant. The breeze parted the robe, and for a moment his legs could be seen, emaciated like two sticks."

The name of the man was not disclosed in this installment, but Soka Gakkai members knew immediately that it was Josei Toda. They were deeply moved to realize that this frail, thin man stood up alone for the noble cause of kosen-rufu and created a brilliant history of the victory of the people, spreading the Daishonin's Buddhism to more than 750,000 households.

It was only twenty years since Toda was released from prison, but given the tremendous growth of the Soka Gakkai in that period, it seemed like an entirely different age. Newer members, who only knew the Soka Gakkai as a large organization, didn't have a true sense of what the early days were like, even though they had heard stories about it from the organization's pioneers. *The Human Revolution* made them keenly aware, however, that the great river of Soka really had begun from a single individual. Conveying that message was part of Shin'ichi's aim. He was also driven by his desire to share the determination and spirit of his mentor with all members.

To grow comfortable and forget the original spirit of President Toda would destroy the spirit on which the Soka Gakkai was founded. Shin'ichi was firmly convinced that in order to eternally preserve the Soka Gakkai, the jeweled citadel of human happiness, he must leave a lasting record of Toda's valiant struggle.

SHIN'ICHI had another gift for Soka Gakkai members at the start of the new year. From January 1, the magazine *Opinions,* which was going to be published three times a month, began carrying selections from Shin'ichi's diary as a young man under the title, "Excerpts from the Diary of My Youth."

Opinions started out as the monthly journal of the Soka Gakkai Writers' Department in November 1962. From 1965, it became a magazine focused on the general readership and published every ten days by the Jiyu Genronsha Publishing Company.

The publication of excerpts from Shin'ichi's diary came about as a result of the persistence of a group of fellow members. Shin'ichi would often tell the youth division members that he had kept a diary from the days of his youth. He also encouraged them to spend each day of their youth struggling in a way that was true to themselves, creating their own record of golden memories.

Hearing of Shin'ichi's diary, youth division leaders begged him to allow them to read it. But diaries, by their very nature, are not meant to be shown to others. Though it recorded events long past, Shin'ichi was still quite reluctant to make his diary public. He therefore continued to refuse their requests, saying: "I cannot publish my diary. Its content is subjective and I'm sure there are many parts that won't make sense to others. There is also a chance that it could cause trouble by encroaching on the privacy of certain individuals."

But Eisuke Akizuki, head of the youth division, continued to press Shin'ichi on the matter, urging: "*Opinions* is going to be released every ten days, and we would very much like to include excerpts of the diary of your youth. It would be a great source of joy and inspiration for the youth members. Please consider it for the sake of the youth who will shoulder the future."

In the face of such a plea from the youth division leader, Shin'ichi could no longer refuse. He genuinely felt like an older brother to those younger members and thought that it might be good for them to know what he had been like in the past—just as he was, without any adornments.

He eventually agreed to cooperate, on the condition that the series would be limited to thirty-six installments and that any portions of the diary that might infringe on the privacy of others would be excised.

THE FIRST INSTALLMENT of "Excerpts from the Diary of My Youth" was Shin'ichi's entry for May 31, 1949, when he was twenty-one.

Tuesday, May 31. Light rain.

One meets too many hypocrites in this world. Youth especially must revere the truth. Whoever pursues the truth throughout life is a great person.

Half a year has passed since I went to work for Mr. Toda's company. Stormy and eventful days. All I can do is steel myself to meet hardships cheerfully. Must advance toward the dawn, never wavering in my conviction, following my lifelong—no, my *eternal* mentor.

Finished the July issue of *Boys' Adventure*. My maiden work. I advance in the cultural vanguard, in company with pure-hearted children. Will develop my editing to the limits of my ability, treating it as my dearest friend, or as my lover.

"Fulfill your mission for today"—for by doing so, you will make the future glorious... .[1]

From January 1949, Shin'ichi started working at Josei Toda's publishing company, Nihon Shogakkan. In May, he became the editor-in-chief of the boys' magazine, *Boys' Adventure,* and he had just completed the first issue the day of this entry. At the same time, he was taking night classes at Taisei Gakuin[2] working his way through school.

The reaction to the publication of "Excerpts from the Diary of My Youth" was greater than Shin'ichi had anticipated. Many of the young members of the Soka Gakkai had not gone very far in school, nor were they particularly socially or economically privileged. They were all nameless, ordinary citizens.

Reading Shin'ichi's diary, these members learned that President Yamamoto, struggling in circumstances very similar to their own, had worked and studied and experienced financial hardship. This made them feel very close to him. Catching a glimpse of Shin'ichi's life in this way, with a strong awareness of his lofty mission to realize kosen-rufu and a readiness to undergo hardship, struck a chord in their hearts and gave them hope and courage for their own future.

One young man shared his impressions: "This diary is filled with self-reflection and determination for the future. In its example of strict self-examination and the spirit to always challenge oneself, I feel that it is laying down the requirements for developing into a leader of kosen-rufu.

"I also learned the meaning of the path of mentor and disciple. I am going to make this a model for my own life."

AT THE NEW YEAR'S DAY gongyo meeting held on the morning of January 1 at the Soka Gakkai Headquarters, Shin'ichi Yamamoto delivered a New Year's greeting, saying: "Life is eternal. From that perspective, our current life is but a momentary dream.

"Whatever wealth and luxury we may be enjoying now, it will not last forever. Nor will such things necessarily bring us happiness. The only way to accumulate boundless good fortune that will last across the three existences is through dedication to the Mystic Law, the genuine Buddhist practice. Carrying out that Buddhist practice in this fleeting lifetime determines our eternal happiness.

"Therefore, in order to attain enlightenment in this life and realize eternal happiness, you must never recoil from any storm of hardship that befalls you. I hope you will strive courageously and boldly, leading the way for victory in our movement for kosen-rufu. Our struggle for kosen-rufu is not aimed only ten or twenty years hence. It is a struggle to lead all people to happiness of the ten thousand years and more of the Latter Day of the Law. It is a movement to realize the lasting peace that humanity longs for.

"Engraving deep in our hearts the conviction that what we do with this life, this year and this day will decide our eternal future, let us achieve total victory in all our endeavors."

The actions we take in each moment decide our eternal future—this was also the credo Shin'ichi strove to live by each day.

Shin'ichi determined that year once again to pour his energies into visiting members around Japan and offering guidance. He would start mid-January, traveling to the Kyushu, Kansai and Chubu regions. He knew that encouragement imparts strength and hope, and serves as the springboard for dynamic growth in people's lives. Thus, he wanted to make a special effort on this tour to encourage district leaders, whose role in Soka Gakkai activities was crucial.

Shin'ichi was constantly thinking about how to encourage the members and rouse their spirits. For example, when the promotion of discussion meetings was set as one of the guidelines for Soka Gakkai activities the coming year, he immediately decided that he would do something to support this endeavor. He then announced a plan to inscribe the words "Eternal Buddha Land" on the flyleaf of the eleventh volume of the *Collected Lectures of the President* and present a copy to each family across Japan who made their homes available for discussion meetings.

Soon after the activities of the new year had commenced, Shin'ichi received news that Director Hiroshi Yamagiwa, former young men's and youth leader, had died of cancer at noon that day. Yamagiwa's health had begun to decline in spring of the previous year. After a period of hospitalization, he was discharged to continue his treatment at home. He later died on January 10.

YAMAGIWA was forty-nine years old when he died. His was the second death of a top leader in close succession, following the passing of General Director Koichi Harayama in December. Nothing made Shin'ichi sadder than losing a comrade-in-faith who had struggled at his side. As soon as he received the news, he went to pay his respects to the Yamagiwa family.

Having joined the Soka Gakkai in 1947, Yamagiwa began practicing the Daishonin's Buddhism at about the same time as Shin'ichi and the two had been close friends ever since. Before being elected to the House of Councilors (Upper House), Yamagiwa had been a lecturer in the engineering department of Tokyo Metropolitan University. He had suffered from a weak constitution from childhood, and as an adult he endured eight years of medical treatment for tuberculosis. Shin'ichi felt the fact that Yamagiwa had lived an active life as long as he had was indeed a manifestation of the principle of extending one's life through faith taught in the "Life Span" chapter of the Lotus Sutra.

In autumn of the previous year, 1964, soon after returning from his trip to Europe, Shin'ichi learned that Yamagiwa had been diagnosed with cancer. He immediately went to visit him in the hospital. The cancer appeared to be considerably advanced, but Shin'ichi would never forget how Yamagiwa smiled and said that the doctors were amazed that he wasn't in any pain.

Yamagiwa was also strongly determined to attend the New Year's Day gongyo meeting, and sure enough, there he was at the Soka Gakkai Headquarters to celebrate the occasion. He died nine days later.

Now, kneeling by his deceased friend's bedside, Shin'ichi observed that Yamagiwa's expression was gentle and peaceful; that he looked as if he had fallen into a deep sleep. Thinking that anyone who could see Yamagiwa now would be convinced that he had attained enlightenment, Shin'ichi spoke to him softly: "Thank you so much for your long years of hard work. Please enjoy a good rest."

To Yamagiwa's eldest son, a second-year high school student, he said: "The thing that will make your father happiest is for you to grow into a fine leader for kosen-rufu. I hope you will dedicate yourself to that mission throughout your life."

"I will!" the young man replied. He bore a strong resemblance to his father.

Shin'ichi then turned to Mrs. Yamagiwa. "Life is eternal," he said. "Your husband will be reborn very soon. Please be sure of that."

Yamagiwa left behind five children. Shin'ichi was determined, as Yamagiwa's comrade in the struggle for kosen-rufu, to continue to look after his family and make certain that they became happy.

Shin'ichi also attended the funeral service on January 12, on which occasion he offered further encouragement to the Yamagiwa family.

ON THE AFTERNOON of January 16, Shin'ichi Yamamoto attended the completion ceremony for the new Kyushu Headquarters building in Fukuoka Prefecture, Kyushu. The three-story reinforced-concrete structure was built next to the old headquarters, facing the Genkai Sea.[3] It was from here that President Yamamoto was beginning his regional guidance tour for the "Year of Victory."

After the ceremony, Shin'ichi attended a district leaders meeting held in the new Headquarters building. He then made an appearance at a young men's and young women's division meeting. Everywhere he went, he offered the members wholehearted encouragement.

On January 17, he traveled to Osaka, where he attended a chapter leaders meeting in the afternoon and then delivered a Gosho lecture for student division members in the evening. The following day, he hastened to Yonago in Tottori Prefecture[4] to attend a district leaders meeting at the Yonago Community Center.

Shin'ichi was very concerned about Yonago. In July of the previous year, Shimane and Tottori prefectures had been hit by torrential rains that killed 110 and injured more than four hundred, and Yonago suffered serious damage.

Nevertheless, the members there vowed together to set in motion a great wave of propagation, determined that now was the time to transform the fate of their community. Then in August, the following month, Yonago Chapter Leader Isamu Ishizaki was killed in a traffic accident. He was only forty-two. People in the community began to question the Soka Gakkai's validity, asking why, if the teachings upheld by the organization were correct and produced benefits, did its local leader die that way? More than a few Soka Gakkai members began wondering the same thing. Distrust mounted, causing many of them to be swayed by doubt and even to start criticizing the Gakkai themselves.

Discussion meetings were gloomy and lacked enthusiasm. Everyone knew that something had to be done, but unfortunately there was no leader equipped to offer clear guidance on the subject of the chapter leader's death. This was because they lacked conviction in faith and a thorough understanding of Buddhist principles.

Throughout his writings, Nichiren Daishonin speaks of the three obstacles and four devils, one of which is the hindrance of death. This devilish function serves to arouse doubt and confusion through the death of practitioners of Buddhism. People have their own karma but ordinary people cannot see the depth of their karma. Therefore, even should one die young, if one carries through with diligent faith, one's death represents the Buddhist principle of lessening one's karmic retribution.

IT IS CERTAIN that people of genuine faith who work to advance kosen-rufu will absolutely attain enlightenment no matter how their lives come to an end.

An early Buddhist scripture tells the following story about a lay follower named Mahanama. Mahanama asked the Buddha to explain where and what kind of life he would be born into should he meet with a fatal accident at the moment when, distracted by the hustle and bustle of the city, his thoughts become diverted from the three treasures of the Buddha, the Law (the Buddhist teachings) and the Buddhist Order (community of believers).

The Buddha said: "For instance, Mahanama, if a tree bends to the east, slopes to the east, tends to the east, which way will it fall when its root is cut?"

"It will fall whither it bends, slopes and tends, lord," Mahanama replied.[5]

The Buddha then went on to say that people who had faith in Buddhism and practiced the teachings in earnest would be reborn into good circumstances due to the flow of the Law in their lives, even if they were to meet an unexpected, accidental death.

Nichiren Daishonin also sent a letter to Nanjo Tokimitsu on the death of his younger brother, writing: "Since he [Shichiro Goro] had profound faith in Shakyamuni Buddha and the Lotus Sutra, his death was also magnificent" (GZ, 1568). He is saying that those who exert themselves in faith are sure to attain Buddhahood.

But the Yonago members did not have such conviction. Conviction is the driving force of kosen-rufu. Without it, we will cease to advance. Even four months after Ishizaki's death, efforts to introduce Buddhism to others in Yonago stalled.

When Shin'ichi received reports of this from the leaders in charge of the Chugoku Region, of which Tottori Prefecture was a part, he sent vice general directors Hiroshi Izumida and Hisao Seki to the area. On January 17, the two of them held separate Gosho lectures for the members in Tottori and Yonago cities and on January 18 they were both scheduled to attend a district leaders meeting at the Yonago Community Center.

On the evening of the 17th, after flying from Kyushu to Osaka, Shin'ichi received a call from Seki, who led the Yonago lecture. "I tried to speak about the meaning of a fellow member's death from many different angles based on the Daishonin's teachings," Seki said, "but the mood is still dark. I will do my best to clear their doubts once and for all at the district leaders meeting tomorrow."

Hearing this, Shin'ichi decided to go to Yonago in person, and he flew there from Osaka the next day. His philosophy as a leader was to always go to the most troubled places himself.

ON THE PLANE to Tottori Prefecture, Shin'ichi Yamamoto recalled his first visit to the area on February 22, 1960, a little more than two months before he became the third president of the Soka Gakkai. He had traveled by train from neighboring Okayama Prefecture to attend a general meeting in the Municipal Gymnasium in Gyotoku, Tottori City. That trip had been the result of a promise he had made to a member.

In March of the previous year, 1959, during a question-and-answer session at a meeting held in Fukuchiyama, Kyoto, an elderly gentleman raised his hand and directed a question to Shin'ichi, who was then the general administrator of the Soka Gakkai.

"I'm Daizo Moriyama from Tottori and I have a favor to ask of you," the man began. "Our membership in Tottori is increasing. I'd very much like to invite you to come to Tottori to meet the members and offer encouragement." It was an earnest plea.

Shin'ichi replied immediately, "Certainly. I promise to visit."

Eleven months later, Shin'ichi fulfilled that promise. The train platform at Tottori Station was packed with members awaiting his arrival. Seeing Moriyama in the crowd, Shin'ichi called out to him: "Hello, there! It's great to see you looking so well! I came to keep the promise I made you."

Moriyama's face revealed his deep emotion. "Thank you so much," he said. "Welcoming you here is like a dream. But as a matter of fact, I have another request. I'd like to ask that a chapter be established here in Tottori."

At the time, members in Tottori belonged to outlying chapters, such as Osaka Chapter, or Tsukiji and Adachi chapters in Tokyo. There was no local chapter in the prefecture.

"I came here intending to do just that," Shin'ichi remarked with a smile. "By all means, let's establish a chapter. Though you may be advanced in years, Mr. Moriyama, I hope that you will be like Okubo Hikozaemon[6] and do your best to protect and support everyone to ensure that activities proceed smoothly."

At the general meeting in Tottori, Shin'ichi spoke with the members, offering them guidance as if he were talking with each of them individually. After the meeting, he met with local district leaders to discuss the prospect of establishing a chapter in Tottori.

Shin'ichi laid the foundation for Tottori's growth during that visit.

THE NEXT DAY, Shin'ichi visited the famous Tottori Sand Dunes,[7] accompanied by about ten leaders from the area. The sky was clear, but patches of snow sparkled on the dunes and the wind was cold. In the distance a camel—a local tourist attraction—could be seen. Shin'ichi proposed that they sing "Desert Moonlight," and they strolled along happily, singing together.

Sitting in a circle atop one of the dunes, they began to talk. Shin'ichi said: "Looking out at this vast landscape gives one a sense of grandeur. With that noble spirit, why don't we each compose a *waka* poem conveying our determination to carry out kosen-rufu. We can preserve them in a safe place and then open them again ten years from now. What do you say?"

Everyone nodded and smiled, then began composing their poems. After about five minutes, Shin'ichi asked: "Are you ready?"

Some replied "Yes!" in energetic voices while others scratched their heads in chagrin. They presented their poems one by one. Shin'ichi then recited his:

> *Resolutely advance*
> *To realize*
> *Kosen-rufu in Asia,*
> *No matter how rough the waves*
> *Of the Japan Sea.*

It was almost two years since the death of second Soka Gakkai president Josei Toda, who called for the realization of kosen-rufu in Asia. Since that time, many of Toda's disciples had unconsciously forgotten the vow they made to their mentor. Shin'ichi, however, continued to strengthen his resolve to stand up and actualize his mentor's vision.

Everyone listened intently to Shin'ichi's poem, deeply moved by the profound commitment of a genuine disciple.

Rising to his feet and gazing out at the sea, Shin'ichi said in a determined voice: "Buddhism means to advance headlong into the raging waves, into the storm. Kosen-rufu cannot be achieved if we are cowardly. Each of us was born into this world with a mission. Let us all play out our roles in this grand drama of life as true champions of kosen-rufu."

Tottori Chapter was established at the Twenty-second Headquarters General Meeting on May 3, 1960, just a little more than two months after Shin'ichi's visit to the prefecture. This meeting at the Nihon University Auditorium, which saw Shin'ichi inaugurated as the Soka Gakkai's third president, marked the organization's departure toward a new era. The members of Tottori Chapter and Shin'ichi thus made their fresh start into the future together.

Later, in August 1962, Yonago Chapter was established. And in September of the following year, it was divided into two chapters. One chapter kept the original name of Yonago, while the other was called Hoki.

ABOARD the plane en route to Yonago, Shin'ichi chanted earnestly in his heart. He was determined to do everything he could to dispel the clouds of doubt that were shrouding the minds of his beloved fellow members in Yonago.

From one o'clock in the afternoon, the district and chapter leaders of the four divisions gathered at the Yonago Community Center for a district leaders meeting led by vice general directors Hisao Seki and Hiroshi Izumida.

At the start of the meeting, Seki stood up and enthusiastically announced: "I have good news, everyone. I have just received word that President Yamamoto is on his way to the Yonago Community Center, and he should be here in an hour."

The room stirred with excitement, yet no one could believe what they had heard. Then, at 2:10 PM, Shin'ichi arrived.

The community center had just opened in December of the previous year, 1964, and little more than a month had passed since then. It was common across Japan that, whenever a community center was completed, the members in the surrounding area would rejoice and propagation efforts there would increase dramatically. Though the Yonago members were happy to have a new place to do activities, they were not overjoyed. Their lingering emotions over the death of their leader blocked the feeling of pure joy they would have experienced under other circumstances.

Offering guidance removes such impediments and replaces them with courage and hope in people's hearts. Shin'ichi was profoundly resolved to transform the inner state of the Yonago members' lives.

Fierce blizzards had ripped through the area up to two days before the meeting, and just thirty minutes before Shin'ichi's arrival it had been raining. By the time he drove up to the Yonago Community Center, however, the sky had cleared and the sun was shining brightly.

"Hello! Thank you for coming!" Shin'ichi called out in a cheerful voice. The members responded with lively exclamations and applause.

"Let's do gongyo together," he said, "and pray for the prosperity, health and long life of your families."

As the sutra recitation and chanting of Nam-myoho-renge-kyo progressed, the members' voices grew stronger. Shin'ichi prayed with all his heart that his dear comrades-in-faith of Yonago would not be defeated.

When they finished, he spoke to a woman in the front row, Toshiko Ishizaki, the wife of the late chapter leader: "Your husband was a true pioneer who made great contributions to kosen-rufu in Yonago. I am deeply grieved by his death. But as long as you remain steadfast in your faith in the Mystic Law, your family will be protected without fail. You have nothing to worry about."

SHIN'ICHI then addressed all the leaders in attendance: "I am very happy to be here today and to spend some time with my spirited and valiant fellow members of Yonago. Seeing you gives me confidence that our organization in Yonago is sound and rock-solid. Am I right?"

"Yes!" everyone replied vigorously.

"Yonago now has its own community center, though it may be small in size. Soka Gakkai community centers belong to the members and I consider this center to be a gift to you all. Please make free use of it, joyfully carrying out your Buddhist practice and leading lives of great happiness."

Shin'ichi then began to talk about the death of Isamu Ishizaki: "There may be some members who are asking why, given that he practiced Nichiren Buddhism, Mr. Ishizaki was killed in an accident. The causes and effects inherent deep in our lives, the workings of our karma, are strict indeed. That is why, even if we practice Nichiren Buddhism, the manner of our death will occur in any number of ways.

"There may be some who die giving their lives in the

struggle to uphold Buddhism, like Mr. Makiguchi who died in prison for his beliefs. There may be some who die young as a result of illness or accidents. But when viewed through the eyes of faith, we find profound significance in their deaths. Those who dedicate their lives to working for kosen-rufu are Bodhisattvas of the Earth. They are followers of the Buddha. Life is eternal, and in light of the teaching of the Mystic Law, such people will absolutely attain Buddhahood."

Shin'ichi's voice rang powerfully throughout the room: "Furthermore, it is also guaranteed that the families of those who are dedicated to kosen-rufu to the very end will also be protected. I wish to declare that, as long as those left behind continue to persevere in faith, the good fortune and benefit accumulated through their loved ones' dedication to kosen-rufu will pass on to them. They will, without fail, enjoy unsurpassed happiness."

Faced with Shin'ichi's tremendous conviction, the feelings of doubt that had clouded the members' minds evaporated and the sun of hope began to rise in their hearts.

"Being without a spouse or partner doesn't mean that we will never be happy. Prosperity and wealth also do not guarantee happiness. True happiness, absolute happiness, is only found when we awaken to the fact that our lives are the very entity of the Mystic Law, carry out our human revolution and manifest the great life-state of Buddhahood through our Buddhist practice.

"We are born alone and we die alone. Only the Mystic Law has the power to protect us across the three existences of past, present and future."

SHIN'ICHI continued speaking, doing his utmost to touch the Yonago members' lives: "If you devote yourselves fully to kosen-rufu, the Buddhas and bodhisattvas throughout the three existences and ten directions will protect you. Therefore, no matter what happens, no matter what others may say or how they may attack you, you must never be swayed or shaken. If you become cowardly and distance yourself from faith, you will only end up miserable.

"Yonago is far from the Soka Gakkai Headquarters in Tokyo and top leaders cannot travel here so often to offer you support. It may also be difficult for you to win understanding about our organization in your local community. Yet despite these challenges and hardships, you have all wholeheartedly exerted yourselves. Though it may seem as if your efforts go unnoticed, the Gohonzon is aware of everything. So is the Daishonin. All of your struggles will turn into good fortune and benefit. If they didn't, there would be no point in practicing the Daishonin's Buddhism.

"Life is eternal, but this present lifetime flashes by in an instant. I hope you will be aware of your mission in this life, devote yourselves to kosen-rufu and accumulate abundant good fortune.

"If you should reach the end of your lives having done your very best, and kosen-rufu in Yonago and Tottori hasn't yet been realized, then there are still your children and grandchildren to carry on your work. Please raise them into wonderful successors of this noble endeavor. Please become cornerstones for the expansion of kosen-rufu into the eternal future and the source of our movement's history.

"For my part, I will earnestly offer prayers for you from Tokyo. Faith is a struggle between devilish forces and the Buddha. For the happiness and welfare of everyone living in Yonago, let us strive together with all our might and triumph over devilish forces!"

The members enthusiastically responded.

Wanting to encourage them further, Shin'ichi then said: "Today marks the rebirth of Yonago. To commemorate this significant occasion, let's take a photograph together in the courtyard. I will present each of you with a copy with today's date written on the back. I would also like to plant a tree in the courtyard as a symbol that I am always here in spirit, struggling alongside you, my fellow Yonago members."

Looking at Toshiko Ishizaki once again, Shin'ichi said: "Mrs. Ishizaki, I understand that you have three children. Is that right?"

"Yes, a girl of eleven, and two boys, eight and six years old."

"They are still young, so things may be difficult for a while but you will definitely become happy. Please continue to warmly embrace and support your children, always bright and strong like the sun."

AFTER TAKING the commemorative photograph, Shin'ichi said to those present: "Let's do gongyo once again."

Turning to Toshiko, he added: "Let's pray together for your husband's repose." He wanted to help her establish a firm foundation for her life so that she could rise above her grief and surmount all obstacles.

Once again, the room reverberated with Shin'ichi's powerful recitation of the sutra and his chanting of Nam-myoho-renge-kyo. When gongyo was finished, he continued encouraging the members. Rising to his feet, he began to shake hands with all 170 members who had gathered for the district leaders meeting, pouring his heart into inspiring each one. "Let's do our best together," he said to some. To elderly members, he remarked, "Please live a long life" or "Please take care of your health." And to the youth, he said as he gripped their hands tightly, "Struggle with all your might, with an ever-youthful spirit!"

Shin'ichi believed that district leaders, who were central to the Soka Gakkai's daily activities, were a crucial part of the organization and the key to achieving kosen-rufu. He was therefore keenly aware of the importance of encouraging them.

In the five years since becoming president, he had many opportunities to talk with leaders on the chapter level and up. Through these encounters, he came to know their individual personalities and abilities, as well as their family and living circumstances, and offered them appropriate guidance as a result.

Given the vast number of district leaders, however, Shin'ichi had few chances to meet and speak with them in person. But it was these leaders who were the main support of the chapters and who had the most frequent and direct contact with the members working on the organization's front lines. If the district leaders deepened their convictions, grew more capable and developed penetrating insight, kosen-rufu was certain to pick up amazing speed. That is what led Shin'ichi to conclude that encouraging them was vital to making fresh strides in the essential phase of the Soka Gakkai's development.

Shin'ichi's final activity in Yonago before bidding the members farewell was to plant a black pine in the garden of the Yonago Community Center. The Yonago members couldn't help feeling that the winter that had hung over their organization for so long had suddenly turned to spring. Their hearts overflowed with new life, reverberated with the music of hope and blossomed with happiness.

On January 20, Shin'ichi attended the opening ceremony for the Gifu Community Center. He then visited Nagoya, where he spoke of the great significance of kosen-rufu. He continued to throw his entire being into every endeavor, never for a moment thinking of himself.

IN HIS EFFORTS to encourage district leaders, Shin'ichi traveled tirelessly around Japan. He attended district leaders meetings in each area, determined to bring the light of hope to shine in the leaders' hearts like the morning sun. He exerted himself wholeheartedly in inspiring each person, fielding every question they asked and shaking each of their hands.

At the Tohoku No. 1 Headquarters District Leaders Meeting held on March 22 in Sendai, Miyagi Prefecture, he shook hands with every one of the nearly six hundred people in attendance. He believed that each hand was the hand of the Buddha, and when he clasped the members' hands in his, he felt a deep surge of respect and appreciation for them.

His hand gradually grew red and swollen from all this handshaking and began to ache, but still he continued, firmly grasping the leaders' hands as he offered them words of encouragement. He sensed a profound nobility in the sparkling eyes of the district leaders, a testimony to Nichiren Daishonin's teaching that the lives of ordinary people and the supreme state of Buddhahood are one and that common mortals are the Buddhas of the true entity of all phenomena.

When the meeting concluded, Shin'ichi retreated to a waiting room and wrapped his hand in a cold towel. With a smile, he said to those who were with him: "Everyone's handshake was so firm. Each of them looked so happy."

One of the leaders who heard this blurted out: "Sensei, it's too much for you to try to shake hands with every district leader!"

"Thank you for your concern," Shin'ichi responded, "but I don't have that many chances to meet and talk with district leaders across the country. I want our encounter to serve as a prime point they can return to throughout their lives."

There was nothing that the leaders present could say to that.

The pain in Shin'ichi's right hand eventually grew so bad that he couldn't even hold a pen to write. Due to heavy writing commitments, which included installments for *The Human Revolution,* as well as editorials for the study journal *The Daibyakurenge,* he decided to limit the amount of handshaking.

Shin'ichi was scheduled to attend a Nagano Headquarters district leaders meeting eight days later, on March 30, but as the day approached, the pain in his hand had not subsided. He had to think of some other way to encourage the leaders. He had received many letters from members who had participated in the commemorative photo session in Yonago, Tottori Prefecture, who said that the occasion had been the memory of a lifetime and that they look at the photo every day and feel renewed. Shin'ichi thus decided to do the same in Nagano.

The Nagano members were also overjoyed to be able to take a photo together with Shin'ichi.

MAY 3, 1965, the fifth anniversary of Shin'ichi's inauguration as president of the Soka Gakkai, was fast approaching. In Tokyo in April and May, district leaders meetings were held in each headquarters to mark this new departure. Shin'ichi was determined to attend them all, and he constantly thought of what he could do to encourage the leaders to make a fresh start toward the next five years with joy and courage.

Remembering how inspired and happy the members in Yonago and Nagano were by the commemorative photos he took with them, he decided to do the same in Tokyo. Exuberant Tokyo district leaders meetings began from the middle of April. When it was announced at each meeting that a commemorative photo would be taken that day, the members would erupt in cheers and enthusiastic applause.

The response to the photo sessions was enormous. When members received their photos later, they were delighted and renewed their vow to work for kosen-rufu. The photos became a kind of badge of honor for the nameless champions who engaged in struggle after struggle for kosen-rufu alongside Shin'ichi Yamamoto, the hallmark of heroes living in accord with the profound principle of cause and effect that governs life. They were also regarded as great personal and family treasures.

The commemorative photos were a tremendous challenge, however, for the *Seikyo Shimbun* cameramen who took them. They chanted earnestly before each session and took each picture as if their lives depended on it. Realizing the photos' significance, they determined not to make a single mistake.

Meetings for the larger headquarters might have more than a thousand participants. In such cases, the members were divided up into many smaller groups. After the photos were taken, the photographers developed the film and made a copy for each person. They frequently worked through the night but they did so filled with pride at the rare opportunity to participate in such a meaningful undertaking.

The Twenty-eighth Headquarters General Meeting marking the fifth anniversary of Shin'ichi's presidency was held on May 3, amid the members' joy at the commemorative photo sessions. Above the platform of the meeting venue at the Nihon University Auditorium in Ryogoku, Tokyo, a sign read in big, bold letters "Congratulations on the Fifth Anniversary of the President's Inauguration."

It had been raining since the previous night, making it the first time in five years that it rained during a general meeting, but the members' spirits soared. Viewing the rain as a symbol of the many difficulties that lay ahead in the endeavor to realize kosen-rufu, they strengthened their resolve not to be defeated.

IN HIS SPEECH at the Headquarters general meeting, Shin'ichi began by expressing his deep gratitude to the leaders of the Soka Gakkai, saying: "I am firmly confident that we have succeeded in constructing a strong foundation for kosen-rufu in these five years. I would like to convey my most sincere admiration and respect for all of you, the leaders who supported me, inexperienced as I was, in the great spirit of establishing the correct teaching for the peace of the land based on Buddhist ideals. Day after day, month after month, year after year, you have selflessly devoted yourselves in the struggle to spread the Daishonin's Buddhism. Thank you very much."

Shin'ichi then touched on the progress the Soka Gakkai had made since that time. When he assumed the presidency, there had been 1.4 million member-households. That number had now increased 3.8 times to 5.4 million households—an increase of four million members. The growth of the youth division had been particularly dramatic. The young men's division had expanded from 158,000 to 1.8 million and the young women's division from 119,000 to 1.3 million—a roughly eleven-fold increase, respectively. Meanwhile, the student division had grown from 2,200 to 71,000, or nearly thirty-two times.

In conjunction with the increasing membership, the organization itself had also seen tremendous growth and expansion. When Shin'ichi became president there were sixty-one chapters—now there were 1,210. Overseas membership increased from 441 member-households to 50,000—a dramatic one hundred-fold increase. And membership in the Study Department had grown from 17,000 to 850,000, a fifty-fold increase.

Touching on this remarkable development, Shin'ichi said: "The Soka Gakkai, which has carried out this sacred undertaking, is the living embodiment of the Buddha. It is a great and harmonious community of practitioners with faith as its marrow and compassion as its blood, a community that is acting in complete accord with the golden words of the Buddha.

"In iron-clad unity we advance, working tirelessly to bring happiness to all people. This strength makes our organization comparable to a solid, unsinkable battleship for peace. I hereby name that mighty ship the *Many in Body, One in Mind*.

"I wholeheartedly believe that our movement for worldwide kosen-rufu, transcending ethnic and national barriers, is proof that the time has come for the great life philosophy of Nichiren Daishonin to rise like the sun from Japan in the east and illuminate the vast skies of the world. The Soka Gakkai is not only the pillar of Japan, it is the hope of the world; it is the sun, the pioneering light leading the way into the twenty-first century. Do you agree?"

Shin'ichi's words were met with thunderous applause.

AS THEY LISTENED to Shin'ichi's speech, the meeting participants, burning with seeking spirit, were deeply impressed by the phenomenal development of kosen-rufu during the last five years. Wanting desperately to find solutions to their own individual problems, many of them had simply thrown themselves into Gakkai activities in line with the guidance of the Soka Gakkai. Now, however, looking back, they could see that through their own efforts a lofty record of kosen-rufu unprecedented in history had been created.

Some were deeply moved to think that they themselves were included among the noble envoys of the Buddha spoken of in the teachings of Buddhism. They were all keenly struck by the realization that devoting one's life to kosen-rufu along with the Soka Gakkai was to live in accord with the teaching that "the green ivy that twines around the tall pine can grow to a thousand feet" (WND, 17). Waves of joy and hope surged afresh in their hearts at the wondrous fact that they were members of the Soka Gakkai and at the profound significance of walking life's quintessential path.

Historians would no doubt one day write that in the three thousand-year history of Buddhism, there had never been such a global network of ordinary people working for world peace with the perseverance and sense of mission as the Soka Gakkai.

Shin'ichi then went on to report the steady progress being made on accomplishing the goals for the next seven years that he had articulated at the Headquarters general meeting on May 3 of the previous year. They were: the construction and donation of the Grand Main Temple to the head temple; achieving a membership of six million households; and the construction of a Soka Culture Center adjacent to the Soka Gakkai Headquarters.

As far as the membership goal was concerned, Shin'ichi announced that, given that the organization's numbers had increased more than 1.1 million in the last year—rising from 4.3 million to 5.4 million—the goal of six million households would probably be realized early the following year. This would mean that a goal originally set for seven years would be reached in less than two.

Sharing his honest thoughts on this point, Shin'ichi said: "Thus I believe that there is no need for us to be impatient when introducing Buddhism to others. Rather, we should steadily carry out our efforts with confidence and joy.

"At the same time, however, when we shift our gaze to the world arena, we see the fires of war raging in Vietnam and upheaval afflicting many areas around the globe. The only way to build true peace is to spread a true philosophy of life. The quicker the Soka Gakkai advances, the sooner peace will come. Mr. Toda once composed this poem:

*Death awaits
All of us one day;
Thus, be fearless,
Leaving unchallenged
Not a single enemy of the Buddha.*

"Let us forge ahead resolutely, never relaxing our struggle against the devilish nature that threatens humanity, as we continue striving for kosen-rufu until the very end!"

SHIN'ICHI then touched on the upcoming House of Councilors (Upper House) elections in July, mentioning the plans on the part of some established Buddhist schools and new religions to field candidates: "These religious groups have up to now harshly condemned the Soka Gakkai for sending members into government, calling it a case of religion meddling in politics. Now, without the slightest compunction, they are attempting to do the very same thing they criticized us for. What's more, the majority of these candidates will be running on the ruling party ticket.

"During the Daishonin's lifetime, there were slanderous priests, such as Ryokan of Gokuraku-ji temple, who conspired with the military government and persecuted the Daishonin. These religious groups I have just mentioned are now plotting similar schemes.

"Let us of the Soka Gakkai, however, continue to advance as steadfast allies of the people, together with the people, and for the victory of the people, no matter what!"

Enthusiastic applause rang throughout the hall.

Shin'ichi's spirit in making his appeal echoed that of Napoleon when he handed out banners to his troops and called on them to give their lives in defending their banner with courage along the path of victory.[8]

Since the Soka Gakkai established the Clean Government Party, and the party had announced its plans to field candidates for the House of Representatives (Lower House), the established political parties had increasingly come to regard the Gakkai as a threat to their existence.

Conservative political parties, seeking a new means of survival, had begun to form alliances with various religious organizations in an attempt to gain their supporters' votes. Meanwhile, these religious groups vehemently wished to remove the Soka Gakkai from the scene for fear that it would convert their own members. They were therefore strongly opposed to the Clean Government Party, whose main supporter was the Soka Gakkai, and wanted to obstruct its progress in any way they could.

Thus, drawn together by self-interest and hatred for the Gakkai, these political and religious forces announced their intent to field candidates for the upcoming Upper House election. Observing this development, Shin'ichi became concerned that before long the Soka Gakkai would become the target of attack from all sides.

In "Letter from Sado," the Daishonin writes of priests of erroneous teachings colluding with an evil ruler to destroy the correct teaching (see WND, 302). In light of the situation today, "evil ruler" refers to corrupt authorities. The Daishonin thus indicates that when those authorities try to destroy the correct teaching, "priests of erroneous teachings" will join forces with them and together they will pool their energies to attack those who uphold the correct teaching.

"ONCE YOU HAVE determined to fight," Napoleon said, "you must persist in that determination; there can be no 'if' or 'but.'"⁹ These words hold true in our struggle for kosen-rufu as well.

The pattern of certain religious groups clustering around authority and conspiring to attack the correct teaching—a pattern that has existed since the Daishonin's time—will never change. Shin'ichi was well aware that the more Clean Government Party representatives were elected to office and the greater the party's influence grew, the more the resentment of the established political parties and various religious groups would be roused. He also knew that, because of this, it was only a matter of time before those groups began launching harsh attacks on the Soka Gakkai.

The Headquarters general meeting marking the fifth anniversary of Shin'ichi's presidency drew to a close. Filled with fresh inspiration, the members pledged together to set out anew.

Also in commemoration of May 3, a book by Shin'ichi titled *Science and Religion* was officially released. The book elucidated that, at their core, science and religion are in no way contradictory, and that the Buddhist philosophy of life is crucial if science is to contribute to the happiness and peace of humanity. The first volume of *The Collected Works of Tsunesaburo Makiguchi* was also published on this day.

Since spring of the previous year, 1964, when the curtain rose on the essential phase of the Soka Gakkai's movement, the organization's publishing activities had accelerated at an astonishing rate. On April 2, the seventh memorial of Josei Toda's death, a volume of Shin'ichi's lectures on "On Repaying Debts of Gratitude," one of the ten major writings of Nichiren Daishonin, was published.

In fact, publishing lectures on the ten major writings had been a cherished dream of Josei Toda. Soon after becoming the second president of the Soka Gakkai on May 3, 1951, he set to work on an edition of a compilation of the Daishonin's writings, which was published on April 28 of the following year. Then, wishing to enable members to accurately grasp the Daishonin's true intent and build an unshakable foundation in faith, he began working on a series of lectures on the ten major writings. In December 1952, a lecture on "On Establishing the Correct Teaching for the Peace of the Land" was published as the first volume in the series, followed by those on "The Opening of the Eyes" and "The Object of Devotion for Observing the Mind." He next began composing his lecture on "The Selection of the Time," but died on April 2, 1958, before he could complete it.

AFTER President Toda's death, Shin'ichi Yamamoto felt a keen sense of responsibility to carry on publishing lectures on the major writings that his mentor could not cover during his lifetime. He gave serious thought to the most appropriate time to embark on this endeavor, and finally settled on April 2, 1964. In the spirit of showing his profound appreciation to his mentor, he decided to start with a lecture on "On Repaying Debts of Gratitude."

Once that project was completed, Shin'ichi went to work on a lecture on "The Selection of the Time," which Toda had started but not completed. The volume was published seven months later, on November 17. On the same day, Shin'ichi's book *Politics and Religion* and the first volume of the Soka Gakkai Study Department's *A Comprehensive Dictionary of Buddhist Philosophy* were also published. Only a little more than half a year had passed since the publication of *Science and Religion*.

Shin'ichi's writing took place amidst the rigorous demands of his daily schedule as president. In the meantime, his various other writing commitments, such as submitting installments for *The Human Revolution* and monthly editorials for *The Daibyakurenge*, also required his attention.

But Shin'ichi was firmly and deeply determined. "Kosen-rufu is a struggle of words," he thought. "Without words that encourage people, without words that demonstrate the truth of Buddhism and the correctness of the Soka Gakkai's movement, kosen-rufu will never advance. Words that move the spirit are the weapon of the peaceful revolution—the human revolution—to realize a fundamental transformation in the life of each individual. Words are life. They are light; hope. I will continue to pour every ounce of my being into speaking and writing until the last moment of my life!"

It was Shin'ichi who served as the motivating force behind the Soka Gakkai's publication activities, which had taken on increasing momentum since the organization entered the essential phase of its development.

At about this time, the *Seikyo Shimbun,* the Soka Gakkai's organ paper, was also gearing up to make great new strides forward. From autumn of the previous year, preparations had been under way to make it a daily paper.

The *Seikyo Shimbun* first went into print on April 20, 1951, just before Josei Toda's inauguration as second president of the Soka Gakkai. It started out as a two-page broadsheet printed front and back and was published once every ten days. Two years later, in September 1953, it became a weekly paper, gradually increasing over the years to four, six, then eight pages. In September 1960, the year Shin'ichi became president, it switched from a weekly eight-page paper to a biweekly published on Wednesdays and Saturdays, with four and eight pages, respectively.

IN JANUARY 1962, the *Seikyo Shimbun* became a triweekly paper, publishing four pages on Tuesdays and Thursdays, and eight on Saturdays. A year later, every issue became eight pages. The readership also grew immensely. At the start in 1951, only five thousand copies were printed, but ten years later, in 1961, more than a million copies were coming off the press. Three years later, in September 1964, with the publication of the one thousandth issue, circulation had surpassed the two million mark.

With the sudden growth in circulation it became difficult, both in terms of time and quantity, to print and distribute the paper from the single location of Tokyo, where it was centered. Regional printing centers were therefore set up. The first was established in Sapporo, Hokkaido, in October 1961. In January of the following year, printing began in Osaka, and in July, it started in Fukuoka in Kyushu. In April 1965, printing facilities opened in Nagoya, Aichi Prefecture, and Takamatsu, Kagawa Prefecture, making a total of six around the country.

Finally, the *Seikyo Shimbun* began full-fledged preparations to go daily. This was a wish long cherished by members across Japan, who wanted more than anything to read the paper every morning just like any other newspaper so that they could start the day with fresh joy and confidence in faith. For some time, both the *Seikyo Shimbun* office and the Soka Gakkai Headquarters received many such requests. In addition, Shin'ichi strongly felt that in order to initiate a great struggle of words in the new era, it was crucial that the newspaper go daily. Speed was everything in the effort to convey news and information for the sake of kosen-rufu.

The *Seikyo Shimbun* had published its one thousandth issue on September 12, 1964. Immediately prior to that, Shin'ichi had said to Eisuke Akizuki, the managing editor of the paper: "We're about to reach the one thousandth issue—congratulations! Our next goal is becoming a daily paper. It is with this transition that the Soka Gakkai's publication activities will also enter their essential phase. I know there is much to be done in preparation for this step, but let's do our best to realize it next year. The readers are eagerly looking forward to it. I'm counting on you!"

Akizuki seemed ready for this. "Yes, I agree completely," he said, with a smile and a nod of affirmation.

EISUKE AKIZUKI had known for a while that Shin'ichi planned to make the *Seikyo Shimbun* into a daily newspaper. Now Akizuki felt the time had come at least.

At the beginning of 1965, the *Seikyo Shimbun* management decided to initiate making this change in October. Then, at a conference of top Soka Gakkai leaders at the end of May, Shin'ichi asked Akizuki: "How are the preparations for switching over to daily publication coming along?"

"Fine," Akizuki replied. "We're planning to begin daily publication in October."

"October?" Shin'ichi asked. "Couldn't we move it up a little earlier? The Soka Gakkai's momentum is accelerating every day. We've reached a point where triweekly publication cannot keep up with the organization's development.

"Requests for this from members are also coming regularly now. The Clean Government Party's paper, the *Komei Shimbun,* will go daily as of June 15. The sooner the *Seikyo Shimbun* does so, the better."

After serious consideration, it was thus decided that the *Seikyo Shimbun* would go into daily circulation on July 15.

But a mountain of problems lay in the way of meeting that goal. As if guessing Akizuki's thoughts, Shin'ichi said, "If you have any concerns, don't hesitate to talk to me."

Akizuki mentioned the need to increase the number of reporters and also to buy equipment like cameras for the branch offices. After listening to Akizuki's requests, Shin'ichi declared in a firm voice: "All right, the struggle begins from now!"

Soon after that, on June 8, Shin'ichi visited the *Seikyo Shimbun* Headquarters. He wanted to encourage the staff and inspire them with fresh energy for advancement as they proceeded with their preparations. After doing gongyo with representatives of the newspaper staff in the Gohonzon room at the *Seikyo* Headquarters, he said: "It's a beautiful day, so let's go up to the roof to talk."

On the roof, everyone sat around Shin'ichi and a discussion ensued under blue skies. "At long last, the *Seikyo Shimbun* is making its debut as a daily paper," Shin'ichi began. "For a while, you will all be very busy and things will be quite difficult. I hope, however, that you will never forget the spirit of continuous challenge, always striving to study hard and develop your skills.

"The degree to which you can polish and strengthen yourselves when you are young will be a deciding factor in the direction of your lives. All the hardship you experience now is important training to enable you to do just that.

WITH MOUNT FUJI visible in the distance, Shin'ichi Yamamoto continued: "Mr. Toda wrote a poem that goes:

Can you not see Fuji's summit?
Rally now, quickly, in growing numbers!

"I hope that all of you will develop into great lions of kosen-rufu who, as champions of the pen, can blaze that noble path even if you must do it alone. Leaders must have strength, wisdom and a sense of responsibility. Those who possess a strong sense of responsibility, who can surmount the most difficult of circumstances and continue to do their best to the very end are able to become great leaders. This is an eternal and unchanging formula.

"I hope you will also be broad-minded leaders who can raise your juniors to be even more capable than yourselves. To do that you must lead by example. Your spirit and actions will serve as true inspiration for others. People will not grow under an authoritarian leader who only gives orders and finds fault with others. The future of the *Seikyo Shimbun* rests on your shoulders. Everything comes down to the actions of the people involved in any given endeavor.

"What is the enemy that can impede the progress of our precious *Seikyo Shimbun?* It is the inertia that creeps in and takes over one's heart. It is laziness and the willingness to give up and forget the spirit of challenge. Unless each of you becomes a reporter who constantly overflows with fresh vitality, wisdom and courage, the *Seikyo Shimbun* will not enjoy success or a glorious future.

"Now, if you have anything you'd like to ask me today, please feel free."

A young man sitting in the front, who was as an editor on the paper, immediately raised his hand and said, "Sensei, I'd really like to hear your opinions and evaluation of each section of the paper so that we can make it the best it can be."

"All right," Shin'ichi replied. "Let's go back to the editorial office and have a look."

Shin'ichi led the others to the editorial office on the second floor of the building and opened the day's paper. "I'd give this story about youth division discussion meetings sixty-eight points out of one hundred. The content isn't bad, but the layout makes it difficult to read."

He turned the page. "This editorial on the second page, I'd give seventy-six points. It's fairly well written as a whole, but the introduction is weak. It's vital to capture the readers' interest in the opening lines. No matter how good the rest of the article is, if the beginning has no impact, no one will want to continue reading.

"How do we grab the reader's attention? One way is to start with a famous quote or to place the conclusion at the beginning. At any rate, I hope you will make an effort to learn how to make the opening lines of an article original and attention-grabbing."

SHIN'ICHI'S critique of the newspaper continued. He looked at each page and assigned scores to the articles and photographs, as well as the layout, sharing his views on writing and photography as he went.

"When reporting on people's experiences in faith," he said, "it's important to paint a vivid picture of their situation. How you describe a person's actions is one way of doing this. Writing 'He was sad and he cried' is flat and dull. But by saying 'He wiped his falling tears with a muddy fist,' you've created a clear image. And the word *mud* even brings color to it. These kinds of little touches make all the difference.

"Given the nature of a newspaper article, there is a limit to how much can be written about a person's experience in faith. It's therefore necessary to delve into the story and hone what you want to convey. If you treat it like a biography and try to put in everything about the subject's life, the article will lose its focus and no one will grasp what you're trying to say.

"A faith experience must be logical and comprehensible to the average person living in society. If you only report superficially that someone recovered from an illness or that their business improved, there is a chance you will promote a distorted understanding of faith."

Shin'ichi's advice was extremely pertinent.

"Above all," he added, "accuracy is the lifeblood of a newspaper."

Turning to Susumu Aota, he then said, "What's that slogan you're always emphasizing, Mr. Aota?"

Susumu Aota was the head of the First Editorial Department, which was responsible for editing the *Seikyo Shimbun* and other publications. As a university student, he was a member of the Tokyo University Lotus Sutra Study Group, where he received training directly from second Soka Gakkai president Josei Toda. After graduating from the university, he worked for a time at a petroleum company, before eventually becoming a staff member at the Soka Gakkai Headquarters.

Aota blushed and said: "It's 'Confirm, reconfirm and reconfirm again. Confirm the facts with your own eyes and your own hands.'"

"That's exactly right," Shin'ichi remarked. "A single mistake completely can undo the reputation of a newspaper."

Shin'ichi continued giving scores to the *Seikyo Shimbun* pages. It was a tense but joyful moment. Most of all, however, it was one of great enjoyment for all who were there. When Shin'ichi gave a high mark, their faces broke out in smiles.

Finally, Shin'ichi said: "On the whole, I'd say the paper is somewhere between seventy-nine and eighty-two points. I hope you'll all study hard and work together to produce the best newspaper in the world. The *Seikyo Shimbun* must become a wellspring of philosophy, an indomitable bastion of the pen foremost in the entire world.

SHIN'ICHI'S encouragement inspired a deeper awareness in the *Seikyo Shimbun* staff of their role in the movement to realize kosen-rufu. From that day forward, they engaged in an all-out effort toward making the

Seikyo Shimbun a daily paper. The June 12 issue was designated to carry an official announcement informing readers of this new development. The article would cover a space of four columns under the headline, "A Daily at Last—Starting July 15."

At the time, articles for publication were sent to a printing plant in Minato Ward, Tokyo, which the Soka Gakkai had contracted to handle the platemaking and printing of the paper. There, in an editorial office established on the third floor of the plant, a team of *Seikyo Shimbun* employees went to work fixing the paper's layout and proofreading the copy.

On the day the announcement was typeset, the manager of the printing plant came rushing into the office, his face pale. He held the galley proof of a part of the announcement in his visibly shaking hand. Approaching Hiroaki Komori, head of the layout section, he appeared somewhat distressed as he looked at the proof and said: "Mr. Komori, I heard that you were planning to become a daily, but I beg you to give up the idea. It's simply impossible. You need at least two or three years' preparation to make this change.

"I've been invited to a number of Soka Gakkai meetings and culture festivals, and I have a good idea just how great the organization's potential is. But publishing a daily paper is no easy matter. I'm afraid you won't last three days. I'm saying this out of utmost concern. I really think you should reconsider."

Such was the advice of the printing plant manager, who had had many years of experience with newspaper publishing.

Komori knew that the man spoke with the best of

intentions, but that didn't change anything. "The July 15 date has already been set," he said. "We can't put it off."

The manager tried to convince him to at least refrain from printing the announcement and to give the date for the switchover more serious thought.

To this, however, Komori responded: "We're definitely going to make it a success. Just you watch."

There was nothing more the printer could say. With an expression of resignation, he replied: "All right. We'll do our best to support you."

LESS THAN a month remained before the *Seikyo Shimbun* would become a daily newspaper. The greatest concern of managing editor Eisuke Akizuki was a shortage of staff. The paper would more than double in size, and finding capable people to work on it was proving difficult.

The *Seikyo Shimbun* office was responsible for the organization's publications, and all of its members were Headquarters staff. For that reason alone, there were a number of important requirements to take into consideration when hiring reporters for the paper. Not only did they need the requisite skills of their craft but, as Headquarters employees shouldering the work of kosen-rufu, they also needed to have strong faith and a sense of personal integrity that the members could rely on. The process of hiring new staff proceeded with great deliberation and took a considerable amount of time. Even without new staff, however, once the change to a daily format was initiated, the paper would have to go to print each day.

Up to this time, new Editorial Department staff had been required to undergo a three-month training period, but this had been reduced first to one month and then just three days. Now new employees were assigned to a particular department almost from the start and had to be trained on the basics of the job.

It also became necessary to obtain more than double the amount of advertisements for the paper, and that would not be easy. Kurazo Tateyama, the head of the Advertising Department, rallied his staff: "It's now or never. Let's go out there and not come back until we get those ads!"

Everyone shared his determination. The Advertising Department had a brilliant record of correcting prejudices and misunderstandings about the Soka Gakkai in society and winning the organization understanding and trust.

For a while after the paper's inception in 1951, the advertising revenue of the *Seikyo Shimbun* came mostly from members. The only other advertising at that time was for products such as Buddhist altars, incense and candles.

When Josei Toda went on a guidance tour to Osaka in 1956, he spoke to the staff of the *Seikyo Shimbun* Kansai regional office's Advertising Department. He said: "You can judge how trusted a newspaper is by its advertising. You are fortunate to have the ads placed by members, and you must continue to show your appreciation for them. If you rely solely on that support, however, you won't be fulfilling your real mission. You need to go out and solicit the big companies, tell them what kind of an organization the Soka Gakkai is, what a wonderful newspaper the *Seikyo Shimbun* is and get their advertising. A person who can't succeed in business can't succeed as a leader."

This guidance was also communicated to the Tokyo Advertising Department.

AFTER HEARING Toda's words, *Seikyo Shimbun* Advertising Department staff members across Japan renewed their determinations. Realizing that it was their mission to open a new path of kosen-rufu, they resolved to win understanding for the Soka Gakkai in the business community.

But they faced a very thick wall of resistance. The head of one company's advertising department, picking up the *Seikyo Shimbun* and seeing the numerous ads for candles and incense, wrinkled his brows and said sarcastically: "I can feel the smoke of incense rising from the pages."

A pharmaceutical company representative replied to their sales pitch with extreme ignorance, saying: "Don't Soka Gakkai members cure their illnesses through prayer? What's the point of advertising medicines and medical equipment in your paper if none of your readers will buy them?"

An employee of a certain automobile manufacturer asked them scornfully: "Are there any Gakkai members who can afford to buy a car? Motorcycles are expensive enough, you know."

But the more resistance they faced, the more fiercely the advertising staff's determination burned. They persevered in visiting company after company, giving their all to sweep away misunderstanding and prejudice. Gradually, their sincerity and steadfast efforts to convince prospective advertisers of the value of putting their ads in the *Seikyo Shimbun* paid off. Companies began to change their opinions of the Soka Gakkai and advertisements from major industries began to adorn the newspaper's pages.

Now, Kurazo Tateyama called on his staff to return once more to that fighting spirit and undertake a fresh challenge. The hearts of the advertising staff were filled with pride at being a part of creating a new history as the *Seikyo Shimbun* went daily, and they rose enthusiastically to the task.

In a short period of time and with astonishing speed, they succeeded in breaking new ground in their endeavor. Everything was ready to go by the deadline. In the meantime, the Business Affairs Department of the paper, which handled such things as shipping, delivery and collections, was also working tirelessly toward the July 15 goal.

A mild-mannered young man named Takafumi Yashiro was in charge of shipping. At first, when the initial projected date for going daily had been October, he had planned to contact Japan National Railways in mid-July to start negotiations for securing transporting arrangements. This was because JNR usually began revising its schedules for October in the month of July, and there was nothing he could discuss with them until then. But when the new deadline of July 15 was set, he had to rush into negotiations with the railway company.

NO MATTER how prepared the newspaper's sales agencies and local delivery networks were, if a smooth transportation route wasn't secured, all efforts would be in vain. Determined that somehow the paper would reach its readers the same day it came off the press, Takafumi Yashiro studied freight schedules and negotiated with Japan National Railways.

Even so, he wasn't able to secure a freighter on the Tohoku Main Line to carry the papers from Tokyo to Aomori Prefecture in northeastern Honshu. He continued to pore over the extremely detailed train schedules as if trying to unlock a puzzle. At last, on July 14, the day the presses started running for the first daily edition of the *Seikyo Shimbun,* the problem was solved.

The same issue was also being tackled in Kansai, where Koichi Towada, the head of the Business Affairs Department of the paper's Kansai office, struggled to pin down transportation routes for the Osaka edition. The last problem he faced was finding a way to deliver papers to areas that didn't even have bus access. There weren't enough copies of the paper being sent to justify truck delivery. Chanting sincerely, he personally traveled to the areas in question in search of a solution.

Then he found a local fish store that sent a truck to Osaka on a daily basis to buy fresh fish. He successfully negotiated with the owner, who agreed to transport the newspapers back to town along with the fish. It was a victory that came from wisdom born of pure determination.

On July 15, the long-anticipated first daily edition of the *Seikyo Shimbun* appeared. The front page carried an article on the Student Division's Eighth General Meeting held at the Nihon University Auditorium in Tokyo. An article about the fresh departure of these intelligent and passionate youth, it was the perfect story to mark the start of the Soka Gakkai's struggle of words in its essential phase of growth.

From this issue, the *Seikyo Shimbun* also began to carry general news and weather, and from July 20, television and radio program listings. With the changeover to daily publication, the editing room became as tense as a battlefield. It was a fierce struggle against the clock. When the paper had been put to bed for the night, many reporters and staff had time for only a short break before setting to work on meeting the next day's deadlines.

A number of reporters, busy gathering information and writing articles, ended up spending most nights in the office. Sleep consisted of little more than a nap on some chairs lined up to form a makeshift bed. One of the staff became well known for his special talent of being able to sleep sitting up. He was First Editorial Department Chief Susumu Aota. His colleagues, impressed with his gift, dubbed it "perpendicular sleeping."

ALL THE STAFF members, from the paper's top executives to the newest employee, determined to get the new daily up and running smoothly, even if they had to do it completely on their own. Their hearts soared with hope.

Although managing editor Eisuke Akizuki worried about the physical condition of his staff and urged them to go home early and get some rest, no one did. The reporters were filled with resolve to work even harder, thinking of how their writing might encourage readers at the start of each day. In addition, as Headquarters staff whose basic spirit was to serve the members and devote themselves to kosen-rufu, they believed it only natural that they strive as hard as they could to create a newspaper that brought cheer to its readers.

With the *Seikyo Shimbun*'s transition to daily publication, Shin'ichi's workload increased immensely as well. Instead of writing three installments of his novel *The Human Revolution* per week, he now had to write seven. He would read reference materials for the novel while traveling from place to place and sketch out the unfolding plot, which he would then set down on paper early in the morning or late at night. This was a demanding personal challenge, but he continued writing as if he were composing letters of encouragement to his fellow members; all the while, he communicated in his heart with his mentor, Josei Toda.

The people most delighted and enthusiastic about the *Seikyo Shimbun*'s transition to daily publication were the newspaper deliverers. Before the changeover was initiated, meetings were held for them across Japan to explain the new system. Ready and eager to take on the challenge, everyone felt tremendous pride and joy to be supporting the *Seikyo Shimbun* as it lifted the curtain on a new phase of kosen-rufu.

In addition, many people living in remote places, where the paper had previously only been received by mail, began volunteering as deliverers. Papers sent by mail arrived a day or two late, but if they were delivered by hand, readers could get them on the day of publication. Requests to become delivery staff came from members who had a deep understanding of the significance of the

Seikyo Shimbun's transition and wanted to offer their time to serve their fellow members.

For members living in remote areas who were isolated from other members and didn't have many opportunities to meet with leaders to receive guidance, reading the *Seikyo Shimbun* on a daily basis was a source of immense encouragement. Gazing up at the glorious morning sun, the deliverers proudly made their rounds, carrying their "letters of kosen-rufu" for the sake of their friends and the Law.

HITACHINAI in Animachi, Akita Prefecture, was one area where both local and national newspapers arrived only by mail. To get there required transferring at Takanosu Station on the Ou Main Line to the local Aniai

Line and traveling about ninety minutes. Hitachinai Station was the final stop, nestled deep in the mountains.

Thanks to the efforts of the local deliverers, however, the *Seikyo Shimbun* reached even here within the day of its publication. Every morning, the delivery person would pick up the papers that had been sent to Hitachinai Station. After covering her route near the station, she would then board a bus and travel as long as forty minutes to deliver the paper to other readers. She was proud that the only newspaper in the town to be received on the same day it came off the press was the *Seikyo Shimbun*.

Tokujicho in mountainous Saba County, Yamaguchi Prefecture, was another area that switched from mail to hand delivery soon after the *Seikyo Shimbun* went daily. The delivery person would pick up the papers at six o'clock in the morning in Hofu City and then head for neighboring Tokujicho, a journey of about ninety minutes one way by motorbike. There he would make his rounds to each of the subscribers' homes, which were scattered throughout the town.

Few of the roads were paved, and it was very hilly. He rode through mountains and rice fields, stirring clouds of dust as he made his way on a journey that took more than one hundred miles a day. When it rained, he became drenched in spite of his raincoat. Even so, he made sure that at least the newspapers stayed dry, wrapping them in several layers of plastic.

For the Soka Gakkai members in Tokujicho, the *Seikyo Shimbun* was a great source of energy and inspiration for sustaining their daily Buddhist practice. And when the delivery person saw the happy expressions on the readers' faces as they waited for their papers, any exhaustion he felt just disappeared.

Whenever Shin'ichi heard of the earnest struggles of the delivery staff across Japan, he was filled with deep gratitude and pressed his palms together in reverence for their efforts. He chanted sincerely each day for the deliverers and the managers of the local sales outlets, praying for their safety and protection. He also asked the leaders to make sure that Soka Gakkai activities ended early, so that the delivery staff could get enough sleep.

Unable to stop thinking about the deliverers, Shin'ichi frequently awoke in the middle of the night. And he would be kept awake by the realization that the staff at the outlets would soon be starting their day.

He was also very concerned about the weather across Japan. If it was raining when he got up in the morning, he worried tremendously about the deliverers. On such days, he would chant with even more intensity.

SINCE the *Seikyo Shimbun* went to daily distribution, Shin'ichi made suggestions and offered encouragement so that the managers of the newspaper outlets and the delivery staff could joyfully fulfill their responsibilities. One such suggestion was that they start a bulletin that would enable them to inspire one another as well as provide guidelines for their work. The bulletin thus began publication as a monthly in July 1966, a year after the *Seikyo Shimbun*'s changeover.

In response to members' requests, Shin'ichi named the bulletin *The Uncrowned*, in reference to uncrowned champions—a perfect description of the spirit of the outlet managers and delivery staff. Seeking neither power nor glory, these members burned with pride as Bodhisattvas of the Earth, struggling earnestly as champions protecting the "bastion of the pen" for the sake of the people.

The circulation of the *Seikyo Shimbun* rose dramatically when the paper went daily, until eventually it reached a par with Japan's three major newspapers, the *Asahi, Yomiuri* and *Mainichi*. Wanting to surpass their competitors, managing editor Eisuke Akizuki and the other reporters studied the basics of newspaper creation, including how to write articles, placement of headlines and layout design.

One day, Shin'ichi met with Akizuki and the other executives to discuss the paper. Akizuki said: "In an effort to make ours the best newspaper in Japan, the editorial staff has been studying hard, looking even to the other daily papers for reference. But we've received feedback from some readers that, though the paper looks more professional, it's lost some of the conviction of the old *Seikyo Shimbun*. Could you share with us your ideas about the direction the paper should take?"

Shin'ichi replied: "That's a very important question. It's necessary to learn from the techniques of the regular dailies, but you mustn't forget that the *Seikyo Shimbun* is a paper for kosen-rufu. Ordinary newspapers are supposed to report on events in an objective and nonpartisan manner. For a newspaper affiliated with a particular organization, however, the struggle is how to convey the organization's message, inspire its readers and widen the circle of understanding for its cause.

"That means that you don't need to imitate ordinary

papers or take their example as your goal. The *Seikyo Shimbun* must remain true to itself and blaze its own trail." Shin'ichi's reply was crystal clear.

"WHAT DOES IT MEAN for the *Seikyo Shimbun* to remain true to itself?" Shin'ichi Yamamoto spoke passionately, "First of all, it is a newspaper dedicated to kosen-rufu. It should fill its readers with a desire to stand up and work for the happiness of others and for peace. It is also crucial that the paper overflows with the spirit to resolutely challenge and refute injustice.

"Second, it must be a newspaper that helps people understand the correct teaching of Buddhism. To read the *Seikyo Shimbun* is to come into contact with Buddhism. It is important that the paper apprehend all things accurately from the standpoint of the great philosophy of life taught by the Daishonin and offer a means by which people can solve their problems.

"Third, it must serve as a letter of encouragement that gives hope and courage to its readers. The *Seikyo Shimbun* is already being read by people who are not Soka Gakkai members and has come to be widely appreciated as a people-focused newspaper. Thus, it should also be a paper from which readers can learn the best way to live and that serves as a font of life force and energy."

Akizuki inquired further: "Since becoming a daily, we've begun including in our pages general news articles and other columns that aren't directly related to faith, such as those dealing with arts and culture and home life. How should we treat these pages?"

Leaning forward in his seat, Shin'ichi replied: "From now on, those pages are going to become very important. Reports on meetings, articles offering guidance and accounts of members' experiences in faith are unique to the *Seikyo Shimbun,* but news and specialty columns appear in other papers as well. Readers will compare those parts of the paper with other newspapers, which means they have to be outstanding.

"For example, since there is only enough space for a limited number of general news articles, what does appear must be very well organized and easy to grasp. In the arts and culture and home life columns, it's important to plan the articles and make comments from a humanistic perspective based on Buddhism. These are the pages that will determine society's evaluation of the *Seikyo Shimbun* and that will demonstrate the paper's excellence. The reporters in charge of those sections must therefore constantly be studying, learning and coming up with new ideas.

"If those pages are inferior to their counterparts in other papers or fall into a rut, it will harm the reputation of the *Seikyo Shimbun* and expose it to ridicule. I hope that those responsible for the paper will strive to make those pages a model for other papers, aiming to make them the best in Japan and the world."

AT JUST ABOUT the time that the *Seikyo Shimbun* was becoming a daily paper in Japan, organ newspapers were beginning to appear one after another in Soka Gakkai organizations around the globe. It was the sincere wish of local members to read guidance and study

Buddhism in their own language, rather than hearing everything through the Japanese members living in their respective countries. Aware of this, Shin'ichi proposed that, as a start, an English-language newspaper be published in the United States.

In August 1964, the *World Tribune* was first published for the members in the United States. It was a four-page, tabloid-sized semimonthly English newspaper that included some articles in Japanese. There were many Japanese members living in the United States who still had a difficult time with English but the publication of the *World Tribune* enabled them to step up their efforts in sharing Nichiren Buddhism with Americans.

There was even the case of a youth who contacted the paper after reading an experience in faith of a U.S. member printed in the *World Tribune* and, struggling with similar problems, wanted to find out more about Buddhism. The publication of an English newspaper did much to spread understanding of the Soka Gakkai in the United States.

Following this, in October 1964, the French organization published its own newspaper, *L'avenir*. Though in the beginning it was just a four-page mimeographed monthly pamphlet, it served as a great source of spiritual nourishment not only for members in France, but also in other regions where French was spoken, such as Switzerland and Belgium.

In May 1965, a Portuguese-language paper, *Nuova Era,* was published in Brazil. It also began as a typed, mimeographed, four-page newspaper but later grew into the *Brazil Seikyo*. In December of the same year, the mimeographed *Seikyo Zeitung* began to be published in German, with sections in Japanese, on a monthly basis in West Germany.

In January 1966, the Chinese-language *Li Ming Sheng Bao* was published in Hong Kong as a four-page, tabloid-sized monthly. And in April, the Spanish-language *Peru Seikyo* began publication in Peru using the same format.

SHIN'ICHI spared no effort in his support of the various publication activities taking place around the world. Whenever he was asked to name a publication or send a congratulatory message, he gladly obliged.

The publications' editorial staff members in each country were all inexperienced. They were Soka Gakkai members who, after finishing their day jobs and Gakkai activities, would assemble in their respective editorial offices and set to work. In fact, these editorial offices were often actually nothing more than a corner in the office of the local community center, or a room in a member's home. These members would work far into the night writing articles and coming up with headlines, arranging the layout, typing text and cutting stencils for mimeographing.

In the case of the *World Tribune*, meeting the deadline for typesetting the articles proved difficult, and the paper would often end up arriving at the printer after the typesetter had gone home for the night. If they waited until the next day, publication would be delayed. Inevitably, there were occasions when the editorial staff had to set the type themselves, blackening their fingers as they selected each letter and lined them up on the printing plate.

The Hong Kong publication, meanwhile, faced other challenges. The printer they were using often didn't have the Chinese characters required for expressing Buddhist terminology. This meant that the editorial staff would have to dash around to other printers in search of what they needed in order to meet their publication deadline.

But the biggest problem for the editorial staff in every country was translation. The papers carried many articles translated from the *Seikyo Shimbun,* including explanations of Buddhist teachings and Shin'ichi's lectures, and this presented enormous difficulties. Most of the Japanese staff were, at best, only conversationally fluent in the language of their adopted country and most of the native staff did not understand Japanese. This alone made the translation of Buddhist terms incredibly time-consuming.

Though the Japanese staff would give their all to this endeavor, the native speakers usually couldn't understand what they had written. As a result, the native staff had to retranslate every article to make it intelligible.

These publications were the result of the painstaking efforts of members all over the world. Yet these struggles enabled the members to deepen their faith and increase their comprehension of Buddhist teachings. In addition, efforts to send the publications to different cultural institutions and university libraries in each country eventually paid off and mistaken notions about the Soka Gakkai were gradually replaced with a correct understanding of the organization.

ON JULY 4, 1965, amid the *Seikyo Shimbun*'s hectic preparations to go daily, the seventh House of Councilors (Upper House) election took place. Since the official beginning of the election campaign on June 10, all the parties canvassed vigorously. The Clean Government Party fielded nine candidates for the national constituency and five for the prefectural constituency.[10] It was the first national election since the party's establishment the previous year, and it was running candidates in the prefectural constituencies of Aichi, Hyogo and Fukuoka—areas where its predecessor, the Clean Government Political Federation, had never done so.

Soka Gakkai members had worked hard to make this debut election of the newborn Clean Government Party a resounding success. Consequently, all nine national constituency candidates were elected along with the prefectural candidates for Tokyo and Osaka. Though the candidates for Aichi, Hyogo and Fukuoka failed to gain seats, the fact that the Clean Government Party won eleven of the total number of seats available when initially only four of its seats were up for reelection was proof of the party's rapid development. This meant that in one stroke, the total number of Clean Government Party representatives in the House of Councilors increased from thirteen to twenty.

A total of 5,097,000 votes were cast for Clean Government Party national candidates. This surpassed, by almost a million, the 4,120,000 votes that had been cast for Clean Government Political Federation candidates in the previous election. Furthermore, in spite of the defeats in Aichi, Hyogo and Fukuoka, those candidates had all come in second place, helping build a solid foundation to achieve victory next time.

In the midst of this campaign, on June 14, the Tokyo Metropolitan Assembly was dissolved and on July 8, four days after the House of Councilors election, the date for the assembly election was officially posted. The previous election for the assembly was held in April 1963, two years earlier. Normally, the next election would take place in the spring of 1967, after the representatives' four-year terms had come to an end.

There had been a scandal, however, surrounding the election for speaker of the metropolitan assembly, which had been held on March 9. A number of Liberal Democratic Party assembly members were arrested for vote-buying, finally resulting in the assembly's dissolution and the calling of an election. This scandal had been exposed through the determined efforts of Clean Government Party assembly members to eliminate bribery and corruption from the assembly.

The first arrest occurred on March 15. The suspect was accused of giving a large sum of money to a fellow assembly member in an attempt to collect votes in the lead-up to the LDP's nomination for a new metropolitan assembly speaker. Then, on March 16, two more LDP candidates were arrested on suspicion of taking bribes. By April 7, seven people were arrested on charges related to this election.

ON APRIL 16, the assembly speaker was finally arrested on suspicion of bribery. This was the first time since the establishment of the metropolitan government that an incumbent assembly speaker had been arrested. The Clean Government Party representatives immediately held a conference to discuss how to respond to this turn of events.

The arrest of so many metropolitan assembly members was unprecedented in the history of the Tokyo government. As a result, the government lost the trust of the people, and its reputation and authority were seriously undermined. Under these circumstances, any matters taken up by the assembly would not likely have the people's support. Above all, the Clean Government Party assembly members agreed, the wrongdoing and corruption in the government had to be exposed and measures taken to clean up and reform it.

The Clean Government representatives called for an extraordinary session of the assembly to discuss the following four resolutions: first, a call for the resignation of those representatives who had been arrested; second, a no-confidence motion to be brought against the assembly speaker; third, the submission of a motion to dissolve the assembly; and fourth, a no-confidence motion to be brought against the governor of Tokyo.

The third of these would mean the resignation of all metropolitan assembly members. Under Japanese law, local governing bodies could not be dissolved by a simple majority vote; unanimity was required. The assembly also could be dissolved by the Tokyo governor as a countermeasure against a vote of no confidence. One other way it could be dissolved was by a citizen recall.

The newspapers on the morning of April 17 extensively reported the arrest of the assembly speaker. Headlines blazoned "Metropolitan Assembly Gone Mad; Speaker Seat Can Be Had for a Price" and "Start Afresh Metropolitan Government! Corruption Reigns!" The general populace was outraged at the corruption, with public opinion growing for the assembly to dissolve and make a fresh start.

With the exception of the Japan Communist Party, a meeting was held among the secretary-generals of the major political parties, including the Liberal Democratic, the Japan Socialist and Clean Government parties. The ruling Liberal Democratic Party, to which all the arrested suspects belonged, did no more than call for the assembly speaker's resignation. The Socialist Party—the LDP's leading opposition—shared almost the same opinion as Clean Government but it did not take a clear stance on the issue of the assembly's dissolution. The reluctance of the LDP and the Socialists to accept this proposal must have stemmed from the fact that an election would likely result in a loss of seats for both parties.

The Clean Government Party assembly representatives, on the other hand, were ready to go to the people. They thus handed in their resignations to their party's secretary-general with a stronger resolve to dissolve the assembly.

SEEING the way the Liberal Democratic and Socialist parties ignored the sentiments of the people, Clean Government representatives were deeply struck by the thought that such behavior would permanently alienate the Tokyo Metropolitan Assembly from its constituents. They were determined not to permit that to happen.

On April 24, the Clean Government Party unavoidably turned to their last resort and decided to initiate a signature campaign for a citizen recall in an attempt to dissolve the assembly. This entailed collecting the signatures of more than one-third of the registered voters in Tokyo and then filing the petition with the Tokyo Election Administration Committee. A local referendum would then be held and a simple majority would determine the assembly's fate.

With this move on the part of the Clean Government Party, the Socialists finally set forth their own plan to dissolve the assembly by way of en masse resignation. They were against a recall, however, asserting that it would take too long. The Communist Party, which held only two seats, followed in the wake of the Clean Government Party and announced that it would implement a recall but refused to agree to dissolution of the assembly any other way.

At this point, the LDP was thrown into a panic. So many of its members had been arrested that if it continued to refuse a dissolution, criticism of the party was certain to mount. On April 28, the LDP consented and set about persuading its assembly members to resign, but several of them stubbornly refused to cooperate. Meanwhile, the two Communist Party representatives also adamantly maintained their opposition to resigning. The route of dissolving the assembly by this means was thus completely blocked.

The anger of the people boiled over; why did the assembly members cling so obsessively to their seats and refuse to take responsibility? In May, several citizens' organizations seeking a cleanup of the government were born, including the Metropolitan Government Reform Federation and the Metropolitan Government Citizen's Reform Committee, both made up of scholars, writers and cultural leaders.

At the same time, the Clean Government Party's recall movement received tremendous support from the people and spread quickly. Other organizations began to start their own movements, and on May 24 they all decided to join forces in an effort to recall the metropolitan assembly members. This united endeavor was promoted by the Clean Government, Communist and Democratic Socialist parties, four labor unions and nine citizens' groups. The Socialist Party, which originally opposed this move, also came on board.

The citizens' anger became a cry for recall that roared through the city like a mighty breaker.

ABOUT two weeks after the initiation of the recall movement by the Clean Government Party, the LDP Headquarters also began seriously considering methods of dissolving the metropolitan assembly. The LDP must have concluded that, after having more than a dozen of its members arrested, its failure to pull together a unanimous resignation and dissolve the assembly would have a major effect on the upcoming House of Councilors election in July.

In the eventuality that the holdout members couldn't be persuaded to resign, the governor of Tokyo could still enforce dissolution if the assembly were to pass a no-confidence motion against him. But the LDP, which maintained a majority in the assembly, wanted to avoid this. Since it had nominated the governor, such a motion would be a demonstration of the metropolitan government's incompetence. At the same time, if they stood by and did nothing, the recall petitions would continue to collect signatures.

A decision was thus made to present national legislation to the Diet that would allow local government bodies to dissolve themselves by a simple majority vote. On May 19, the last day of the extraordinary session of the Tokyo Metropolitan Assembly, the resignation of the arrested assembly speaker was approved. Following this, the Clean Government, Socialist and Communist parties placed a no-confidence motion against the Tokyo governor before the assembly, but it was voted down.

The session was then extended for one day, and after two o'clock in the morning on May 20, the Clean Government, Liberal Democrat, Socialist and Communist parties passed a joint resolution to dissolve the assembly. This move showed the assembly's intent, but it carried no legal force. It had been made on the assumption that the legislation in the Diet would be approved.

On June 1, a special exemption law concerning the dissolution of local government bodies passed, and two days later it was announced and put into effect. Though some saw the new law as an infringement on local autonomy by the national government, most saw it as an unavoidable emergency measure to reinstate the people's faith in the metropolitan assembly. The law required a quorum of three-fourths, and a four-fifths majority of that number for dissolution.

On June 14, an extraordinary plenary session of the Tokyo Metropolitan Assembly was convened and, in accord with the new law, a resolution dissolving the body was approved and carried out.

The Clean Government Party's struggle in starting the recall movement was based on its firm determination to repudiate all wrongdoing. This roused public opinion and served as a great force toward dissolution of the hotbed of political intrigue that the assembly had become.

Clean Government Party representatives fervently believed that it was up to them to restore trust in the Tokyo administration, for trust is the underpinning of government.

THE SOKA GAKKAI members, who had supported the Clean Government Party from the outset, were happier than anyone about the Clean Government representatives' dedication to fighting corruption. When the party announced its decision to resign en masse ahead of the other political parties, they cheered in their hearts.

While the other assembly representatives, wishing to hold on to their posts, feared dissolution and the election that would follow, their Clean Government counterparts unhesitatingly called for this move and placed utmost importance on redeeming the metropolitan assembly. This fact deeply impressed Soka Gakkai members, who were also struck by the Clean Government representatives' profound sense of responsibility and courage to take action without any thought of personal gain.

Seeing the efforts of the Clean Government Party in the process leading up to the assembly's dissolution convinced these members of the party's ability to clean up and reform Japanese government. The Clean Government representatives' commitment to eradicating corruption from government and regaining the trust of the people also gave Shin'ichi a true sense of satisfaction as the founder of the party.

On July 8, the official announcement for the Tokyo Metropolitan Assembly election was made. It would take place on the 23rd of that month. At the time of dissolution, the Clean Government Party had seventeen seats, but it decided to field twenty-three candidates in this election. It was a fierce contest. In the end, however, all twenty-three were elected, with nine of them garnering the most votes in their respective districts. This victory represented a great leap forward for the party.

The ruling LDP, in contrast, which had won sixty-nine seats out of 120 in the elections two years earlier, was sharply reduced to thirty-eight seats this time, far short of a majority. This result clearly indicated the people's desire for a clean and honest government.

Shin'ichi looked forward to the continued efforts of the Clean Government Party. But cleaning up the government and returning it to the hands of the people would not be easy. Without the elimination of money politics, corruption was sure to quickly resurface. It was bound to be a long struggle. In the words of German sociologist and economist Max Weber: "Politics is a strong and slow boring of hard boards. It takes both passion and perspective."[11]

Politics is a realm of greedy power seekers. Because there is such potential for personal gain, there are also various temptations and threats. Everything therefore comes down to what extent each politician is able to maintain their conviction, passion and guiding philosophy for serving the people.

SHIN'ICHI recalled the words of his mentor Josei Toda when the latter first sent fellow Soka Gakkai members into the world of politics: "Those who never forget my spirit will be able to carry out government reform and develop into great political leaders working for the people. If, however, they should become driven by self-interest, they will function as negative forces that destroy kosen-rufu.

"Going into politics is a huge gamble for both me and the Soka Gakkai. I am sending my disciples into that realm with the feeling of a lion pushing its cubs over the lip of a deep ravine to test their survival skills."

Contemplating the future of the Clean Government Party, Shin'ichi prayed long and hard that all Clean Government representatives would remain true to President Toda's intent and become stouthearted lions protecting the people.

With August came the traditional Soka Gakkai summer training course. This year's would take place at the head temple in four two-night, three-day sessions. They would begin on the 2nd, with the men's division session, followed by those for the young men's, women's and young women's divisions, in that order.

In addition, on August 10 and 11, training sessions would be held for the first time for representatives of the high school and junior high school divisions, the future of the Soka Gakkai. Some three hundred members from overseas would also participate in the fourth session of the course with the young women's division.

Shin'ichi determined to give his all to infuse firmly the hearts of his fellow members with the Soka Gakkai spirit. Having entered the essential phase, it was now time for the kosen-rufu movement to further develop its activities in all areas of society, aiming to actualize the Buddhist spirit of humanism. For that reason, it was crucial that all Soka Gakkai members return to the Gakkai spirit that is the prime point of everything.

The Soka Gakkai spirit is having the courage to discard the shallow and seek the profound. It is selfless dedication to propagating the Law even at the cost of one's life. It is to strive with unceasing devotion as taught in the Lotus Sutra. It is to exert oneself bravely and vigorously with passion and resolve. It is to possess the great power of perseverance that enables one to withstand any persecution with composure. It is to practice in accord with the Buddha's teaching, working for kosen-rufu just as the Daishonin instructs. It is the spirit of refuting the erroneous and revealing the true, giving no quarter to injustice. It is the path of the oneness of mentor and disciple, the very lineage of correct faith. It is the firm unity of many in body, one in mind. It is the spirit of showing others the same respect as one would a Buddha.

WHAT IS the best way to communicate this spirit? The answer is clear: through one's actions. One's spirit can only be transmitted by example.

At the summer training course, Shin'ichi poured his energy into encouraging the members who had come from all across Japan. He did everything he could, from posing for commemorative photos with them and conducting question-and-answer sessions, to holding guidance meetings into the early morning hours. He urged the men's division to remain dedicated to the Gohonzon throughout their lives, and called on the young men's division to be revolutionaries of the Mystic Law. He also told the members of the women's division that the Mystic Law is the wellspring of happiness and asked the young women to live a youth with no regrets.

Whenever Shin'ichi met members on the temple grounds, he wholeheartedly spoke with them. His actions were a perfect example of brave and vigorous exertion, of unceasing devotion and of showing others the same respect as one would a Buddha.

On August 8, Shin'ichi attended the fourth session of

the training course, at which he presented chapter and divisional flags to members visiting from overseas. Hisao Kajiyama, the young men's member who was studying at the Chinese University of Hong Kong, and Yoshiko Kato, who worked for a local airline, were also appointed leaders of the Hong Kong young men's and young women's divisions, respectively. Kazuko Ellick, leader of Hollywood Chapter in the United States, received a chapter flag, while the leaders of the Peru young men's division and of the young women's divisions of Los Angeles, Germany and Thailand received divisional flags.

Shin'ichi praised the seeking spirit of the overseas members in traveling so far to learn about Buddhism. He then announced that the Grand Main Temple slated for construction at the head temple would be equipped exclusively with Western-style seating, as was appropriate for a Buddhism intended for the entire world.

Shin'ichi further declared that the members gathered were Bodhisattvas of the Earth and courageous pioneers who would realize the happiness of billions of people around the world. He said: "I hope you will all continue to joyously pursue your Buddhist practice for the sake of your own happiness. I also hope you will cheerfully and boldly carry out faith in order to help those who are suffering. And I hope you will persevere in faith throughout your lives with pride and strong determination toward the realization of lasting world peace."

The overseas members took this guidance to heart, gaining a deeper understanding of their mission. Shin'ichi was keenly aware of the hardships many of these members had surmounted to come to Japan. It had undoubtedly been a huge challenge for them to save for their travel expenses and make arrangements to take time away from their work and families.

UNLIKE past summer training courses, no one had spent weeks traveling to Japan by ship this year. However, the group of eight members from France, led by Europe Headquarters Leader Eiji Kawasaki, had journeyed for eight days, transferring from train to airplane to ship.

They left Paris by train at half past two in the afternoon on July 25. After passing through Belgium, West Germany, East Germany and Poland, they arrived in the Soviet Union. At Brest, their first stop within the Soviet Union, they underwent a check of their passports, personal effects, money and vaccination papers. The officials inspected everything thoroughly, including underneath the beds in the sleeping cars.

The train then made its way through Smolensk and arrived in Moscow at 4:20 PM on July 27, where the members stayed overnight at a hotel. At half past eight the next morning, they flew across the Soviet Union to Khabarovsk aboard a small propeller plane. They reached Khabarovsk at half past four in the morning on July 29, where they transferred to another train that pulled into Nakhodka a little after eight o'clock in the morning on July 30. They then boarded a ship, and at just before five o'clock in the afternoon on August 1, the ship sailed into Yokohama Harbor.

Throughout the trip, the members chanted whenever they could, and while aboard ship they held study exams on the Daishonin's teachings. Of course, the trip would have been faster and much more comfortable had they flown by jet from Paris to Tokyo, but none of them could afford it.

Tears of emotion welled in Shin'ichi's eyes at the profound seeking spirit of these overseas members who had come to Japan in pursuit of the Law. He was certain that they would enjoy great happiness in the future and their countries would see tremendous development.

Seeking spirit is the root that absorbs the nourishment of faith and enables us to grow and develop. If that root is strong, wonderful flowers of happiness will bloom in our lives without fail.

Shin'ichi continued encouraging the overseas members with all his might on their departure from the head temple after completing the training course. As they each requested him to visit their countries, he said: "I will go. I promise to go and meet you there.

"This weekend, I am leaving for the United States. The essential phase is the age of worldwide kosen-rufu. Let us open the door to world peace together!"

A copper-colored Mount Fuji, bathed in summer sunlight, towered majestically in the clear blue sky.

Notes

1 Daisaku Ikeda, *A Youthful Diary: One Man's Journey from the Beginning of Faith to Worldwide Leadership for Peace* (Santa Monica, CA: World Tribune Press, 2000), p. 3.

2 Taisei Gakuin is now Fuji College.

3 Genkai Sea: Arm of the Sea of Japan located off the northern coast of Fukuoka and Saga prefectures in Kyushu.

4 Tottori Prefecture: Located in western Honshu and bounded by the Sea of Japan on the north, Hyogo Prefecture on the east, Okayama and Hiroshima prefectures on the south and Shimane Prefecture on the west. Two of its major cities are Tottori and Yonago.

5 *The Book of the Kindred Sayings*, translated by Mrs. Rhys Davids (Oxford: Pali Text Society, 1994), Part Five, p. 321.

6 Okubo Hikozaemon (1560–1639): A warrior who served the first three Tokugawa shoguns. His spirit and mettle in refusing to curry favor with the powers that be of his day earned him the love and respect of generations to come.

7 Tottori Sand Dunes: Located on the east coast of Tottori Prefecture, bordering the Japan Sea, the dunes have been a prominent feature of the area since ancient times.

8 Count Labedoyere, *Memoirs of the Public and Private Life of Napoleon Bonaparte* (London: George Virtue, 1827), vol. 1, p. 324.

9 Translated from French. Lieutenant-Colonel Ernest Picard, *Précepts et Jugements de Napoléon* (Paris: Berger-Levrault, 1913), p. 105.

10 The House of Councilors has a complex election system. Its members are elected for six-year terms and seats are divided into nationwide and prefectural districts. Elections for the House of Councilors are staggered so that half of the representatives in each district are up for reelection alternately every three years.

11 Max Weber, "Politics as Vocation" from *Essay in "Sociology,* translated by Hans H. Gerth and C. Wright Mills (New York: Oxford University Press, 1946).

Winds of Happiness

A LITTLE before eight o'clock in the morning on August 14, 1965, the telephone rang at the general director's desk at the Soka Gakkai Headquarters. Kiyoshi Jujo picked up the receiver and heard the tense voice of Director Akira Kuroki, who had departed for the United States the day before.

"Hello? General Director Jujo? It's Kuroki. I'm calling from Los Angeles. This place is like a war zone. Shops and stores are ablaze, and the airport is crawling with armed security police."

On the evening of August 11, the anger of residents in Los Angeles toward discrimination had exploded into a massive riot.

Meanwhile, a ceremony marking the start of construction on the first Nichiren Shoshu temple outside Japan, as well as an outdoor culture festival put on by Soka Gakkai members in the United States, were scheduled for the evening of August 15. The temple was to be built in Etiwanda, on the outskirts of Los Angeles, and Soka Gakkai President Shin'ichi Yamamoto and High Priest Nittatsu were set to travel there to participate in the events.

Kuroki had flown to Los Angeles with Vice General Director Ittetsu Okada and others as an advance party, leaving Japan on the morning of August 13. When he arrived, he found the upheaval to be much worse than anticipated.

"As we drove down the freeway," Kuroki continued to tell Jujo, "we could see flames rising from the city and there are reports of repeated looting. They say that the riots are going to spread."

The riots had been triggered when a white police officer stopped a twenty-one-year-old black youth in the Watts neighborhood of South Los Angeles on suspicion of drunk driving and began questioning him. The majority of Watts' residents were African-American. Apparently the police officer's manner was extremely arrogant. An argument ensued and when the officer tried to arrest the suspect, the young man's mother and brother joined the fray.

A crowd of Watts' residents started to gather. Soon, patrol cars were swarming to the scene, their sirens blaring. This incensed the crowd. African-American residents of Los Angeles had suffered discrimination for many years and the hurt and resentment they felt now exploded into a raging inferno.

People in the crowd began to throw stones at the patrol cars and police officers. They overturned cars and set fires. This was how the Watts Riots, which would last six days, began.

THE FOLLOWING day, August 12, normalcy seemed to have been restored to Los Angeles. But when evening came again, an African-American boy threw a stone at a white person and rioting erupted once more. Some seven thousand angry citizens continued throwing stones and wreaking havoc on into the night. Store windows of white shopkeepers were broken and looting resumed. Building walls were spray-painted with graffiti screaming, "Burn it down! Burn Watts down!"

Many buildings, including churches and shops, were set on fire. Some rioters looted guns. Flames scorched the sweltering summer night sky, a symbol of the deep-seated anger and resentment of black Americans against the discrimination they had suffered at the hands of whites.

Akira Kuroki arrived in Los Angeles on the morning of August 13. He waited for daybreak to come to Japan, and then called Kiyoshi Jujo. Jujo clutched the telephone receiver and listened to Kuroki's report, his brow wrinkled with concern.

"Given this development, I think there is a major safety issue with regard to the upcoming visit of President Yamamoto and his party," Kuroki remarked.

"I see," Jujo said. "I was just looking over the morning paper myself and worrying about what's going on there. At any rate, please let me know right away if there are any changes in the situation."

After receiving Kuroki's call, Jujo was troubled. President Yamamoto was scheduled to depart for Los Angeles with High Priest Nittatsu and his wife from Haneda Airport at ten o'clock that night. Jujo would be accompanying them, along with vice general directors Katsu Kiyohara and Hiroshi Izumida, and other leaders.

Jujo immediately met with several top leaders to discuss the matter. They were terribly concerned, and finally decided that, because of the potential danger the situation in Los Angeles posed, it would be best for President Yamamoto and the high priest to cancel that day's departure and postpone the trip. Jujo then headed for the president's office to convey their conclusion to Shin'ichi.

When Shin'ichi saw Jujo's expression, he said: "You've come to talk to me about the disturbance in Los Angeles, haven't you?"

"Yes, that's right," Jujo replied, unable to hide his surprise at President Yamamoto's penetrating grasp of his intent.

SHIN'ICHI smiled. "I had a feeling I'd be hearing from you at any moment."

With a serious expression, Jujo said: "The fact is, I just received a telephone call from Kuroki, who's in Los

Angeles as a member of the advance party. He told me about the situation over there and it seems pretty dangerous."

"I've been watching the reports on the riots in Los Angeles since this morning myself," Shin'ichi responded, "and I've been thinking quite a bit about it. You've come to tell me to cancel my trip, I suppose."

Hearing this, Jujo relaxed and nodded yes. "Even if we don't cancel it, we could at least postpone it. We can go as soon as the situation calms down and we know things are safe."

But Shin'ichi replied firmly: "No, I can't do that. I'm grateful for your concern and I understand your sentiments, but it's precisely because of the events in Los Angeles that I must go there and encourage the members right away.

"Now is the time for our fellow members in the United States to stand up. Why did this crisis occur? It's clearly because of the injustice of racial discrimination. The elimination of such discrimination is the earnest wish of African-Americans. And political leaders of good conscience have worked hard to see this realized. As a result, a law that protects the civil rights of African-Americans has finally been enacted.

"But why is it that discrimination persists, even though equality is now guaranteed by law? The reason is because discrimination resides in people's hearts. In order to become a nation of true freedom and democracy, the United States must move forward from reforming its laws to reforming the hearts of its people."

Shin'ichi's voice grew more forceful: "Only Buddhism

can realize such a reformation of people's hearts, a reformation of their inner state of life.

"August 15, Los Angeles time, the scheduled date of the outdoor culture festival there, marks the twentieth anniversary of the end of World War II. I want to make it the day when we lift high the banner of Buddhism, the philosophy of true happiness and peace for all people, over the land of America.

"Japan's defeat in the war was tragic and painful, but thanks to the United States, in its wake freedom of religion was instituted in Japan and the dawn of kosen-rufu arrived. For that, I want to show my gratitude to the United States."

IN THE TEN years since the Montgomery Bus Boycott sparked by the arrest of Rosa Parks in 1955, the American Civil Rights Movement had grown tremendously and legislation was being passed toward the complete eradication of racial discrimination. In particular, the Civil Rights Act was a significant milestone. This law had been submitted to the U.S. Senate by President John F. Kennedy in June 1963 and enacted in July 1964, after his assassination and during the presidency of his successor Lyndon B. Johnson.

The Civil Rights Act of 1964 clearly prohibited discrimination in public facilities, such as restaurants, theaters, parks and swimming pools, as well as in the workplace. It did not, however, sufficiently abolish discrimination in the area of voting rights.

In 1866, three years after President Abraham Lincoln had issued the Emancipation Proclamation that freed the slaves, the U.S. Congress passed the first Civil Rights Act, which guaranteed full civil rights to all Americans, regardless of race, color or previous condition of servitude. In 1870, the fifteenth amendment to the U.S. Constitution was passed, officially granting African-Americans the right to vote, but this stirred terrible anger and rebellion among the white community.

Lynchings of black Americans were frequent, and those who tried to exercise their voting rights were often forcefully prevented from doing so by whites. Many white Americans feared and loathed the idea of giving the right to vote to black Americans, whom they had dominated and scorned for so long. Some states thus restricted the voting rights of African-Americans by abusing the requirement that all eligible voters register with the local authorities.

In the southern state of Mississippi, for example, voter registration qualifications were made very strict, demanding that registrees provide tax payment certificates, read and explain passages from the Constitution and so forth. The rest of the southern states followed suit.

Some went so far as to require that voters possess a certain amount of land or property. Many African-Americans who had been forced to work as slaves and denied any education were illiterate, and very few of them owned land or anything else of value. It was in this way that the southern states attempted to legally restrict the voting rights of black Americans.

PRESIDENT JOHNSON signed the Voting Rights Act on August 6, 1965, just eight days before Shin'-ichi and his party were due to arrive in the United States. This law banned any qualification or prerequisite to voting, such as presenting tax certificates or taking literacy tests, that denied the right of any U.S. citizen to vote on account of race or color. It had been a long, slow process but steady progress was being made in passing legislation that outlawed racial discrimination. Even so, in actuality this injustice did not abate.

The suffering of African-Americans continued in various forms, with persisting discrimination in employment and promotion practices, as well as in housing and education. Employment discrimination was especially harsh. Finding work itself was difficult and very few people were able to pursue the field of their choice.

Furthermore, black Americans were paid less than white Americans doing the same job, and if business went bad, they were the first to be fired and the last to be rehired. Like a virus penetrating the finest filter, the prejudice residing in people's hearts slipped through the loopholes of the law and gave rise to the cruel act of racial discrimination.

Shin'ichi determined to spread the Buddhist philosophy of the equality of life throughout America in order to eradicate the discrimination inherent in people's lives. He and his traveling companions departed from Haneda Airport at ten o'clock in the evening on August 14, according to the original plan. It was eighteen years to the day that Shin'ichi had encountered Josei Toda at his first Soka Gakkai discussion meeting. In other words, this date was a pivotal prime point of his life. He thus boarded the plane holding the spirit of his late mentor firmly in his heart.

Flying via Honolulu, Hawaii, Shin'ichi and his party

arrived in Los Angeles after eight o'clock in the evening, local time. Because they had crossed the International Date Line, it was still August 14 in Los Angeles. Local members, whom Shin'ichi hadn't seen for some time, as well as Vice General Director Ittetsu Okada and others from the advance party, were at the airport to greet them.

As they made their way to the hotel, America Headquarters Leader Nagayasu Masaki updated Shin'ichi on the situation with the riots.

"Arson, shootings and looting continue in Watts," he reported. "In fact, they are saying that things may get worse."

ON AUGUST 13, the third day of the riots, the California National Guard was called out to assist the police. Yet by this time, two blocks of Watts had been destroyed. On August 14, the day Shin'ichi Yamamoto arrived in the United States, a state of emergency was declared. This allowed the authorities to take a variety of measures aimed at restoring law and order to the area. Among these, an eight o'clock evening curfew was imposed. Casualties nevertheless increased as the shooting continued between rioters and police. The flames of rage spread to other parts of the nation as well, setting off disturbances in Chicago and other cities.

On August 15, the day of the groundbreaking ceremony for the new temple in Etiwanda and the outdoor culture festival, the situation was still out of control. The governor of California declared the riots ended on August 16, the following day. For six days, the night skies of Los Angeles were red with the flames of anger and hatred.

More than ten thousand members of the National Guard, armed with rifles and machine guns, were mobilized to ease the disturbance. Some four thousand people were arrested, more than thirty were killed and nearly nine hundred suffered injuries.

Many African-Americans made serious efforts to mitigate the tensions and end the rioting. Some walked through the neighborhood trying to calm their agitated neighbors. Some risked their lives to rescue white people who were trapped inside collapsed buildings, while others assisted whites who were injured. Even in these terrible circumstances, the light of conscience and goodwill did not die out.

Dr. Martin Luther King Jr., civil rights leader and winner of the Nobel Peace Prize, condemned the riots as a self-destructive act that should be socially abhorred. Violence never solves anything. In fact, it only widens the gap between people, providing them with an excuse to reject each other and drive them into a corner. The Watts Riots did nothing but trample on the dream shared by Dr. King and many other African-Americans of a day when all Americans, regardless of race, could join hands as sisters and brothers.

IN THE MORNING on August 15, Shin'ichi and the other leaders accompanying him visited the Los Angeles Community Center in East Los Angeles. A police station was across the street from the center and police snipers could be seen on its roof. The staff at the center said that they had been stationed there for the last several days as a precaution because of the riots.

Shin'ichi did a solemn gongyo together with the members who had gathered at the community center, praying in earnest for the peace of American society and the safety of its people. Afterward, he accompanied High Priest Nittatsu and his wife to Disneyland, in Orange County, south of Los Angeles. Not wanting to take any chances of something happening to the high priest in the city, Shin'ichi thought it would be better to spend the day elsewhere. The day passed without event and that evening they went to the location in Etiwanda where the new temple was to be built.

After the ceremony, the first Soka Gakkai outdoor culture festival in the United States was held. When Shin'ichi and High Priest Nittatsu arrived at the site at half past six in the evening, they were greeted by a thunderous wave of applause from the five thousand members who assembled. A richly verdant lawn shimmered in the evening light. The members had worked hard amid their busy daily schedules to create this beautiful expanse of grass.

Shin'ichi proposed the construction of the Etiwanda temple on his previous trip to the United States, in 1963. The realization of this proposal was the long-cherished wish of the U.S. members. Nichiren Shoshu temples were meant to be citadels of the Law that led people to happiness and served as centers of activity for the advancement of kosen-rufu.

In the summer of 1964, the site for the temple was purchased in Etiwanda, San Bernardino County. At the time, it was an orange grove and vineyard and the land had to be readied for construction to begin. The members set to work from December of that year, spending their Sundays covered in dirt and grime as they toiled from morning until dusk. It was arduous labor that involved cutting down trees, removing the stumps with bulldozers, smoothing the earth with shovels and then planting grass on the site.

THE TEMPLE grounds covered an approximate area of 9.79 acres. Though some one hundred members participated each Sunday in the effort to clear the land for planting the lawn, completing the project took quite a long time. As summer approached the following year, 1965, blazing temperatures became a major obstacle. Also, the lawn that they eventually planted couldn't be watered during the day because the water would get too hot and damage it, so the work had to be done well after sundown. Nevertheless, the members joyfully exerted themselves in the task, joking that they were like owls.

The time came for the culture festival rehearsals to begin, but there was still work to do on preparing the grounds. Thus, in addition to rehearsing, the performers also pitched in on the endeavor. These noble efforts resulted in the creation of a beautiful, lush lawn.

The groundbreaking ceremony for the first overseas Nichiren Shoshu temple started at 6:45 PM. The summer sun gradually sank behind the ridges of the San Gabriel Mountains, and dusk settled in. A light wind gently blew.

The ceremony was conducted in both Japanese and English. Yasushi Morinaga, head of the Soka Gakkai Headquarters Overseas Bureau, moderated in Japanese, and Tad Fujikawa, vice leader of Los Angeles Chapter, moderated in English. First on the program was the recitation of the sutra and the chanting of Nam-myoho-renge-kyo, followed by the actual groundbreaking, a progress report and greetings from the general director and other leaders.

High Priest Nittatsu announced that the new temple would be named Enichi-zan Myoho-ji. Then, to enthusiastic applause, President Yamamoto took the podium. Shin'ichi said vigorously: "I'm so happy to see all of you, my fellow members in the United States, after so long. I've been told that, in the language of the original inhabitants of this land, Etiwanda means 'Hill of Wind.' What a wonderful and meaningful name that is. In the 'Record of the Orally Transmitted Teachings,' the Daishonin states: 'When Nichiren and his followers chant Nam-myoho-renge-kyo, they are like a great wind blowing' (GZ, 742). Our efforts to spread the Daishonin's Buddhism are indeed like a great wind blowing away all unhappiness and suffering.

"I earnestly hope that from this citadel of the Law in Etiwanda you will send the winds of kosen-rufu, of happiness and hope across this vast land of America. That is the true purpose of building this temple."

GAZING at the faces of the assembled members, Shin'ichi continued: "The Daishonin's Buddhism is for the entire world. In Japan, the Soka Gakkai has undergone all manner of attack and criticism but now it has developed into a force that will have a decisive impact on the direction of Japan's future. I am sure that we are also regarded with some prejudice here in the United States, but we mustn't let that defeat us. There will absolutely come a day when people will praise and appreciate the Daishonin's Buddhism.

"Exactly twenty years have passed since the end of the tragic Pacific War that created a miserable history of conflict between the United States and Japan. But when we ask whether either country has realized happiness and peace, we see that they are both still struggling with various issues. I wish to declare, however, that as the Daishonin's teaching spreads, the path to lasting peace will be opened and problems regarding nuclear weapons, racial discrimination and ethnic conflict will be resolved.

"That is because Nichiren Buddhism is the supreme philosophy that teaches that all people are equal and that, regardless of nationality, race or ethnic background, they possess the most noble and unsurpassed state of life of Buddhahood. Buddhism is the only path that leads to the actualization of enduring world peace and human happiness. I hope you will work together to make this goal a reality, moving forward with 'Friendship' as your motto.

"I close my remarks today with my sincere prayers for your good health and continued vigorous activities."

Joyous cheers and applause echoed in the night air.

After hearing Shin'ichi's remarks conveyed through English interpretation, one young African-American man in the crowd who was a member of the event staff clapped with exceptional enthusiasm. His name was Robert Michael, and he was a twenty-seven-year-old youth. Tears streamed down his cheeks as he vowed in his heart: "I will devote my life to kosen-rufu in order to realize genuine equality for all people in the United States. That is my mission!"

Robert had been discriminated against since childhood because of the color of his skin. He had been subjected to such cruel treatment that there were many times when he felt overcome by rage. His indignation and frustration caused him many sleepless nights.

ROBERT MICHAEL was born in a slum district of New York City. His father worked as the superintendent of an apartment building, but the pay was low and he had a difficult time supporting his wife and their five children. Often they didn't even have enough to eat.

It was when Robert started attending school that he first experienced discrimination. When he walked past the homes of white people as he made his way to and from school, white children sometimes threw stones and bottles at him. He would go home feeling hurt and confused but the cramped living space offered little solace.

His father, unable to lift the family out of poverty no matter how hard he worked, often got drunk in frustration and would yell at and strike Robert's mother. All of the yelling and screaming only aggravated the boy's emotional wounds.

Eventually Robert turned to God for comfort, but one day when he went to church the white pastor shouted angrily at him: "Go home! It's not the time for your kind to be here. Get out immediately!" Even the church had separate worship services for blacks and whites.

Filled with pent-up anger, Robert and his friends spent their days loitering around the neighborhood and getting into fights. He began stealing. With the money he robbed from people he bought marijuana and smoked it constantly, trying to forget the grim circumstances of his life.

He started carrying a gun, was arrested twice and dropped out of high school. When he was seventeen, he joined the army at his mother's urging but found that blatant discrimination between whites and blacks existed there, too. At the start, whites and blacks slept in separate buildings and black recruits were frequently assigned the more dangerous tasks.

In the southern town where Robert was stationed, he accidentally entered a public lavatory restricted to whites and was harshly reprimanded by a white police officer. His life-state spiraled downward.

Robert Michael first encountered Buddhism in June 1958, while stationed in Japan. A friend he made there told him about the Soka Gakkai. Impressed by the confident assurance that his prayers were certain to be answered if he practiced, he decided to join. As he continued chanting Nam-myoho-renge-kyo, he began to experience the benefits of faith. Most of all, however, he felt that his eyes had been opened by the Buddhist teaching that all people equally possess the wonderful state of life of Buddhahood and can find true happiness.

AFTER he was discharged from the army, Robert found a job at a construction-related company in Los Angeles and embarked on a new life. He also continued to be earnestly involved in Soka Gakkai activities. In that realm of faith, he found that indeed there was no racial discrimination—whether African-American, Mexican-American or Japanese-American, all members were completely equal. Soka Gakkai meetings exuded a warmth surpassing family bonds, filled with sincere dialogue, encouragement and friendship. Robert began to see the brilliant light of humanism shining through the darkness that had shrouded his life up until then.

After participating in Gakkai activities for some time, Robert noticed a tremendous change taking place in himself. His views of white people, whom he had hated so fiercely, were transforming. All the animosity he had felt toward those who were prejudiced against blacks grew into pity.

He thought to himself: "If everyone could believe in the great Buddhist principle that all people possess the life-state of Buddhahood, African-Americans would surely feel more confident and white people would surely rid themselves of their prejudiced views. Then both sides would come together based on mutual trust and respect, just as people do in the Soka Gakkai. That's it! I'm going to devote my life to kosen-rufu for that purpose."

With this profound determination, Robert threw himself wholeheartedly into sharing Buddhism with others. He talked to everyone he could, black and white alike. At first no one would listen but gradually people he spoke with started to practice. He sensed a circle of human harmony, transcending the divisions of race, expanding around him.

Robert felt terrible regret about the rioting in Watts. He understood well the pain, anger and frustration of African-Americans, who had suffered discrimination for so long. But he also knew that attacking white people and burning down the neighborhood would change nothing—if anything, it would only bring further suffering to the black community. The failure of Watts' residents to understand this greatly disturbed him.

He was also deeply grateful to President Yamamoto for visiting Los Angeles at such a critical time. Profoundly struck by Shin'ichi's speech at the groundbreaking ceremony, in which he called for an end to racial discrimination, Robert renewed his determination to fulfill his mission.

AFTER the groundbreaking ceremony, a new organizational lineup and leadership appointments were announced, followed by the return of chapter flags by the old leaders and their bestowal on the new ones. Up to this time, America Headquarters had been comprised of two general chapters but with the birth of Hawaii

General Chapter and others, there were now six in total.

The organization also showed dramatic growth with an increase in chapters from fourteen to twenty-three. In addition, Yasushi Muto, who had been the young men's division leader for North America, was appointed vice leader of the America Headquarters. Muto had been working for the Overseas Bureau of the Soka Gakkai Headquarters in Japan but in July of the previous year, 1964, President Yamamoto had sent him to the United States to strengthen the organization.

About six months prior to that, Shin'ichi invited Overseas Bureau staff members to dinner, and it was then that he sounded out Muto about transferring him.

"Mr. Muto," Shin'ichi said, "I would like you to go to the United States. The organization there needs an administrative officer. America is an important base for worldwide kosen-rufu. I would like you to go there and help Headquarters Leader Masaki. How about it?"

Muto replied without hesitation: "Certainly. I'm ready to go anywhere for the sake of kosen-rufu. I promise to do my best!"

Shin'ichi was pleased by Muto's determination. It brimmed with the fundamental spirit of a Headquarters staff to dedicate one's life to kosen-rufu. Muto was a quiet, reliable young man. Shin'ichi felt that his steady character was ideal for the person who would work behind the scenes as the administrative officer for the American organization, which was certain to see rapid development.

"You're the first Headquarters staff to be sent overseas," Shin'ichi said to Muto. "I hope that, rather than thinking of this as a temporary assignment, you'll go with the intention of supporting our members in the United States and working for kosen-rufu there until the day you die.

"Without such a commitment, you'll soon start complaining about this and that and moaning about wanting to return to Japan. You'll also start lording your position over others and placing top priority on your own interests. If that happens, it goes without saying that you won't be able to win the trust of American people, and they probably won't want to have anything to do with you. In that case, you will have failed as both a leader of kosen-rufu and a Soka Gakkai Headquarters staff. What's more, you will become a function of the devilish nature that seeks to destroy the organization of kosen-rufu.

"Your innermost determination is what matters. You must be firmly determined to dedicate your life to kosen-rufu."

"I am!" Muto replied, his voice ringing with energy and resolve.

SHIN'ICHI was also concerned about helping Muto, who was still single, find a marriage partner. He asked General Director Kiyoshi Jujo to support the young man in any way he could. Jujo eventually introduced Muto to Chikako Hayashida, a leader of the young women's division in the United States. The two got married in Japan and left for the States soon after.

Because the Soka Gakkai was already registered in the United States as a religious corporation, Muto was required to resign from his position at the Soka Gakkai Headquarters in Japan and be rehired as an employee of the American organization. Shin'ichi strongly hoped that, with Muto's appointment as vice leader of the America Headquarters, the young man would also assist Headquarters Leader Masaki in organizational matters and demonstrate his abilities to the fullest.

After the chapter flags had been distributed, Shin'ichi took his leave of the event and went to rest for a while in a trailer that had been set up for that purpose on the grounds. The sky over Etiwanda was now dark and filled with sparkling stars. The grounds were illuminated and the green lawn glimmered in the light, waiting for the start of the first Soka Gakkai outdoor culture festival to be held in America.

At that moment, the festival organizers were engaged in a tense discussion. The riots in Watts had resulted in delays or cancellations of buses and many of the festival participants had not yet arrived. Members with cars were rushing back and forth ferrying them to Etiwanda from Los Angeles but this wasn't proving sufficient. Meanwhile, opening time was fast approaching.

Akira Kuroki, who was in charge of the culture festival, came to a decision: "We'll have to hold the festival with those members present now. We can rearrange the groups to compensate for those that are lacking too many of their performers."

At this point, it was the only alternative. The new arrangements were made in a frenzy of last-minute activity. Even the way the performers made their entry was suddenly altered. But with everyone cooperating closely in the spirit of many in body, one in mind, the changes were swiftly and successfully carried out.

The true value of unity is demonstrated in emergency situations. Though the various program participants were slightly thrown off guard by the unexpected changes, they continued to confirm the new plan with each other as they waited for the festival to begin.

Shortly after eight o'clock in the evening, the culture festival opened to thunderous applause.

THE ENTRANCE procession began with the Brass Band appearing first, wearing feathered hats and red uniforms like those worn by honor guards. The Fife and Drum Corps followed, clad in scarlet jackets and white skirts with matching berets. They marched out onto the field vigorously playing Soka Gakkai songs. The spectators sitting in the stands that had been erected on the grounds erupted in applause.

The Brass Band had been started by a group of young men's members who had volunteered to perform at an all-America general meeting held in Chicago two years earlier in 1963. A little more than six months later, a proposal was made to start a Fife and Drum Corps in the young women's division. This was right after it was decided that representative members from the United States would travel to Japan to participate in the dedication ceremony for the head temple's Grand Reception Hall, which had been constructed and donated by the Soka Gakkai. Among this contingent, a group of Fife and Drum Corps members would also be sent to perform at the ceremony to show America's development as well as to encourage the participants.

But there was no one in the United States young

women's division at the time who could give musical instruction. In the end, an experienced drummer in the young men's division Brass Band agreed to teach the young women how to play the drums, and thus the young women's division drum corps was born. Among them, five members went to Japan in April that year—in 1964—to attend the dedication ceremony.

The leader of the group was a young woman named Miyuki Inohashi. Miyuki was a third-generation Japanese-American. After World War II, the family returned to Japan and she and her mother joined the Soka Gakkai in Hiroshima in 1957. Two years later, the family went back to the United States and Miyuki's mother exerted herself in faith steadily and diligently as a district leader.

Miyuki and her mother often talked about going to Japan in the year commemorating the seventh memorial of President Toda's death. With that dream firmly in mind, they both dedicated themselves wholeheartedly to laying the foundation for kosen-rufu in America.

Then, in February 1964, Miyuki's mother had a stroke and died. Miyuki went to Japan for the dedication ceremony carrying her big drum and an urn containing her mother's ashes, which she planned to intern there. She spoke silently to her mother: "Mom, I'm here in Japan, where we promised to go together. I promise to work hard enough for both of us from now on." With this pledge in her heart, Miyuki was determined to give her all to her drum performance.

THE AMERICAN young women's division drum corps gave its first performance in Japan on their arrival at Tokyo's Haneda Airport. Their vigorous drumming dispelled the tiredness of the long journey of their fellow members who had traveled with them from the States. When Shin'ichi heard of the arrival of these young women, he suggested that they perform together with the Japanese young women's division Fife and Drum Corps members, who were also set to perform at the dedication ceremony. He also presented the five Americans with uniforms matching the ones that would be worn by their Japanese counterparts for the occasion. They were overjoyed.

But it was very difficult for the American members, who couldn't even read music properly, to perform the pieces that had been selected by the Japanese Fife and Drum Corps. They did their best to learn but there simply wasn't enough time, so it was finally decided that they would march in the parade just carrying their drums without playing. President Yamamoto sent them encouraging words and presented them with five fifes.

Miyuki Inohashi and the other young women renewed their determination, vowing to become a world-class fife and drum corps and someday perform before President Yamamoto. After returning to the United States, they practiced diligently and recruited members for the corps. But even though their membership increased, they only had the five fifes given to them by President Yamamoto. They couldn't afford to buy any themselves, so at first, some of them practiced using soft drink bottles as their instruments.

At the start of 1965, it was decided that the first outdoor culture festival would be held in Etiwanda that

August. The Fife and Drum Corps rehearsals picked up steam. And then President Yamamoto sent another ten fifes for the corps' members. The corps grew rapidly, and managing to acquire additional instruments, nearly forty members performed at the outdoor culture festival. Aside from the five uniforms given to them by President Yamamoto, they had all made their own scarlet jackets and white skirts.

As the drum majorette, Miyuki Inohashi stood proudly at the front of the corps. A huge smile filled with joy and excitement spread across her face. Following the entrance of the Fife and Drum Corps, representatives of the young men's and young women's divisions, representing each of the chapters in America Headquarters, marched out onto the field.

THE CHAPTER representatives each carried placards indicating their respective area, such as Seattle and New York. The crowd applauded vigorously.

At the time, the America Headquarters included Mexico and Canada, and many members from those two nations also participated in the festival. After the dramatic entrance of the thirteen-hundred-member procession, the young women's division gave a splendid dance performance to the accompaniment of a women's division chorus from the western part of the United States. Next came a gymnastics display by two hundred young men's members. Under the floodlights, the white of their uniforms stood out in vivid contrast to the green of the field.

Blue and yellow flags began fluttering across the field like waves, eventually taking shape as several Japanese folding fans created by teams of five young men each. They were a diverse group of youth, with people of different ethnic backgrounds working together in close teamwork to put on a truly wonderful, artistic performance. For their finale, the young men's division members constructed several four-tier human pyramids, and then in a flash the pyramids came down and their performance concluded.

The young men's performance shone with noble bonds of trust and human harmony transcending all differences. One journalist covering the event referred to it as "a perfect example of true peace and equality for humankind."

Everyone came together across the barriers of race to pray for the success of the outdoor culture festival and to make their rehearsals fruitful. When the trouble broke out in Watts, members in other areas, concerned about the safety of their fellow members living in the riot zone, opened their homes to them and offered them rides to and from rehearsals. This love and friendship resulted in a splendidly unified performance.

In August 1963, during the march on Washington to commemorate the 100th anniversary of the Emancipation Proclamation, Dr. Martin Luther King Jr. had delivered his famous "I Have a Dream" speech from the steps of the Lincoln Memorial. Dr. King had proclaimed: "I have a dream that one day on the red hills of Georgia the sons of former slaves and the sons of former slave-owners will be able to sit down together at the table of brotherhood."[1]

Now, at the outdoor culture festival, Robert Michael stood watching the performances as a member of the event staff. He thought to himself, "We, the Soka Gakkai, are making Dr. King's dream a reality. How amazing this is! We are definitely going to change American society!"

NEXT on the festival program were performances of beautiful Japanese folk songs by members of the women's division. Two hundred women's chapter representatives from the eastern part of the United States performed two numbers and three hundred from the west performed another. Wearing matching summer kimonos and carrying large parasols, everyone did their best to present the Japanese folk pieces. Their costumes all were handmade by the members.

A number of potted palm trees were then carried out

onto the field to serve as the set for a hula dance performed by 250 members of Hawaii General Chapter. The Hawaiian members had chartered two planes and flown across the Pacific in high spirits to participate in the festival. Hula dancers filled the field, swaying in rhythm to the strains of Hawaiian guitars like so many colorful flowers, their green and white costumes accentuated by the leis worn around their necks.

This was followed by a traditional Hawaiian dance of bravery that involved twirling flaming swords. The sweat on the dancers' bodies sparkled under the lights. Shin'ichi Yamamoto leaned forward in his seat and enthusiastically applauded these members who had come from so far away.

Next was a Japanese dance called "Kuroda Bushi,"[2] performed by three hundred members of the Los Angeles women's division. Shin'ichi said to the leaders accompanying him: "Why don't you go and sing along with them? They'll love it."

General Director Kiyoshi Jujo, vice general directors Hiroshi Izumida and Katsu Kiyohara and the other leaders in Shin'ichi's party then went up to the microphone and began singing "Kuroda Bushi" enthusiastically:

If you drink sake, drink it down in one gulp…

With that, the Japanese Americans sitting in the stands also started to sing along. Members who didn't know the lyrics joyously clapped to the rhythm and the dancing on the field became livelier.

It was a wonderful finale that brought the Japanese

leaders, the performers and the audience together as one. The cheerful singing echoed in the night sky over Etiwanda, the "Hill of Wind" of happiness. This marked the end of the outdoor culture festival and President Yamamoto and High Priest Nittatsu left the festival to a great chorus of the Soka Gakkai's "Song of Worldwide Kosen-rufu."

On the way to the car, Shin'ichi stopped to offer encouragement and shake hands with each of the youthful event staff members he encountered, saying, "Thank you! You did a fine job!"

WHILE Shin'ichi was shaking hands with staff members, a young African-American man rushed up to him and extended his hand. Shin'ichi grasped it and the youth began speaking excitedly. Nagayasu Masaki, who was standing nearby, interpreted.

"President Yamamoto, thank you so much for coming to the United States at this dangerous time when riots are happening in Watts. Your actions have shown me what courage really is. You also have taught me the spirit of a leader dedicated to realizing peace for all people. My own courage has increased a hundredfold. Someday we will build, through our own efforts, a peaceful and harmonious society free of racial conflict in America. Please rest assured of that." Tears streaked the young man's face.

Shin'ichi replied: "Thank you! If you have solidified your resolve to achieve kosen-rufu, I can safely say that my purpose in coming to this country has been fulfilled. It's enough for a single individual, for you, to rise up with the same spirit as me. Just as a great river begins from a single drop, a great river of peace in America will begin from you. I entrust America to you."

The young man clutched Shin'ichi's hand in both of his and shook it firmly. Both men's eyes shone with emotion.

On this day, August 15, the rioting in Watts continued and armed police and the California National Guard were called in to quell the situation. It wasn't until the following day that the governor of California declared the riots ended.

On the evening of August 16, Shin'ichi went to the Los Angeles Community Center and did gongyo with the new leaders who had been appointed the day before and other local members. Shin'ichi prayed in earnest to eradicate the devilish function of the human heart that causes people to discriminate against others.

After gongyo, Shin'ichi spoke to the members: "The members of America Headquarters have opened a new chapter in the history of kosen-rufu with this first culture festival outside Japan. You have made a tremendous achievement that is being praised by members around the world. I deeply appreciate your hard work. Congratulations.

"Please be aware that this accomplishment has opened a new frontier in your lives and a new page of history leading to happiness.

"WHY did we hold a culture festival at this time? What was its purpose? Of course, one of the main goals was to show the American people a true picture of the Soka Gakkai and to promote understanding of our organization. But the most important reason was for each of you to create happy lives.

"Various challenges surrounded this culture festival. First you had to clear the land, and then, while preparing for the groundbreaking ceremony for the new temple, you also had to rehearse for the festival itself. Some of you probably considered quitting halfway through. But you fought against that desire, chanted wholeheartedly and worked hard to fulfill your responsibilities.

"First and foremost, all your prayers and the tireless efforts and contributions you made toward laying this important foundation in our movement for kosen-rufu will without fail turn into wonderful benefit and good fortune. This is the power of the Mystic Law of cause and effect. In addition, one by one, you broke through the wall of obstacles and of limitations that makes things seem impossible in order to ensure the success of the culture festival. As a result, I believe you were able to acquire confidence and unshakable conviction in faith. That is most important.

"Life is full of trials. Sometimes we fall ill and sometimes we hit deadlocks in our work. Overcoming these difficulties with composure requires strengthening our life force. We need to have firm conviction in faith, which serves as a spiritual support.

"Through pouring your energies into this culture festival and overcoming all manner of hardship based on prayer, I imagine you have come to understand the truth that there is no stagnation in Buddhism. The more you experience this, the more you will establish unwavering faith and the more you will forge a strong self that nothing can defeat.

"Soka Gakkai activities are the arena where we do this. So are culture festivals. In other words, activities exist to enable us to lay the groundwork for our own happiness."

When Nagayasu Masaki had finished interpreting Shin'ichi's remarks, the members broke into applause. It was an expression of their joy at comprehending fully the significance of Gakkai activities. Shin'ichi then turned to South America Headquarters Leader Yasuhiro Saiki, who was present, and said: "Next year I will visit Brazil. Let's hold a culture festival there, too."

YASUHIRO SAIKI and his wife Setsuko stood up and replied in unison: "We'll do our best!"

In December 1962, Yasuhiro was appointed leader of

the young men's division in South America when the trading company he worked for sent him to São Paulo, Brazil. He had joined the Soka Gakkai at the beginning of September that same year, at the introduction of Setsuko.

The couple had wed in August 1956, but on the evening of their wedding day Setsuko experienced a severe asthma attack. After that, she suffered from attacks several times a day. Two months later, Yasuhiro's company sent him to South America for the first time. He was terribly reluctant to leave his wife behind in Japan, given her condition.

Setsuko had suffered from asthma since she was a child. She joined the Soka Gakkai in her hometown of Kyoto, in the autumn of 1955, following the example of her mother, who had joined out of her urgent wish to see her daughter cured.

After becoming a member, Setsuko exerted herself wholeheartedly in faith and battled against her illness. As a member of the young women's division, she actively participated in the Osaka Campaign of 1956, which under Shin'ichi's leadership, Osaka Chapter achieved the momentous result of 11,111 new member-households in a single month. The encouragement she received from Shin'ichi then was a huge support for her faith.

In the spring of 1956, it seemed as if Setsuko had conquered her asthma, but then it returned on the evening of her wedding day. As she sent Yasuhiro off to his post in South America, she made a profound determination. "This illness is my karma," she thought. "I have no other choice but to cure it through faith. I will definitely overcome this illness and greet my husband in good health when he returns."

Setsuko chanted earnestly and threw herself into Soka Gakkai activities. When Yasuhiro's three-year overseas assignment was completed and he returned to Japan, he was greeted by the smile of a beautiful, cheerful and healthy Setsuko. Seeing this actual proof, Yasuhiro became interested in the organization and joined at his wife's encouragement in September 1962. Around that time, Yasuhiro's company decided to send him back to Brazil, once again without Setsuko. Aiming to learn as much as he could about faith while he was still in Japan, he began to participate energetically in Gakkai activities. And he spoke to others about Buddhism on a daily basis.

YASUHIRO SAIKI applied himself diligently to studying the teachings of Nichiren Buddhism. A month before he returned to Brazil, he met with Shin'ichi at the *Seikyo Shimbun* offices in Tokyo. Yasuhiro was a youth who had just joined the Soka Gakkai but knowing that he was about to go to Brazil, Shin'ichi encouraged him with all his might: "The important thing is that you do your absolute best at work and become a person who is trusted by your coworkers. Those efforts will contribute greatly to kosen-rufu as well."

On the spot, Shin'ichi decided to appoint Yasuhiro the young men's leader of South America. It was an unprecedented and bold move. Shin'ichi placed high hopes on Yasuhiro's future potential.

At the airport on the day of Yasuhiro's departure, the young man received a handwritten card from Shin'ichi that read: "There is no strategy superior to the Lotus Sutra. Shin'ichi." Engraving these words in his heart, Yasuhiro began his valiant struggle in Brazil. He worked twice as hard as anyone else at his company and he came to be trusted greatly by the Soka Gakkai members in the country. When he first arrived in Brazil, the young men's division had only about one hundred members but in two years it grew to between five hundred to six hundred.

Then Yasuhiro received orders from his company to return to Japan. He gave serious thought to this new development. Realizing that if he were to return to Japan he could not accomplish his dream of kosen-rufu in South America, he resolved: "I simply can't leave Brazil. What will happen to the youth here if I do? I will quit my job instead and stay here and work for kosen-rufu until the day I die."

Yasuhiro had graduated from the Tokyo University of Foreign Studies and joined a large trading company, following the elite track in Japanese society. As an employee there, he had a bright future. But he was beginning to see that he had a mission as a human being that was far greater and more important than such personal prosperity and success.

He returned to Japan at the end of 1964 and handed in his resignation. He had both the confidence and the ability to make a living as an independent businessman. His boss tried to persuade him to stay on but Yasuhiro had made up his mind.

After resigning, Yasuhiro went to the Soka Gakkai Headquarters to see President Yamamoto. Shin'ichi warmly greeted him.

WHEN Shin'ichi heard Yasuhiro's story, he smiled and replied: "I see. Please follow your heart. I will support you 100 percent. When you return to Brazil this time, take your family with you and do your best, with the intention of staying there permanently."

At the December 1964 Soka Gakkai Headquarters Leaders Meeting, Yasuhiro and his wife, Setsuko, were appointed the leaders of South America Headquarters. In mid-January 1965, the couple went to Brazil, and for the next eight months Yasuhiro traveled all over South America in his new capacity as the central leader. He would often take bus trips as long as twenty or thirty hours one way to visit and encourage members. As a result, the organization in Brazil and the rest of South America began to make great strides.

A new page of history in the kosen-rufu movement is bound to open in places where people exert themselves to the fullest. Shin'ichi invited the Saikis to the Etiwanda Culture Festival because he wanted to propose that a culture festival take place in Brazil as well.

On August 17, Shin'ichi flew to Mexico with High Priest Nittatsu. He wished to encourage the members of Mexico Chapter, which had been established just five months earlier, as well as to look for building materials for the Grand Main Temple. Accompanying them were vice general directors Kiyoshi Jujo and Katsu Kiyohara, Yasuhiro and Setsuko Saiki of the South America Headquarters and Nagayasu Masaki of the America Headquarters. In addition, Yasushi Morinaga, head of the Soka Gakkai Overseas Bureau, and Kiyoko Yamanishi, leader of the North America young women's division, had arrived in Mexico a day earlier as an advance party ahead of Shin'ichi and the others.

Yamanishi had been a vice leader of the young women's division of the Shikoku region in Japan, but after getting married her husband had been transferred to Mexico by the trading company he worked for. Thus, in November 1963, she went with him as the leader of the young women's division in Central America.

When Emiko Haruyama, the former North America young women's division leader, returned to Japan in August of the following year, Yamanishi was appointed as her successor. With this change, the Central America young women's division merged with its North America counterpart. Soon after that, because of circumstances related to her husband's job, Yamanishi moved to California, very near the border with Mexico. Even after the move, she continued to look after the members in Mexico.

Shin'ichi and his party departed from Los Angeles airport a little past noon. As the aircraft approached Mexico City, situated some 7,349 feet above sea level, Shin'ichi gazed down at the city and thought of Josei Toda.

FOR SHIN'ICHI, this visit to Mexico had special significance. Mexico was a country that Toda had actually dreamt about and longed to visit.

At the end of March 1958, Shin'ichi went to see his mentor, whose ill health was keeping him on a futon on the second floor of the Rikyo-bo lodging at the head temple. This was during a pilgrimage commemorating the completion of the Grand Lecture Hall, which had been built and donated to the head temple by the Soka Gakkai. When Shin'ichi entered the room, Toda began to speak softly: "Shin'ichi, yesterday I dreamt I went to Mexico. They were all waiting. Everyone was waiting. They were all seeking Nichiren Daishonin's Buddhism. I want to go—to travel the world on a journey for kosen-rufu. Shin'ichi, the world is your challenge; it is your true stage. It is a vast world."

Toda reached his hand out from beneath the covers and Shin'ichi silently grasped it in his own. Then, as if squeezing out every last ounce of his energy, Toda said: "Shin'ichi, you must live! You must live as long as you can and travel the globe!"

These words continued to echo within Shin'ichi's heart, ever rousing a new flame of a fighting spirit. Toda had an especially strong interest in Mexico. This was probably because the first organized emigration of Japanese people to Latin America had been to that country.[3]

Toda's interest in Mexico was also piqued by the fact that first Soka Gakkai president Tsunesaburo Makiguchi had mentioned Mexico in his *Jinsei Chirigaku* (The Geography of Human Life), citing it as an example of a nation where mountains function as the sources of water, the regulators of the soil and the moderators of the climate.

Toda read many books on Mexico and often shared his thoughts about it with Shin'ichi. In addition, he would often ask Fumiko Haruki—Kansai General Chapter Leader Seiichiro Haruki's wife, who had spent her childhood years in Mexico because of her father's work in trade—about the lifestyle and customs of Mexico. He would listen happily to her accounts with a smile on his face.

IN THE SUMMER of 1957, shortly before his death, Josei Toda heard from an acquaintance that the well-known scholar of Zen Buddhism Daisetsu Suzuki had been to Mexico that year for the second time and lectured at a university there in an effort to spread the teachings of Zen. Toda remarked in an irritated tone: "That's no good. It will be a terrible shame if people of Mexico do not learn of Nichiren Daishonin's Buddhism, the true teaching of Buddhism for all people. If someone doesn't bring the correct teaching to Mexico, genuine happiness will not be realized for the people there."

Shin'ichi and his party arrived in the capital of Mexico City after four o'clock in the afternoon local time. Around a dozen local members, including Mexico Chapter Leader Raul Iwadate, were at the airport to greet them. Iwadate was a stout gentleman in his mid-sixties. When he went to Japan five months earlier for the three-million-member general pilgrimage to celebrate the completion of the Grand Reception Hall, Mexico Chapter was established and he was appointed its leader.

Iwadate had participated in the outdoor culture festival at Etiwanda in the United States but returned to Mexico early to prepare for the arrival of Shin'ichi and the others. With flushed cheeks, he welcomed Shin'ichi enthusiastically.

Shin'ichi shook Iwadate's hand firmly, and said: "Thank you for everything. I have always wanted to visit

Mexico because it was the cherished wish of Mr. Toda, who actually dreamt about doing so himself. Now we have a chapter in Mexico and I am able to walk on Mexican soil and meet all of you in my mentor's place. I am overwhelmed when I think how happy Mr. Toda must be right now!

"Let's raise the curtain on a new stage of kosen-rufu in Mexico!"

Tears filled Iwadate's eyes. He was a prominent figure in Mexican society. He had come to the country in 1923, leaving Japan with a grand and youthful dream of seeing the world. He headed for Mexico with the thought that he might spend a year or two there but it became the stage upon which his entire life would unfold.

AFTER arriving in Mexico, Raul Iwadate decided to try and establish himself in business. He started with an outdoor fruit stall, carefully saving his earnings until he could open a grocery store. His store was a success and he worked very hard, regretting only that there weren't more hours in the day. The store had an excellent reputation, but someone perhaps envious of his success set fire to it.

Iwadate refused to let this setback discourage him. He started over again and even expanded his business. In addition to a grocery store, he bought a sulfur mine and operated a farm, eventually employing more than five hundred people. He had become one of the most successful Japanese immigrants in Mexico.

But World War II cast a dark shadow over Iwadate's life. As an Allied nation, Mexico declared war on Japan and the assets of Japanese immigrants were frozen by the government. Even so, Iwadate was not defeated. When the war was over, he immediately got back on his feet and started another grocery store. But a third stroke of bad luck came his way. He was cheated and forced to sell his land for almost nothing. This left him with a huge debt. In addition, his health, which had been strong until then, suddenly collapsed. His blood pressure became abnormally high and his poor physical condition caused him to spend a great deal of time in bed. From his sickbed, he heard those around him make half-sympathetic, half-scornful remarks about his dim prospects.

He, too, began to feel that he might not ever make a comeback and his spirit waned. At a complete loss, he thought to himself: "Whenever I start to believe I have succeeded, it seems I fall into one kind of trap or another and become stuck. No matter how much effort I make my labors fail to come to fruition. Why does this always happen to me?"

He decided to send a letter explaining his situation to a relative in Tokyo whom he always trusted. This relative happened to be a Soka Gakkai member. Iwadate soon received copies of the *Seikyo Shimbun* newspaper and *The Daibyakurenge* study journal from this relative. He read the guidance of President Yamamoto, the editorials and the explanations of Buddhist teachings in the publications as if devouring them, and felt a profound resonance with the concepts of *karma* and *good fortune*.

IWADATE thought deeply about his life: "I've always done my absolute best and lived true to my beliefs.

I've worked hard from morning to night and have striven to be socially conscious. I've put forth more effort than most. However, though different people might try equally hard, they don't necessarily all succeed. But among those who do, some remain successful over the long term, while others, like me, become tripped up by unanticipated problems. What accounts for this discrepancy? Do people actually have a destiny, a fate?"

President Yamamoto's guidance and the explanations of Buddhist teachings appearing in the *Seikyo Shimbun* addressed these questions squarely. Iwadate was strongly drawn to the assertion that Nichiren Buddhism taught how to change one's karma. It was a ray of hope in the darkness that shrouded his life.

In June 1963, Iwadate began to practice of his own accord. He did gongyo and chanted Nam-myoho-renge-kyo just as the letters he received from his relative in Japan instructed, and also made an effort to share Buddhism with others. His extremely high blood pressure gradually began to normalize and he recognized this as his first benefit of taking faith.

Two months after Iwadate started chanting, a discussion meeting was held in a waiting area at the Mexico City Airport led by Vice General Director Seiichiro Haruki and Director Hiroshi Yamagiwa, who were on a stopover in Mexico. Eight members from five households gathered and the first Soka Gakkai group was established in Mexico with Iwadate's appointment as the group leader.

In spite of this leadership responsibility, Iwadate's understanding of Buddhism at this stage was still limited. In addition, there were no senior leaders in Mexico, so there was no one from whom he could receive direct guidance in faith. The activities of the new group thus began with the *Seikyo Shimbun* as their only support. Iwadate read the newspaper from beginning to end, nearly memorizing every word. He also passed it around to other members who could read Japanese and they used it to study Buddhism together. These efforts became a source of energy for introducing Buddhism to others and gradually the network of members in Mexico grew.

Having regained his health, Iwadate also threw himself into his work with renewed determination. He began producing and selling Japanese processed foods, including soybeans and pickled plums. He wondered whether pickled plums would sell in Mexico, with its different culture and customs, but against all expectations his products sold briskly.

EVENTUALLY, Iwadate's products could be found on the shelves of every shop in Mexico. His business grew steadily and he was able to pay back all his debts. Filled with joy at having received such benefits, in the spring of 1965, he and three other members traveled to Japan. At the March Soka Gakkai Headquarters Leaders Meeting, he was appointed leader of Mexico Chapter.

Shin'ichi and his party now headed from the Mexico City Airport to their hotel. Shin'ichi aimed to encourage Chapter Leader Iwadate with all his might, as well as to appoint leaders for the women's and young men's divisions, seeing to it that the local organization was in good order.

That evening, a Gohonzon-conferral ceremony was conducted at Iwadate's home on Coyoacán Avenue in Mexico City by a priest accompanying High Priest Nittatsu. Afterwards, Shin'ichi met with vice general directors Kiyoshi Jujo and Katsu Kiyohara, America Headquarters Leader Nagayasu Masaki and others at his hotel to discuss personnel appointments. It was decided that Iwadate's wife Chisako would be made leader of the Mexico Chapter women's division and that Tsunemitsu Nakada would head the young men's division. It was also decided to divide Mexico Chapter into three districts.

The following day, Shin'ichi and High Priest Nittatsu briefly toured Mexico City with Iwadate as their guide. The Olympics were to be held there in 1968, and the city was bustling with preparations. Shin'ichi and his companions walked from Juárez Avenue to Paseo de la Reforma, which the Archduke Maximilian of Hapsburg built in the mid-nineteenth century, modeling it after the Champs Elysées in Paris. This street was the city's hub.

They soon came upon the Independence Monument. A golden angel sparkled at the top of the monument, under which heroes of the independence movement were said to be entombed.

The Paseo de la Reforma was lined with trees and beautiful parks and plazas could be seen. Shin'ichi and the others occasionally came across people wearing sombreros and ponchos. Thinking of how he was actually walking through the streets of the capital of Mexico, which his mentor had dreamt of visiting, Shin'ichi was overcome with emotion. He silently vowed to Toda: "Sensei, I promise to create a brilliant realm of happiness here in Mexico as well!"

SHIN'ICHI and the others entered the famous Chapultepec Park, the site of many cultural institutions, including the National Museum of Anthropology, the National Museum of History—located inside Chapultepec Castle—and the Modern Art Museum. The Museum of Anthropology, built around a courtyard with a pond, had just been completed the autumn of the year before. The building itself was a work of art worth seeing.

Shin'ichi carefully observed all the buildings, intending to use them as references for the construction of the Grand Main Temple.

The group also went to visit the ancient city of Teotihuacan. Situated about thirty-one miles northeast of Mexico City, it is believed to have flourished from about third century BCE to the eighth century CE. The Pyramid of the Sun, some 213 feet in height, is located there. Twice a year the sun is positioned directly at the pyramid's peak, and a halo seems to shine around it.

That evening, a discussion meeting was held at Iwadate's home. Shin'ichi was unable to attend because he had to discuss the construction of the Grand Main Temple with High Priest Nittatsu. He also had pressing deadlines for his writings, including installments for *The Human Revolution*, an editorial for *The Daibyakurenge* study journal and an article for a women's magazine.

Entrusting the discussion meeting to General Director Kiyoshi Jujo and other leaders in his party, Shin'ichi sent a message to the members attending. At the meeting, Jujo announced the new leadership appointments. When he introduced Chisako Iwadate as the chapter women's division leader, enthusiastic applause filled the room. Chisako was shy, but she was always kind and caring and everyone liked her. She stood up and bashfully acknowledged the warm applause with a bow. The purehearted, strong-willed Raul Iwadate and his wife Chisako made a perfect team.

The women's division is the sun of Soka. When the sun shines brilliantly, all surroundings are illuminated by the light of hope, the sad darkness is dispelled and flowers of happiness and smiles bloom fragrantly in one's family and the community.

The appointment of a leader of the women's division

was a manifestation of Shin'ichi's wish that Mexico would become a brilliant realm of happiness.

TSUNEMITSU NAKADA was then introduced as the young men's leader. Nakada was twenty-one years old and from the Kansai Region in Japan, having only arrived in Mexico three months earlier. He had joined the Soka Gakkai at the age of nine, together with his parents. At the time, his father had been suffering ill health, which had placed a strain on the family. After graduating from junior high school in Osaka, Nakada spent some time as a live-in clerk at a store before finding a job in the parts department of a major appliance manufacturer.

It was Shin'ichi's editorial in *The Daibyakurenge*, August 1961, entitled "Youth, Become World Leaders!" that had piqued Nakada's interest in traveling overseas. His determination to get out and see the world grew stronger day by day, but when he spoke to others about it, they laughed at him and called it an empty dream.

Almost every night after returning home he would read "Youth, Become World Leaders!" aloud and chant Nam-myoho-renge-kyo in earnest to encourage himself. Then, one day, a friend asked him if he was interested in working for an appliance manufacturer in Mexico. Though Nakada could speak neither Spanish nor English, he immediately jumped at the offer. His heart leapt with joy and he felt the power of having faith in the Gohonzon.

And that was how Nakada had come to Mexico three months earlier. But now that he was actually living here, he found everything a challenge, starting with his lack of language ability. Mexico City was 7,217 feet above sea level, and he became winded and dizzy if he ran for even a short distance. In addition, the company he was working for was on the verge of collapse and couldn't even pay its workers their full salaries. His living quarters was a storage shed in the company president's home. He wished he could return to Japan, but he didn't have the fare, so he considered taking a job on a cargo ship in order to get home.

The only thing keeping Nakada in Mexico was Iwadate's announcement that President Yamamoto would be visiting the country that coming August. And now, at this discussion meeting, Nakada was appointed Mexico Chapter young men's leader. He stood up when Kiyoshi Jujo called out his name but he couldn't hide his uneasiness. "I don't have a solid foundation for my life here in Mexico and I can't speak the language," he thought, wondering if it was really all right for him to accept the responsibility.

NAKADA'S doubts didn't last long, however. He realized that the reason he had been given a leadership position was because others had high expectations for his future potential. "What matters now," he thought, "is the action I take to live up to these expectations."

Kiyoshi Jujo next announced that three districts— Azteca, Tacuba and Latin America—would be established within Mexico Chapter, followed by the introduction of the men's and women's leaders for those districts.

Nakada was filled anew with fighting spirit. Since

departing Japan he strongly wished to devote himself to kosen-rufu in Mexico. To him, doing so meant demonstrating the validity of the Daishonin's Buddhism by becoming successful in society. Nakada had neither social position nor personal wealth but what he did possess was a burning passion to dedicate his life to kosen-rufu.

His struggle began from the day of the discussion meeting. Praying wholeheartedly to become strong to fulfill his mission, he threw himself into his work. But his employer went out of business and he was forced to find a new job, this time at an automobile repair shop. He built a reputation of hard work and trust there and would later go on to establish an automotive parts dealership of his own.

A person who makes a firm determination to work for kosen-rufu is strong. From such determination wisdom, life force, success and victory in life are born.

Having concluded all of his announcements, Jujo said: "President Yamamoto asked me to relay to you that due to an important meeting with High Priest Nittatsu, he is unable to attend this discussion meeting but he sends you all his best regards. He also asked me to give you the following message: 'In the realm of faith, all are equal. Instead of making distinctions based on how long or short one has been practicing the Daishonin's Buddhism, I hope you will all advance together in unity centered around your chapter leader. The true spirit of Buddhism is found in working together in friendship and harmony. Mexico has tremendous future potential, and with the Olympics coming up in three years, it is certain to become an even greater focus of world attention. I would like to suggest that you make a goal of having a membership of five hundred people three years from now. What do you think?'"

THE ROOM erupted in thunderous applause. If the present twenty-six member-households were going to achieve a goal of five hundred members in just three years, each and every person would have to struggle with the strength of a thousand. Shin'ichi's suggestion inspired the Mexico Chapter members to make a great determination to realize that goal.

Jujo closed by saying: "I truly feel the tremendous expectations President Yamamoto has for Mexico. Let us all work together to create a wonderful history of kosen-rufu and happiness in this land."

Following this, the leaders accompanying Jujo each said a few words and offered encouragement to those in attendance. The members were then presented with such mementos as square pieces of cloth for wrapping prayer beads and placards on which Shin'ichi had written the Chinese characters for peace and security. The discussion meeting thus came to an end amid great joy.

After the meeting, Mr. and Mrs. Iwadate and Tsunemitsu Nakada went to the hotel where Shin'ichi was staying. It was raining but their steps were light. Not wanting to impose on President Yamamoto by all three of them going to the room together, Nakada decided to wait in the lobby while the Iwadates went up together.

Shin'ichi was happy to see them and cordially invited them in. They began to talk, together with Kiyoshi Jujo and Nagayasu Masaki, who were also there. When Shin'ichi asked about how he had come to live in Mexico, Iwadate shared his story. Iwadate then said with deep feeling: "Somehow the couple of years I planned to stay here has stretched into forty. Along the way, I came to love Mexico. Many of the people here actually resemble the Japanese, which may have helped me feel at home.

"Mexico also has one of the most stable governments in Latin America and I have been attracted to it because of its opportunities for those who are willing to work hard."

Shin'ichi nodded and said: "I see. That's very important. If you don't like the place you're living in, you can't fully carry out your mission. If you are unhappy, you will always be wishing you could go somewhere else or return to Japan —thus, you'll have a negative attitude and won't really apply yourself to your work. You can begin to create value when you strive to look for the good points that will enable you to like and appreciate the place where you are."

SHIN'ICHI then asked Raul Iwadate: "Are you having any particular problems?"

"There is one thing," Iwadate replied. "Soka Gakkai publications are the sustenance of our faith but the cost of having the *Seikyo Shimbun* alone sent from Japan is so high that none of our members can afford to subscribe. Right now we all take turns reading one copy of the paper, passing it around from member to member until it is falling apart."

"I see," Shin'ichi said. "I'd like to help. I will have several copies of the *Seikyo Shimbun* sent to you here in Mexico at my own expense."

Iwadate's face lit up. "Thank you so much! I know that will make everyone very happy!" he said, bowing his head repeatedly in gratitude.

Gesturing for him to stop, Shin'ichi continued: "I will also do my best to send you books and other Gakkai publications. I wish to assure that Mexico, the country that my mentor dreamt of visiting, experiences great development. The Olympics will be held here in three years; let's build a firm foundation for kosen-rufu by then. Mr. Iwadate, the time has come. Forty years have passed since you arrived here in Mexico. What were all those years for? From the standpoint of Buddhism, they were the period when you prepared yourself to stand up and realize kosen-rufu in Mexico. The true stage of your endeavors lies ahead. Let's do it! Let's work together! Let's cause the winds of genuine happiness to blow in Mexico!"

Iwadate nodded, his face flushed with excitement. Shin'ichi then turned to Chisako and said: "I hope that from this point on you will demonstrate your abilities fully as women's leader. The power of women is the driving force for the advancement of kosen-rufu. Such power was clearly exemplified in the activities of Doña Josefa in the movement for Mexican independence."

Josefa Ortiz de Dominguez was a heroine of the Mexican independence movement. Mexico had been conquered and colonized by Spain in the first half of the sixteenth century. The Spanish called it Nueva España, or New Spain. But in the early nineteenth century, after Spain was invaded by Napoleon's armies and the Spanish monarchy were forced from power, a movement for Mexican independence gained momentum. Josefa Ortiz de Dominguez played a crucial role in this struggle.

JOSEFA ORTIZ DE DOMINGUEZ and her husband Don Miguel Dominguez, the chief magistrate of Querétaro, threw themselves into the independence movement. They gave their support to the movement's leader, Miguel Hidalgo y Castilla, parish priest of the town of Dolores. Doña Josefa was a wise and courageous woman of spiritual fortitude. She and her comrades gathered in the parlor of her home under the pretense of being a literary academy and steadily forwarded their plans for the uprising.

If they succeeded, they were determined to replace the humiliating name "New Spain" with "Mexico." One theory has it that "Mexico" is an Aztec word meaning "the place of Mexitli," a god of the Aztec Empire, which was built by the indigenous peoples of that land. They also decided that the new nation of Mexico would be a republic, slavery would be abolished and all citizens would enjoy equal rights.

The revolt was finally set for October 1, 1810. Before they could carry it out, however, their plans were secretly exposed. In mid-September, the authorities moved to arrest Miguel and Josefa Dominguez. Learning of this, Doña Josefa understood that if she didn't act quickly, the dream of independence would fade and never be realized. Now was her chance! Just before she was imprisoned, she sent word through a comrade to the priest

Hidalgo telling him that their plans had been uncovered and that they mustn't wait until October but begin the uprising immediately.

When Hidalgo heard this message, he went into action in the town of Dolores. On September 16, he gathered the people together and called out to them: "Long live Independence! Long live Mexico!" And the people responded in turn. This was the famous "Cry of Dolores," the torch that ignited the independence movement. The first thing they did was free Mexican prisoners from jail and put the Spanish authorities in their place.

At first, only a few hundred gathered around Hidalgo but in a matter of days their numbers had swelled into the tens of thousands. This struggle fought by ordinary citizens was long and hard but independence from Spain was finally achieved eleven years later in 1821. It is fair to say that the courageous and sagacious decision of Doña Josefa led the way to Mexico's liberation.

SHIN'ICHI said to Chisako: "I hope you will become a Doña Josefa of the Mystic Law and protect your fellow members in Mexico as she did her comrades."

"I will!" Chisako replied, her voice ringing with energy.

Then Shin'ichi turned again to Raul and said: "Mr. Iwadate, life is short. What matters is how we use this limited life. One way is to pursue our own small desires that we think will bring us happiness. You, however, have a mission to work for kosen-rufu in Mexico and realize happiness for this country's citizens. In light of the

Daishonin's writings, it is clear that you have appeared as a Bodhisattva of the Earth for that very reason. I hope that you will devote your life to kosen-rufu as a pioneer and leader bringing peace and happiness to the people of Mexico."

Iwadate nodded enthusiastically and shook Shin'ichi's hand firmly, tears welling up in his eyes. "I'll do my best," he replied. "I'll do my absolute best, as long as I live and breathe."

It was a moment of profound life-to-life communication. And it was the moment when the pillar of kosen-rufu in Mexico was firmly secured.

Mr. and Mrs. Iwadate left Shin'ichi's hotel room, their hearts filled with strong determination. Nakada waited for them in the lobby. Seeing Raul Iwadate with tears in his eyes, Nakada wondered what had taken place in President Yamamoto's room. He had never seen Iwadate cry before. Iwadate said nothing, however, only murmuring "Let's go" as he headed for the hotel entrance.

Outside it was still raining but Iwadate didn't open his umbrella. Nakada and Chisako walked behind him. The rain felt good on Iwadate's face, which glowed with joy. Stopping before the Independence Monument topped with the shining golden angel, Raul spoke softly: "Now I understand the real significance of my coming to Mexico. In fact, I now know the true reason why I was born in this world. I am going to dedicate the rest of my life to kosen-rufu here in Mexico. Meeting President Yamamoto made this decision possible. The only thing left to do is take action. Tsunemitsu, I hope you'll work with me."

IWADATE gripped Nakada's hand firmly. Nakada squeezed back, tears of emotion filling his eyes as he said: "Let's do it, Mr. Iwadate! I also came to Mexico with the determination to realize kosen-rufu here. I'll do my best. I'll give it my all." Standing beneath the angel statue illuminated atop the Independence Monument, the two men shook hands and nodded in solemn agreement. Chisako, who was nearby, also nodded as she dabbed her eyes with a handkerchief.

That night was one in which the three leaders of Mexico Chapter made a historic vow. It was already after eleven o'clock in the evening, and the rain had stopped.

Shin'ichi Yamamoto was scheduled to leave Mexico the following day, August 19. At four o'clock in the afternoon, he and his traveling companions left the hotel. When they arrived at the airport, about twenty or thirty members were there to see them off. Overseas Bureau Chief Yasushi Morinaga introduced Nakada to Shin'ichi, explaining that he had just been appointed leader of the young men's division in Mexico.

Shaking hands with Nakada, Shin'ichi said: "The power of youth creates the future. That is why I have such high hopes for the youth division. There are only a few youth members in Mexico, but if you stand up and make an effort, that's enough. Just as a single spark can set an entire field aflame, everything starts from one person. The success or failure of kosen-rufu will be determined by the actions of pioneering members. That is why you must never be defeated, no matter what difficulties or hardships you encounter. I hope you will do your best to overcome your own weaknesses and to surmount all personal suffering and that you will boldly and resolutely take action for the sake of Mexico's future."

These words struck Nakada deeply. "I will!" he said, his voice brimming with a fighting spirit.

Shin'ichi then took a commemorative photograph with the members who had come to see him off. After that, his flight's departure was announced.

"Please do your best, working closely together in joy and high spirits," Shin'ichi said. "I am praying every day for your good health and happiness. Let's meet again." With these final words of encouragement, Shin'ichi bade farewell to the members of Mexico Chapter.

SHIN'ICHI'S visit to Mexico set off a joyous wave of advancement there. "Let's greet the Mexico Olympics with a membership of five hundred" became the members' byword. Chapter leaders Raul and Chisako Iwadate and Tsunemitsu Nakada strove especially hard to actualize this goal. Each person was determined to fulfill their vow to President Yamamoto, even if they had to wage a solitary struggle. Each rose with a stand-alone spirit.

When everyone stands up and works toward a shared goal, true unity and strength are born. This is an eternal and unchanging principle. On the other hand, no matter how well the members of a group may appear to get along, if they are only co-dependent, they are nothing but an aimless crowd and cannot reveal their full potential.

Wishing wholeheartedly to share the philosophy for realizing true happiness in Mexico, the members prayed sincerely and went from town to town to introduce the

Daishonin's Buddhism to their friends. Gradually, not only Japanese immigrants but also Mexican people began taking faith in the Daishonin's Buddhism. After a year, membership had grown to one hundred households—a remarkable fourfold increase from the original twenty-six households.

Members were always bringing new faces to Iwadate's home to learn about Buddhism and fruitful Buddhist dialogue took place there almost daily. Iwadate and the other leaders enthusiastically traveled from one place to the next to talk about Buddhism and teach new members gongyo. Sometimes they would travel more than 621 miles by car, a journey that would take a full week.

One district leader's car—no doubt because it had been driven so hard—overheated every time he drove into the mountains. He often had to make several trips to the valley below to fetch water for the steaming radiator.

But everyone was always in the highest of spirits. Their hearts burned with the determination to transform their beloved Mexico into a garden of peace where the winds of happiness blew.

Two years after Shin'ichi's visit, Mexico Chapter had grown to 250 households, and in May of that year, 1967, it was expanded into a general chapter.

Then came the year of the Olympics in 1968. A general meeting was scheduled for May 25, and when that day arrived, the membership had reached an astonishing seven hundred households. Calculated as individual members, the number was more than twice their original goal of five hundred. The members in Mexico had fulfilled magnificently their promise to Shin'ichi.

AFTER leaving Mexico, Shin'ichi and his traveling companions headed for San Francisco via Los Angeles. While Shin'ichi was still in Mexico, Soka Gakkai Director Akira Kuroki and the other three leaders who had been dispatched from Japan, went to San Francisco as an advanced party to oversee district leaders meetings and study examinations.

Shin'ichi arrived in San Francisco on August 19, and the following day, August 20, priests sent from Japan conducted Gohonzon-conferral ceremonies. Since the opening of the community center in San Francisco at the end of 1963, the activities of the members had gained momentum and membership was growing quickly, resulting in an increased demand for Gohonzon conferrals. At first only two conferral ceremonies were scheduled, but so many people were requesting to receive the Gohonzon that ultimately six were held.

While in San Francisco, Shin'ichi was determined to give his all to encouraging newly appointed San Francisco Chapter Leader Tad Ozaki, slated to be Shin'ichi's driver in the city. Shin'ichi landed at San Francisco Airport after ten o'clock in the evening, and when he got to his hotel, he spoke privately with Ozaki. He was tired but this would be his only opportunity during his stay to talk with him at length.

Tad Ozaki was a second-generation Japanese man in his mid-thirties. He was a captain in the United States Air Force and had joined the Soka Gakkai a year earlier. Before taking faith, he had been extremely skeptical of the organization. He first encountered Buddhism when his wife Aiko, who was suffering from a serious kidney disease, joined the Soka Gakkai. Although doctors said she had only a year or two to live, a Gakkai member had adamantly told Ozaki that his wife would regain her health through faith and urged him to become a member.

Ozaki was put off by such a suggestion. He felt that, in light of the doctors' dim prognosis, it was irresponsible of the member to make such baseless assertions and give his wife false hope. Ozaki detested irresponsible words and actions. He was an air force captain, and had attained his rank through his own hard work and effort. His mother had died of tuberculosis when he was ten. The following year, World War II started and Japanese-Americans were detained in internment camps. Ozaki and his family were sent to a camp in Oregon, where they were forced to stay for five years.

AFTER the war, because there was no real school in the camp, Ozaki returned to school, this time with students much younger than he. Working all the way, he finally managed to enter high school but then his father died in an accident. Though he was constantly beset by difficult trials, he persevered with firm determination and did his absolute best, eventually graduating from high school and then joining the air force.

Knowing that during the war, the 442nd Division, largely made up of Japanese-American soldiers, had been praised and highly distinguished, he thought it likely his abilities would be evaluated fairly, regardless of his family or ethnic background. A hard and diligent worker, he advanced steadily in the ranks.

Subsequently, he was posted to Japan, where he met

and married his wife, Aiko. Then her chronic kidney condition worsened and became life threatening. Ozaki was terribly disheartened by this turn of events, but as a person who had always made his way through life by remaining true to his convictions, he could not accept the possibility that illness could be cured through religious faith. Further, he was angered by what he saw as an attempt by a Soka Gakkai member to exploit the desperation of others.

Aware that the Soka Gakkai had established the Clean Government Political Federation in Japan and was venturing into the realm of politics, Ozaki also concluded that it must be a religious organization with sinister ulterior motives. He decided that it was his duty as part of the military personnel to expose what he was certain were dark plots of the Gakkai. Though he was generally an amiable, peace-loving man, he also possessed a strong inner passion for truth and justice.

Ozaki started by attending a Soka Gakkai discussion meeting, where he heard members sharing various experiences of faith. Some talked about overcoming financial difficulties, while others spoke of triumphing over illness. Some members became so emotional and choked up while talking that they had difficulty finishing their stories. Listening to them, he couldn't help but feel that they were telling the truth.

Ozaki also noticed the bright expressions of the participants and their lack of affected piety. The man leading the meeting seemed sincere, without any air of dubious mysticism or the arrogant authoritarianism that one often found in leaders of religious groups.

A question-and-answer session began and the leader

answered everyone's frank questions clearly, politely and confidently.

One of the participants asked: "Earlier, someone spoke about curing illness through faith, but I wonder, how is that possible?" It was a question that Ozaki himself had wanted to ask.

THE LEADER replied to the participant's question: "In short, faith enables us to bring forth the supreme life-state of Buddhahood, which gives us strong life force to overcome even illness. For example, while there may be people with the same illness or injury who take the same medicine or receive the same medical treatment, some heal quickly while others don't. This is because of a difference in their life force. And faith is the wellspring of life force."

The leader then went on to use various examples to explain that our bodies and minds exist in an inseparable relationship, and he emphasized the importance of our mental attitude or determination.

"Buddhism does not, however, in any way deny the efficacy of medicine," he added. "When we fall ill, we should of course seek medical treatment. Buddhism is reason, so it is only natural that we make full use of the power of medicine. But the fundamental power for conquering illness comes from our own life force."

This made sense to Ozaki. He continued to attend Soka Gakkai meetings. The thing that surprised him most was the consideration the members displayed for others. In one case, an elderly member had been diagnosed with cancer. Fellow members visited her on a daily basis to offer her encouragement and support, as well as to pray for her recovery. One member said to Ozaki: "I found happiness through Buddhism, which is why I want to share it with everyone I know. I believe that bringing happiness to a single individual and creating world peace both stem from the same source."

Gradually, Ozaki's attitude toward the Soka Gakkai underwent a profound change. Until then, he had thought that a dubious religion that promised things such as faith healing must be alienated from normal society and conduct strange rituals but the Gakkai was not like that at all. Discussion meetings were held regularly, serving as open forums for dialogue, and members all sought to be good citizens who played leading roles in their places of work and society.

Ozaki also thought that the Soka Gakkai was guided by the arbitrary teachings of some guru, but he found instead that it was based on a compilation of the writings of Nichiren Daishonin—as well as the teachings of Buddhism.

It was true that the members deeply admired their youthful leader President Yamamoto but it seemed to be largely a matter of being inspired by his character. And everyone said that President Yamamoto was a person who placed great emphasis on dialogue.

AFTER observing the Soka Gakkai for himself, Tad Ozaki decided to join. He had discovered that rather than sinister ulterior motives, the organization was dedicated to the pure and noble ideal of constructing a world of happiness and peace for all.

Ozaki thus threw himself wholeheartedly into Gakkai activities. Firmly resolved to spread the Daishonin's Buddhism, he would often drive two or three hours from his home in San Francisco to such places as Sacramento, Monterey and Fresno to open the path for kosen-rufu in the United States. Then, on the day of the Etiwanda Culture Festival, he was appointed the leader of San Francisco Chapter.

After listening to Ozaki's account of how he had joined the Soka Gakkai, Shin'ichi said in a firm voice: "As a second-generation Japanese-American, you must have a good understanding of the thinking of both Japanese and American people. Japanese people tend to comprehend Buddhism in the context of their own culture and traditions and try to transmit it in the same way to Americans. This often confounds American people, who find it difficult to understand such cultural elements, which are really extraneous to Buddhism. It is therefore crucial that Buddhism is communicated to Americans in a way they can readily grasp and accept. I would like to entrust this task to you.

"There is no need at all to rush with propagating Buddhism in the United States. The important thing is for each individual to feel that there is no more enjoyable, fulfilling or wonderful realm as that of Buddhism. If that is accomplished, those individuals will develop into core leaders from whom the Daishonin's teaching will spread widely.

"If we become caught up only in the glitter of activities and forget these fundamental points, then although we may seem to be making great strides, kosen-rufu in

WINDS OF HAPPINESS • 143

the United States will fail. We need to proceed at a steady pace and build an organization in which every member appreciates just how amazing the Daishonin's Buddhism is. Leaders bear a heavy responsibility in this endeavor. Whether or not our movement succeeds here will become clear thirty or forty years from now."

Ozaki listened with great concentration to President Yamamoto's words, as if to engrave them in his heart.

"Please take care of San Francisco in my stead," Shin'ichi said finally and shook Ozaki's hand. He then signed a copy of his book *Science and Religion*, which he had brought with him from Japan, and presented it to him.

AFTER two nights in San Francisco, Shin'ichi made stops in Seattle and Honolulu before heading home to Japan on August 25. In both cities, he gave his all to fostering the core leaders and spent many hours offering personal guidance. In each place Shin'ichi visited, Gohonzon-conferral ceremonies were conducted by priests sent from Japan, with a total of 1,170 people ultimately receiving Gohonzon.

When Shin'ichi first set foot in the United States in October five years earlier in 1960, the largest gathering he attended was one of one hundred people for the establishment of Los Angeles Chapter. During this trip, the number of people receiving Gohonzon alone exceeded one thousand. A new age had clearly arrived. Who could have envisioned such a rapid expansion of worldwide kosen-rufu?

Stirring fresh winds of happiness in every place he went, Shin'ichi's visit to the United States and Mexico came to a close.

After returning to Japan, Shin'ichi threw himself immediately back into encouraging the Japanese members. Before his overseas trip, in April and May, he had taken commemorative photographs with district leaders of all the headquarters in Tokyo. Seeing how greatly this had inspired them, he decided to do the same with district leaders throughout Japan.

Next, group leaders of the men's and women's divisions wanted to take commemorative photos with President Yamamoto, and hundreds of letters of request poured into the Soka Gakkai Headquarters. At the time, the unit was the frontline organization for Gakkai activities. Several units made up a group, several groups made up a district and several districts made up a chapter.

If Shin'ichi were to take commemorative photos with

the group leaders, it would require much more time and energy than he expended so far. General Director Kiyoshi Jujo and other leaders at the Headquarters considered the group leaders' requests, but given President Yamamoto's schedule, they deemed it impossible to carry out.

When Shin'ichi learned of their conclusion, he said: "Is it really impossible? Isn't there any way we can work it in? I believe that the president exists for the sake of members, and that serving members is the foremost duty of the Soka Gakkai Headquarters. Please don't worry about my health and reconsider the matter. I would very much like to take commemorative photos with the group leaders."

AT THE VERY least, Shin'ichi was determined to take photographs with the men's and women's group leaders, who were the main source of support for the district leaders. The staff at the Soka Gakkai Headquarters thus met again to deliberate about how to make this happen.

In the end, Shin'ichi's schedule was adjusted and a plan was made for commemorative photographs with group leaders starting in the Kansai Region on October 3. Preparations in Kansai got under way immediately and the municipal gymnasium in Fuse City[4], Osaka, was secured for the photo-taking sessions.

Even though this project was limited to group leaders belonging to local headquarters within Osaka Prefecture, the total number of participants still came to twenty-four thousand. If each session were to include fifty members, it would take 480 sessions to photograph everyone. And if it were to take just five minutes for each group to enter the gymnasium, get positioned and have their photo taken, some forty hours would be required to complete the endeavor.

Realizing this wouldn't work, the Kansai members in charge racked their brains to come up with a solution. The only alternative was to increase the number of members in each photograph. But even if the photographer used large film, he would only be able to capture the faces of a few hundred members clearly.

Finally, they decided to have five hundred members in each photo, standing on bleachers twelve tiers in height, which would be made especially for the occasion. Three sets of bleachers would be built on three sides of the gymnasium, so that 1,500 members could be accommodated at one time. They wanted to speed up the process as much as possible.

They also decided to use special lighting to ensure a sharper image. About one hundred young men's members volunteered to construct the bleachers, working on the project for two full days and nights. Six hundred wooden poles, one thousand wooden planks and six hundred sheets of paneling were used.

The bleachers were completed at half past three in the morning on the day of the shoot. At five o'clock that morning, staff members coordinating the event met at the gymnasium to discuss arrangements. The completely unprecedented photography session for twenty-four thousand members was about to begin.

THOUGH the photo shoots were not scheduled to begin until noon, by ten o'clock the park that had been prearranged as the meeting site was filled with participants. They were all dressed in their best attire, hair neatly combed and arranged, with bright and cheerful faces. When told that they would have a commemorative photograph taken with President Yamamoto on October 3, they nearly leapt with joy.

Believing that a photograph captures one's state of life, the group leaders were determined to appear having given their all to sharing the Daishonin's teachings with others. They felt that if they didn't, their faces would forever be recorded as lifeless images, which would be a terrible shame. With that spirit, they threw themselves into telling others about Buddhism and chanted abundantly. Now the day had finally arrived.

Shin'ichi, on the other hand, had a cold a few days before the photo shoot and wasn't at all well. His throat was red and swollen, he felt feverish and sluggish. But when he thought about the group leaders who were working so hard on the front lines of the organization, how eagerly they had been looking forward to this day and all the efforts they had made leading up to it, he could hardly fail to attend.

Shin'ichi arrived at the gymnasium just before noon. The three sets of bleachers were each filled with five hundred men's group leaders, their faces tense with anticipation. Most of them were meeting President Yamamoto in person for the first time.

When he entered the gymnasium, Shin'ichi smiled as

he addressed the waiting members with a traditional Osaka greeting in the local dialect. "How's business?" he asked. Smiles spread across the members' faces and from a corner of the room came the traditional reply: "Booming!" The hearts of Shin'ichi and the Kansai members immediately became one.

The photographer's flash brightly glimmered. It seemed particularly harsh to Shin'ichi, who wasn't feeling well. After the shoot was finished, Vice General Director Seiichiro Haruki picked up a portable microphone and began asking members how long they had been practicing. This was in preparation for distributing gifts that Shin'ichi had brought to present to them.

"First, will those who have been practicing for twelve years or more please raise their hands?" he asked. Only two or three members did so. "All right, who is in their eleventh year of practice?" This time no one raised his hand.

"Has anyone been practicing for ten years?" With this question, about one-fourth of the members in the gymnasium raised their hands.

THESE men's group leaders had joined in 1956, the year President Toda had sent Shin'ichi to Kansai to create a new history of the victory of the people. In May of that year, under Shin'ichi's leadership, Osaka Chapter achieved the unprecedented golden record of 11,111 new member-households in one month and laid the foundations of ever-victorious Kansai.

Many of the members who joined as part of the great wave of expansion that Shin'ichi initiated were now valiantly striving for kosen-rufu as men's and women's group leaders and their lives overflowed with benefit.

Smiling warmly, Shin'ichi said: "Unfortunately, there isn't much time to talk today but I want to say that I hope you will all live long and chant abundantly throughout your lives.

"In particular, I want to encourage those of you facing serious difficulties to pray to the Gohonzon earnestly and diligently, chanting Nam-myoho-renge-kyo five hundred thousand, one million or two million times to overcome them. The Gohonzon is the embodiment of the great fundamental Law of the universe. There is no reason that our problems should go unresolved. Life is full of difficulties, but if we let our problems get the better of us, it is because of our inner weaknesses.

"I am determined to open the way forward so that your children will freely take action in all fields of endeavor toward the realization of peace for Japan and the entire world. The future is secured. Please rest assured and do your absolute best.

"Lastly, since we have taken a photo together here today, let's make a pledge that we will make our way to the Land of Eternally Tranquil Light together as well!"

"OK!" the members energetically replied. Some blinked away tears, while others dabbed their eyes with handkerchiefs. Everyone's face shone with excitement.

At the end of each photo session, Shin'ichi wholeheartedly encouraged the members. When the first session was finished, it was time for the three groups of five hundred to leave and the next fifteen hundred to come in. At first the plan was that while one group of five hundred was having its photo taken, the other two groups would enter and get in position; but the movement of so many people shook the gymnasium floor and interfered with the photo taking. They then switched to a system of having all three groups move in and out at the same time. The interval could have offered Shin'ichi a valuable moment to rest, but instead he headed outside to encourage the waiting members.

ONCE outside the gymnasium, Shin'ichi said to the members: "I'm sorry to keep you waiting. There are just so many people here today."

When the members saw Shin'ichi, they exclaimed with joy. He spotted a man about fifty years old on crutches and approached him. "Did you injure yourself? Please get well soon and live a long and healthy life." He presented the man with some prayer beads.

Soon the next session began. After each photo was taken, Shin'ichi would pick up the microphone and encourage the members with all his strength. He spoke to them as if wringing every ounce of energy from his being. His sore throat ached when he talked.

The photo sessions for the men's group leaders ended at two o'clock in the afternoon. Because of his fever, Shin'ichi was dripping with sweat and his breathing labored. In the room provided for him to rest, he changed his underclothes and sat down on the sofa with a cold towel pressed to his forehead. He felt faint. The others in the room were only two or three leaders who had accompanied him from Tokyo.

Seeing Shin'ichi's condition, one of them cried: "President Yamamoto! Are you all right?"

"I'll be fine," Shin'ichi replied. "I'm just resting. I don't want the members to worry about me."

Moved by his strong sense of duty, the other leaders prayed that the photography sessions would finish without incident. Just then, one of the Kansai leaders opened the door to the room and said: "President Yamamoto, we're ready!"

"All right, let's go!" Shin'ichi thumped the arm of the sofa and rose energetically; he seemed transformed. It was time for the women's group leaders' photo shoot to begin.

As he entered the gymnasium, Shin'ichi called out to the members, once again in the Osaka dialect: "Sorry to keep you waiting. Thank you so much for coming today."

The room erupted in applause.

"You all look so beautiful and youthful," he continued. "I can see that you have been chanting earnestly since morning. I hope you will do this every day, chanting as much as possible and cheerfully and vibrantly living out your lives.

"YOU have all made great contributions to building the noble foundations of ever-victorious Kansai. I will never forget you as long as I live. I plan to keep a copy of each of the photographs we took today in my office, as a symbol that we are always striving together. Please know that I will be sending prayers for you."

At that moment, the sweet voice of a child rang out from a corner of the gymnasium: "Sensei!" It belonged to a boy of about five who had come with his mother.

Shin'ichi waved the boy over and told him with a gentle smile: "We'll finish soon, so just wait a little longer, all right?" And he gave the boy some grapes that had been set out on the table for him.

Shin'ichi then picked up the microphone again and continued: "I hope you will all do your best to raise your children into fine young people who will be active on the stage of kosen-rufu.

"Mothers are the supreme example of faith for their children. If mothers have sincere faith, their children will follow suit. Mothers are the sun. No matter how deep the darkness of suffering, when the sun shines, everything is bathed in the light of hope. No matter what happens, as long as the mother is strong, her family will be safe and secure and her home a splendid garden of happiness."

Noticing some elderly women among the participants, Shin'ichi addressed them and presented them with handwritten calligraphy, prayer beads and books.

In spite of his enthusiasm, each time a session ended, Shin'ichi returned to the waiting room and slumped on the sofa as if he was about to collapse. His face grew more and more flushed with fever and his eyes were bloodshot. Though he was hot, he also had the chills. But after a few moments' rest, he summoned up his strength and stood up resolutely, saying: "Let's go! Everyone's waiting!"

As he walked to the gymnasium, he remarked to the leaders with him: "At the end, let's take a photo with the youth who have been working as event staff. They've all done a great job."

Given Shin'ichi's condition, the leaders were taken aback by this suggestion, but when they thought about his determination they didn't dare object. They were all deeply touched by the sight of President Yamamoto encouraging the members with the spirit that each moment of his life might be the last.

In the end, forty-eight groups of men's and women's group leaders had commemorative photos taken with Shin'ichi.

THE MEMBERS of the event staff were photographed in two groups. Scanning the faces of the young people standing on the bleachers, Shin'ichi Yamamoto said: "I sincerely appreciate all your efforts today, getting up early on a Sunday and exerting yourselves behind the scenes to make sure everything ran smoothly. Thank you for your hard work.

"Who are the greatest champions? They are the ones who always protect the people. Who are the noblest? They are those who silently toil to support the precious children of the Buddha. That is why you are the most honorable and worthy of people. As an expression of tremendous respect for you, I would like to join you in a commemorative photograph."

The final flash of the day released a burst of light. The photography shoot ended just before five o'clock. It had lasted four hours and fifty-five minutes and involved fifty groups in total.

Perhaps because of the successive flashes, Shin'ichi's eyes ached and he continued to see flickers of light even after he closed them. Though he had suffered from a burning fever throughout the day, none of the Kansai members had noticed.

The following day, Shin'ichi traveled to Nagoya and took commemorative photographs with twelve thousand Aichi Prefecture men's and women's group leaders. For about ten years after that, commemorative photo sessions with group leaders and other members working on the front lines of the organization took place all over the country, ranging from Hokkaido in the north to Okinawa's Miyakojima and Ishigakijima islands in the south. Over those years, Shin'ichi had a number of health problems due to his demanding work schedule but he persevered through it all. He wanted to create something eternal out of these fleeting moments together with his beloved fellow members, as well as offer them words of encouragement.

Kosen-rufu is a noble endeavor that can only be achieved when all comrades in faith stand up as lions. That is why Shin'ichi was determined to light the everlasting flames of commitment, joy and courage in the hearts of his fellow members. Fire is sparked when stones are struck together. Shin'ichi fully was aware that it was heart-to-heart inspiration that would ignite the flame of kosen-rufu.

Every photo session was an exciting drama of communication and exchange between Shin'ichi and fellow members. Many of those members still cherish their commemorative photographs today and speak of them as their greatest treasure and a symbol of the prime point of their lifetime vow.

The connections that Shin'ichi forged with the tens of thousands of members he took photographs with became the driving force for dynamic fresh growth in the movement for kosen-rufu.

Notes

1 Martin Luther King, "I Have a Dream," speech delivered in Washington, D.C. on August 28, 1963. From *The Penguin Book of Twentieth-Century Speeches,* edited by Brian MacArthur (New York: Penguin Books, 1993), p. 334.

2 "Kuroda Bushi": A Japanese folk song from Fukuoka Prefecture that is known as a sake-drinking song.

3 Takeaki Enomoto (1836–1908), who had served as Japan's Minister of Education, Minister of Agriculture and Commerce, and Foreign Minister in the Meiji government, originally promoted the idea. In 1897, he sent the "Enomoto Emigration Group," comprised of more than thirty Japanese citizens to Mexico. This was eleven years before the voyage of the *Kasato Maru* carrying the first Japanese emigrants to Brazil.

4 This is present-day Higashi-Osaka City.

A New Course

BRIGHT AUTUMN skies stretched over Japan. It was as if the protective functions of the universe praised and smiled upon the sincere faith of Soka Gakkai members. The date was October 9, 1965, and for the next four days through October 12, the long anticipated contribution campaign for the construction of the Grand Main Temple was to take place at sixteen thousand district collection centers across Japan. Contributions were being accepted from nine o'clock in the morning through eight o'clock in the evening each day, but on this first day of the campaign, members stood waiting outside the centers long before they opened, wanting to make their contributions before anyone else. Their faces shone with joy.

Understanding that the Grand Main Temple would be what Nichiren Daishonin had referred to as the sanctuary of the Temple of the Essential Teaching to be built at the time of kosen-rufu, the members regarded the opportunity to contribute to its construction as the greatest good fortune and highest honor. It was with this belief and conviction that they threw themselves into the contribution campaign.

The plans for the Grand Main Temple's construction were announced on May 3 of the previous year, 1964. On that day, at the Twenty-seventh Headquarters General Meeting held in the Nihon University Auditorium, which marked the beginning of the essential phase of the kosen-rufu movement, President Yamamoto introduced the construction and donation of the Grand Main Temple to the head temple as one of the Soka Gakkai's goals during the next seven years. The Grand Main Temple was to serve as the main edifice of the head temple and the place where the Dai-Gohonzon would be enshrined. President Toda, Shin'ichi explained, had instructed that it should be built after the construction of the Grand Reception Hall had been completed.

Shin'ichi further expressed his wish to collect stones from all over the world and inter them in the building's foundation as a symbol of humanity's prayer for lasting peace, and voiced his intention to adorn the structure with fine building materials from each of the five continents. The special contribution campaign, he announced, would take place for four or five days in 1965, culminating on October 12.

Since that meeting, members were actively involved in preparations toward the upcoming contribution campaign. Shin'ichi, meanwhile, on his travels around the world, had collected stones from each country and purchased special construction materials.

On January 21, 1965, the Grand Main Temple Construction Committee was established and High Priest Nittatsu formally appointed the committee's chairperson, vice chairpersons and members. At its inception, the committee had fifty members excluding the chairperson: twenty priests and thirty Soka Gakkai members. (Later, five members of the National Hokkeko Federation, a group of Nichiren Shoshu lay supporters, were added to the committee.)

Shin'ichi was appointed chairperson and four priests and nine Gakkai leaders were made vice chairpersons.

THE CONSTRUCTION COMMITTEE held its first meeting on February 16, 1965, in the conference room of the Grand Reception Hall at the head temple. There, High Priest Nittatsu clarified the significance of the Grand Main Temple, saying:

> The most important issue regarding the Grand Main Temple is what Gohonzon should be enshrined in it....
>
> In the two transfer documents entrusted by Nichiren Daishonin to Nikko Shonin, it is stated: "When the sovereign accepts this Law, the sanctuary

of the Temple of the Essential Teaching should be established at the foot of Mount Fuji" (GZ, 1600). Fundamentally, this injunction elucidates that the construction of the sanctuary of the essential teaching is our objective. This is a significant instruction for the realization of kosen-rufu.

In this regard, it seems to be generally held that the sanctuary of the essential teaching itself will be erected on the premises of the Temple of the Essential Teaching but this is incorrect. To build the hall of the sanctuary of the essential teaching within one of the temple buildings or as one among many structures of a grand temple is a precept of earlier Buddhist teachings. Though sanctuaries of earlier Buddhist teachings and the theoretical teaching of the Lotus Sutra were like this, in the Latter Day of the Law the only precept is to have faith based on the chanting of Nam-myoho-renge-kyo. Therefore, the hall where the Dai-Gohonzon is enshrined is itself the sanctuary of the essential teaching. It follows then that constructing the sanctuary at the great Temple of the Essential Teaching does not require that the Gohonzon of the sanctuary of the essential teaching be enshrined in some specially built sanctuary hall but within the main hall of the temple itself.

The Daishonin clearly transmits this in the "One Hundred and Six Comparisons," when he states: "The most excellent place to establish the Three [Great] Secret Laws will be at the main hall of Hommon-ji temple at Mount Fuji" (GZ, 867). The postscript to this document reads: "The mandala I directly transferred to Nikko should be enshrined as the object of devotion in the main hall [of the Temple of the Essential Teaching]" (GZ, 869)....

It is therefore correct that the Gohonzon of the sanctuary of the essential teaching should be enshrined in the Grand Main Temple where people may come to worship it. Because many who slander the Law still exist today, in the age of the Latter Day of the Law, I would like to state that [the Dai-Gohonzon] should be open to the public at the time of kosen-rufu.

In this statement, which was published in the February 20, 1965 edition of the *Seikyo Shimbun,* High Priest Nittatsu thus confirmed that the Grand Main Temple was the very building that would be the sanctuary of the essential teaching at the time of kosen-rufu, and that its construction was, in fact, the construction of the sanctuary of the essential teaching.

WHEN Shin'ichi initially announced the Soka Gakkai's plan to construct the Grand Main Temple and donate it to the head temple at the Headquarters general meeting on May 3, 1964, he had in mind that the sanctuary of the essential teaching would be the next building to be constructed. That is why at that meeting he declared that after the Grand Main Temple, all that would be left to be built was the sanctuary of the essential teaching. But then later, High Priest Nittatsu asserted that at the time of kosen-rufu the Grand Main Temple would itself be the sanctuary of the essential teaching.

To convey the significance of the Grand Main Temple's construction as revealed by the high priest's statement at the Grand Main Temple Construction Committee meeting, as well as to call on members to participate in the contribution campaign, the committee produced and distributed a leaflet dated March 26 entitled "On the Significance of Offerings for the Construction of the Grand Main Temple."

The leaflet introduced High Priest Nittatsu's words at the committee meeting, stating that the construction of the Grand Main Temple was itself the construction of the sanctuary of the essential teaching and that it represented the achievement of kosen-rufu. It read:

> The significance of the construction of the Grand Main Temple is indeed profound, and our tremendous good fortune in participating in donating it to the head temple is beyond measure. It is our sincere wish that the priests and laity will work together in unity to realize this grand endeavor.
>
> The Grand Main Temple will be built in the deep recesses of the head temple grounds beyond the Grand Reception Hall in accord with the instruction that "the Dai-Gohonzon be placed deep in the back of the reception hall." It will represent the very best of contemporary architecture, using fine materials from the five continents, and have stones from all over the world interred in its foundation. Based on the principle that pure water always springs forth where the True Law flourishes,

there will be a large fountain built in the front courtyard area. The Grand Main Temple will be one of the architectural masterpieces of the twentieth century.

We would like to hold the contribution campaign for four days, beginning on October 9 and culminating on the auspicious day of October 12, the anniversary of the Dai-Gohonzon's inscription. This will no doubt be the last occasion to contribute to a building project of this scale at the head temple. It is indeed a golden opportunity.

Participating in the great work of constructing the Grand Main Temple that will enshrine the Dai-Gohonzon, the true object of devotion for realizing happiness for all humanity—not only for the ten thousand years of the Latter Day of the Law but for all time—is an eternal honor and a source of wonderful good fortune. It is our great hope that all believers will participate in this glorious effort in the most sincere spirit of faith.

When they read the leaflet, members were overcome with emotion at the thought of participating in the construction of the Grand Main Temple that would be the sanctuary of the essential teaching. They were determined to give their all to making the most meaningful contribution possible.

IN RESPONSE to members' requests, in addition to the leaflet, coin banks were distributed to each member. The coin banks were small, plastic blue cubes, decorated with a picture of the head temple and Mount Fuji. Filled with a spirit of gratitude, the members thus enthusiastically began saving.

The year 1965 was said to be the worst economic recession to hit Japan since the end of World War II. From the start of the year, there was a succession of bankruptcies of medium-sized companies, including Dainichi Machine Manufacturing Company and Nippon Textiles. In March, Sanyo Special Steel collapsed, becoming the largest bankruptcy in Japan's postwar era.

The September closing reports of the First and Second Sections of the Tokyo Stock Exchange. Based on statistics gathered from 546 listed companies, they were the worst of the postwar era as well, with a mere 1 percent increase in revenue and a more than 20 percent decline in profits. Companies cut back drastically on hiring and the job situation became very tight. Yet in spite of the economic downturn, commodity prices continued to rise, with consumer prices jumping 7.6 percent in one year. This placed heavy pressure on people's standard of living.

The Soka Gakkai Headquarters sought to minimize the financial burden on its members so that they could participate in the Grand Main Temple construction project without worry despite the harsh economic times. The Headquarters itself, also faced with straightened circumstances due to the increasing expense of building community centers around Japan, made great efforts to cut costs and consequently reduced all other expenses to a minimum. One measure was the temporary suspension of the well-received film series *Seikyo News* after the release of its forty-eighth edition in May 1965.

But even in the face of these severe economic conditions, the determination of members to make contributions only burned brighter. They knew they were presented with a rare chance. Had they been born in a different age, they thought, they would never have been given this opportunity, and they thus regarded it as the greatest good fortune.

The members were resolved not to let tough economic times stop them. Instead, they felt spurred on by the challenge. Thinking of how the wealthy merchant Sudatta in Shakyamuni's day and Nanjo Tokimitsu in the Daishonin's time had made donations even in the midst of terrible hardship, the members were determined to make sincere offerings themselves. They wanted to make the best contribution they could so that they would feel not the slightest sense of regret.

Sharing their determinations with one another, members set high contribution goals for themselves and then poured their energies into achieving them, their hearts aflame with vibrant joy.

FILLED with a sincere spirit of faith, some members of the men's division even gave up smoking and drinking in order to put the money they saved toward their donation. This thrilled their wives, who could see the positive effect the campaign was having on their husbands' health. Some women began sewing their children's clothes in an effort to cut household expenses so they could make their contribution goal. High school students took on paper routes and elementary school students saved their allowances to do their part.

Many who made donations filled coin banks or tin cans to the brim with one hundred-, ten- and one-yen coins, cradling them carefully in their arms like great treasures. The actions of these humble members shone with a sincerity that no amount of money could ever measure. The solid weight of their coins was the weight of their pure faith.

In one case, three siblings from Fukuoka Prefecture, all in their teens, traveled a distance of twenty-five miles for three hours by bicycle to hand in their contribution. Their plan was to add what they saved on their roundtrip train fares to the amount they had already. In some regions, it was not at all unusual for members to walk six to twelve miles to the nearest collection point. A group of twenty-six members in Toyama Prefecture journeyed by boat down the Shogawa River from Gokayama in Higashitonami County to get to the collection center in Inamimachi. And in the Tsushima islands, members also traveled by boat to make their donations.

The members' excitement reached its peak on October 4, five days before the start of the contribution campaign, when an artist's depiction of the Grand Main Temple appeared on the front page of the *Seikyo Shimbun*. The headline read in big, bold letters: "Plans for the Epochal Grand Main Temple," and the image filled the top half of the page.

The entrance hall was shown stretching out spaciously across the front. A supporting pillar extended upwards from the building's rear, while the roof sloped downwards on either side, depicting the shape of Mount Fuji. The text explained that the tower was 216 feet in height, about twice that of the Grand Reception Hall, and that the number signified the generation of the current sixty-sixth high priest, Nittatsu. The width and depth of the building were each approximately 330 feet.

Everyone was deeply impressed by the structure's contemporary and grand appearance, and they were moved by the awareness that the Grand Main Temple would soon become a reality. The realization that this magnificent edifice was being built through their own efforts filled the members with tremendous joy.

THE DEPICTION of the Grand Main Temple that appeared in the *Seikyo Shimbun* was copied onto large pieces of paper that were hung at collection points.

Though there existed many palaces, temples and other grand buildings in the world, members were proud of the fact that the Grand Main Temple would be built through the efforts of ordinary people.

The contribution period—taking place for four days and starting on the morning of October 9—ended at eight o'clock in the evening on October 12 and was carried out joyously and without incident. On October 14, Shin'ichi Yamamoto called a meeting of the vice chairpersons of the Grand Main Temple Construction Committee and made an interim report on the campaign. The next day, he met with High Priest Nittatsu at the head temple and gave him a detailed update as well.

The October Soka Gakkai Headquarters Leaders Meeting was held shortly before two o'clock in the afternoon on the seventeenth at the Nihon University Auditorium in Ryogoku, Tokyo. There, President Yamamoto first offered his gratitude for the contributions that were made to the Grand Main Temple construction project, saying: "Thanks to the sincere efforts of the more than eight million people who participated in this contribution campaign, we have far surpassed our goal. Thank you very much!

"I'd like to now report on the breakdown of the donations. The Association of Priests and Their Families donated 157,878,265 yen; the National Hokkeko Federation contributed 313,820,162 yen; and Soka Gakkai members contributed 35,064,305,882 yen, for a grand total of 35,536,004,309 yen."

Cheers and applause rang throughout the auditorium. It was a victory of faith and the power of the people.

At the outset, the Soka Gakkai Headquarters set a goal of three billion yen in contributions, because President Toda had designated that as the amount that should be used for construction. In order to accommodate as many people as possible, however, the scale of the original plan had to be doubled. And, in addition to the extra cost in building materials such a change would require, prices in general had risen steeply since President Toda's day.

But the sincere donations made by Soka Gakkai members alone surpassed ten times the original goal, meaning that the finest building could be erected without worrying about the cost.

Shin'ichi continued: "Contributions will be collected overseas for four days from November 12 through November 15. I would like to announce the results of that campaign at the November Headquarters leaders meeting."

AFTER announcing the results of the Grand Main Temple contribution campaign, Shin'ichi read the list of items being donated to the head temple. He then presented the list to High Priest Nittatsu, who stood behind the podium facing the audience. The high priest chanted three times as he accepted the ceremonial wooden tray on which the list was placed. He then read aloud the official document of acceptance and handed it to Shin'ichi.

Once more the auditorium erupted in applause. High Priest Nittatsu next delivered remarks, saying: "As you have just heard, I have been presented with an offering that far exceeds what anyone could have imagined." He went on to comment on the significance of President Yamamoto's pledge to construct the Grand Main Temple as the hall that would enshrine the Dai-Gohonzon of the sanctuary of the essential teaching, in accord with the Daishonin's instruction.[1]

High Priest Nittatsu then quoted the words of the twenty-sixth high priest Nichikan: "Just as the smell of incense is equally delightful to the one who sells it, the one who buys it and the one standing nearby, the benefit received by teacher, disciple and all who respond with joy is equally unsurpassable."[2] In this way, he said, by pledging to build and donate the Grand Main Temple and encouraging others to make the same pledge, President Yamamoto is the teacher, while the members of the Soka Gakkai and the Hokkeko Federation, as well as the priests and their families who participated in this campaign, are the disciples.

Commenting on the report that President Yamamoto had chanted Nam-myoho-renge-kyo 3.5 million times for the success of the contribution campaign, the high priest remarked that President Yamamoto's prayers had turned into thirty-five billion yen in contributions. And he declared: "From ancient times, the act of making a vow itself has been regarded as more than half the battle toward a goal's actualization. With this contribution of thirty-five billion yen, we have indeed overcome the greater part of the struggle to realize the construction of the Grand Main Temple."

High Priest Nittatsu further stated that in Buddhism, this world is considered the realm of Mount Sumeru, and that there are said to be ten billion such realms throughout the cosmos. The construction of the Grand Main Temple, he added, will bring benefit to the people of all those ten billion Mount Sumeru realms. This is because the benefit of chanting Nam-myoho-renge-kyo with sincere faith to the Dai-Gohonzon will definitely extend to the far reaches of the entire universe, he said.

The high priest closed his remarks by saying that he wished to entrust President Yamamoto with the task of ensuring that the full amount of contributions be put toward the Grand Main Temple's construction as well as other activities and facilities to be used toward achieving kosen-rufu. He then handed Shin'ichi an official document charging him with this duty.

Thunderous applause rang throughout the auditorium and continued for some time.

It was a historic moment. Joy and pride shone on the faces of the members who had given their all to the contribution campaign.

SHIN'ICHI took the podium next, his heart filled with profound gratitude for his fellow members. He said: "Nichiren Daishonin's mandate that the sanctuary of the essential teaching be established is now effectively coming to fruition seven hundred years later, in our time, by our hands, with our contributions. Congratulations!"

Applause shook the auditorium once again.

"Let us have the conviction that making this wonderful offering means that we have accumulated great good fortune in our lives. The benefit that accrues from making contributions is clearly spelled out in the Gosho. If we were to contribute to kosen-rufu just as the Gosho teaches and then failed to receive actual proof, then Buddhism would be false. The Gohonzon has tremendous power. I'm sure you are all well aware of that through your own experiences in faith until now.

"Confident of the good fortune we are attaining, let us continue to advance joyfully, harmoniously and in high spirits toward our next goal, bracing ourselves for the struggle ahead. Also, let us remember that the amount of one's contribution is not important; it is one's sincerity that matters. The Gohonzon is witness to everything, which means that the benefit we receive is determined by our attitude in faith. Accordingly, I would like to say that it is inappropriate to talk about the amount contributed by individual members."

Shin'ichi then announced that High Priest Nittatsu would present all who had participated in the contribution campaign with a cloth for wrapping their prayer beads. In closing, he said: "Up to now, the Soka Gakkai has been criticized and ridiculed as a gathering of the poor and sick. But the fact that we have achieved such a great amount of contributions in the midst of these tough economic times is evidence that the Soka Gakkai has become an unrivaled organization in Japan. I wish to declare that this is proof of the tremendous benefit that comes from having faith in the Gohonzon.

"I hope that you will continue to accumulate good fortune in your lives and that you will one day declare you are the happiest people in all Japan. Lastly, I would say that this is a right of all of you who have participated wholeheartedly in this contribution campaign."

The Headquarters leaders meeting came to a close

amid the members' great joy at their successful campaign. The wheels were thus set powerfully in motion.

THE GROUNDBREAKING ceremony for the Grand Main Temple took place on October 12, 1967. Five years later, on October 1, 1972, the completion ceremony was held. For a week after, a number of events took place in high spirits to celebrate and commemorate this important occasion. The Dai-Gohonzon transfer ceremony took place on October 11; the ceremony to officially announce the Grand Main Temple's completion on the 12th; the fountain-jetting ceremony was held in the courtyard on the 13th; the Grand Main Temple inauguration ceremony on the 14th; and the world peace prayer ceremony on the 15th, along with a World Peace Culture Festival and other events.

In accord with High Priest Nittatsu's instruction, everyone regarded the Grand Main Temple as the sanctuary of the essential teaching. With the aim of creating a magnificent structure that would endure as a cultural legacy of humanity and a masterpiece of aesthetic beauty, the building's architecture was designed and constructed using state-of-the-art techniques.

But after the death of High Priest Nittatsu, Nikken Abe, who became the sixty-seventh high priest, suddenly declared in January 1991 that the Grand Main Temple was "not the actual sanctuary of the essential teaching in the ultimate sense." This was just eighteen years after the building's completion. He also began to make statements to the effect that it was President Yamamoto who had arbitrarily designated it as the sanctuary of the essential teaching.

This was clearly a declaration that completely went against the instructions of High Priest Nittatsu. It was an insidious betrayal not only of Soka Gakkai members but also of members of the Hokkeko Federation, as well as the priests and their families. It was precisely because Gakkai members believed that the Grand Main Temple was the sanctuary of the essential teaching that they had given their all to the contribution campaign, even cutting back on food if they had to.

Furthermore, in April 1998, Nikken without warning transferred the Dai-Gohonzon from the Grand Main Temple to the Hoanden Hall and announced that the Grand Main Temple would be torn down. Claiming that the building was old, in June of that same year, he ordered that its demolition begin. In doing so, he trampled on the sincere spirit of eight million followers.

It was an act motivated purely by envy of the Soka Gakkai, the organization that was making tremendous contributions to the advancement of kosen-rufu. No doubt because of his arrogance and overweening ambition to make a mark for himself, Nikken also sought to completely destroy the noble legacy of his predecessor, High Priest Nittatsu. This was truly the act of someone who had been taken over by the devil king of the sixth heaven and whose head had been "split into seven pieces" (LS26, 310), and who as a result was destined to fall into the hell of incessant suffering.

In contrast, the sincere faith of the members who contributed to realizing the Daishonin's injunction would without a doubt adorn their lives with eternal good fortune.

ON OCTOBER 19, 1965, two days after the October Headquarters Leaders Meeting, Shin'ichi left for Europe to purchase construction materials for the Grand Main Temple and to offer encouragement to members there. He would visit four countries—France, West Germany, Italy and Portugal—accompanied by vice general directors Akizuki, Okada and Nishimiya; women's vice leaders Okada and Haruki; and his wife, Mineko.

While discussing arrangements before their departure, Shin'ichi said to his traveling companions: "Let's make a conscious effort to promote cultural exchange on this trip. While advancing world peace is the mission of Buddhists, I believe that linking the hearts of people from different countries is what forms the solid foundation for such peace. Cultural exchange forges those bonds and promotes mutual understanding.

"The activities of the Min-On Concert Association here in Japan are well under way now and I think the time has come for the association to start taking a more active role on a global scale."

With Shin'ichi's words in mind, the leaders set forth on their trip to Europe determined to initiate cultural exchange.

The group arrived in Paris shortly after half past nine in the morning on October 20. Shin'ichi went directly to the hotel where he met with Europe Headquarters Leader Eiji Kawasaki and discussed the expansion of the European organization. A ceremony to mark the opening of the Soka Gakkai Europe office was scheduled for the afternoon—although the office was actually just the Kawasaki family home. Until now, the Kawasakis had lived in a one-room apartment, but they moved to a two-room apartment on Rue Pascal near Eiji's workplace at the Collège de France. They also decided to use the place as the European office for the Soka Gakkai.

When Shin'ichi and his party arrived, the Kawasakis' apartment overflowed with members. After enshrining the Gohonzon they had brought with them from Japan, Shin'ichi led everyone in a solemn gongyo. Although not all of the members were Japanese, their voices fused together in perfect harmony.

When gongyo was completed, Shin'ichi said: "Congratulations! Opening this European office, humble though it may be, is a huge first step. In the future, we will build a magnificent center here in France as well, so please look forward to that day."

The members' eyes sparkled with anticipation.

SMILING, Shin'ichi continued: "In April last year, the Europe Headquarters was established with 209 member-households but I understand that in the nearly eighteen months since then membership has grown remarkably to 446 households. For this reason, and taking into consideration the future growth of Europe, we would like to divide the current headquarters into Europe No. 1 and Europe No. 2 Headquarters.

"Europe No. 1 Headquarters will mainly include France, England, Italy, Switzerland and Belgium, while No. 2 will mainly consist of Germany, Norway, Sweden, Denmark, the Netherlands and Austria. We would also like to announce the establishment of the Europe General Headquarters at this juncture."

Applause filled the room.

At the time, the Soka Gakkai in Japan was organized into chapters, general chapters, headquarters and general headquarters in order of ascending size. The general headquarters system had started in January of the previous year with the formation of Kansai General Headquarters. Other general headquarters were subsequently established across Japan, until they numbered twenty-five. This, however, was the first to be formed overseas.

"In Japan," Shin'ichi continued, "a general headquarters is made up of two hundred thousand member-households on average. There aren't so many members in Europe right now, but in anticipation of tremendous growth in the future, we've decided to establish a general headquarters at this stage with Vice General Director and Youth Division Leader Eisuke Akizuki as its head. Meanwhile, Eiji Kawasaki, who has until now been in charge of Europe Headquarters, will be the leader of Europe No. 1 Headquarters, and Koichiro Sada, who has been head of Germany Chapter, will be the leader of No. 2.

"Paris Chapter will also be divided, creating a new Champs-Elysées Chapter. Shinsaku Haruno will be the leader and Shotaro Hasebe the vice leader of this new chapter.

"How does that sound? Do these appointments meet with your approval?"

Cheers and applause again spread throughout the room.

"I am very happy that you agree with these appointments. This is the most important thing. If leadership appointments were determined solely by the opinions of local members, they could easily turn into mere popularity contests. Of course leaders need to be well liked. But it may happen that leaders who do not fight injustice win the support of the members because they are perceived as tolerant.

"I'M SURE some of you are thinking that since the tide of democracy is sweeping the globe, all decisions made within the Soka Gakkai should also be reached by a majority vote," Shin'ichi continued. "I completely agree that it is important to discuss things thoroughly with everyone involved before a decision is made but in the realm of Buddhism, not everything can be decided by majority rule.

"During World War II, when the priesthood, out of

fear of the military government, suggested that the Soka Gakkai accept the Shinto talisman like it had, first Soka Gakkai president Makiguchi staunchly refused. The priesthood's decision to obey the authorities itself was no doubt reached through the deliberation of the senior priests at the head temple.

"In Buddhism, however, even if a decision is made by consensus, if that decision goes against the teachings or the spirit of the Daishonin, it must not be followed. The Mystic Law is the basic criterion for everything. To stand up even alone, and guide things back on the right track when everyone starts heading in a mistaken direction—this is a requirement of a genuine leader.

"It therefore follows that leadership appointments must not be made through popularity contests where the one with the most wins. At the same time, however, if top leaders arbitrarily make personnel appointments without consulting those whom the decisions will directly affect, the end result will likely be failure.

"That's why top leaders must first listen to the opinions of local members and then carefully observe each leadership appointment candidate's faith, which is their fundamental qualification.

"Until now, I have spoken with many of you on several different occasions to hear your input. Both before leaving Japan and since arriving in Paris we have carefully considered the prospects for leadership appointments from a number of perspectives. That is why we have made appointments that everyone can support."

Shin'ichi added, with increased vigor: "Incidentally, the reason Europe Headquarters has been divided into two is because without friendly rivalry, inertia sets in. A good rival can inspire us to greater development. With such a healthy spirit of competition, I hope you will realize great advancement."

Among the participants in the meeting that day, Shin'ichi saw many faces for the first time. This was eloquent testimony to the progress of kosen-rufu in Europe.

WHEN Shin'ichi finished talking, Eiji Kawasaki introduced to him a woman sitting toward the back of the room.

"President Yamamoto," he said, "I'd like to introduce a member who has traveled from Africa to be here today. This is Mrs. Fujie James." A woman with a slender face and a refined air rose and bowed.

Shin'ichi bowed deeply in return and said: "Thank you for coming from so far away. Please, come up front."

When she had made her way to the front of the room, Shin'ichi inquired: "Where in Africa have you come from?"

"From Kaduna in Nigeria," she replied.

"How many members are there in Nigeria now?"

"Thirty-four. Thirty are native Nigerians, and the other four, including myself, are Japanese. The Japanese members there are engaged in various kinds of work, such as offering technical support and guidance."

"Is that right? That many!" Shin'ichi said with great emotion.

Five years earlier, in 1960, he had visited the U. N. Headquarters in New York and sat in on both committee and plenary sessions of the General Assembly. He would never forget the dynamism with which the youthful representatives of the newly independent African nations spoke out. They showed no trace of the arrogance and cunning that often characterized the leaders of the great world powers. They displayed a fresh and vital energy and were filled with self-confidence and pride.

At that moment, Shin'ichi keenly felt that the twenty-first century would be the century of Africa. Now, he was overjoyed to hear that Bodhisattvas of the Earth were actually appearing on that continent and working to spread the teachings of Buddhism there. And thirty-four members were certainly sufficient to form a base for the future of kosen-rufu.

Shin'ichi then inquired how it was that Fujie had come to be in Africa and what kind of activities members were engaging in there.

Fujie joined the Soka Gakkai in 1957 at a friend's introduction, and from that time had participated diligently in young women's activities in Japan. In 1963, she married an Englishman working as a manager for an airline company and they moved to Birmingham, England, to begin their new life together. Hearing that there was a member named Eiko Rich living in London, Fujie contacted her immediately and then went there to visit her. As she had no friends in England except her husband and communicating in English was still quite difficult, Fujie found Eiko to be a tremendous source of support and comfort.

ABOUT SIX MONTHS after their marriage, Fujie's husband was transferred to Nigeria. Fujie was anxious and worried about the move. All she knew about Nigeria was that it was a newly independent nation in the tropics very near the equator. She decided to pay a visit to Eiji Kawasaki.

After listening to Fujie describe her feelings, Kawasaki said: "You may be feeling lonely now but from a Buddhist perspective you are going to Nigeria to fulfill your mission as a pioneer of kosen-rufu in Africa. This is a promise you, yourself, made to Nichiren Daishonin in the remote past.

"It's true that it will probably be hard adjusting to a climate, environment and culture that are all unfamiliar to you. But I hope you will think of this as the opportunity to finally carry out your mission from the distant past. Whatever may happen, you mustn't be discouraged. When things are tough, just chant abundantly."

Once she realized that going to Nigeria was her personal mission, the clouds of uncertainty that troubled her evaporated and she was full of hope. "Alright, I'll do my best!" she thought. "I'll plant the seeds of happiness in Africa!"

She and her husband first moved to the city of Kano, Nigeria. Her new living situation could not have been more different from that in England, and Fujie felt disoriented. The highest buildings in the city were the airport and a few three- or four-story hotels. Leaving the city, one was surrounded by a vast expanse of red earth.

Fujie was especially surprised to encounter chameleons. Disguised by their ability to change colors, they could be found not only in trees but everywhere. She was also troubled by the geckos that scampered about the walls and ceilings of the house. The prevalence of malaria also alarmed her.

But knowing that she had chosen this as the place to carry out her mission, she began to chant in earnest as if to saturate the very earth of Africa with her chanting. Sitting on a blanket spread out on the concrete floor, she studied the map of Africa, concentrating on the names of cities and praying for each of them. She also began to introduce Buddhism to others in her newly acquired English but no one she spoke to started practicing the Daishonin's Buddhism.

Eventually, she and her husband moved to the town of Kaduna. According to news she received from Eiko Rich in London, a Japanese member had been sent to the same town from a spinning factory in Japan to offer technical advice. Fujie was overjoyed to learn this and contacted him immediately.

THOUGH he was not very good at English, the official language of Nigeria, he had been teaching some of the locals he knew from work to chant Nam-myoho-renge-kyo. This encouraged Fujie. Her English was also far from perfect but she began to explain to those who started chanting why Buddhism was so wonderful. Thus, these two members from Japan combined their energies and started promoting Soka Gakkai activities in Nigeria.

Gradually, more people began to practice. They held discussion meetings once a week on Saturday evenings at the homes of local residents. On occasion, as many as thirty or forty people would attend, overflowing the room.

In early October 1965, Fujie received a letter from Eiko Rich in the United Kingdom saying that President Yamamoto would soon visit Europe, though apparently Eiko did not yet know the exact dates. Fujie decided she wanted to meet President Yamamoto during his trip and she prayed in earnest. Then, on the 16th of that month, her husband proposed that they take a trip to South Africa. When Fujie heard his offer, she asked if they might go to Paris instead. She assumed that if President Yamamoto were going to Europe he would be sure to visit Paris where Eiji Kawasaki, the central leader of the Europe organization at the time, was located.

Her husband happily agreed to her suggestion and they arrived in Paris a few days later on October 19. Immediately, Fujie contacted Kawasaki and asked whether President Yamamoto had reached the city yet. Kawasaki replied that he would not be there until the following day. So it was that Fujie joyfully attended the meeting with Shin'ichi on the evening of October 20.

Hearing her story, Shin'ichi was thrilled to know that members with a shared mission were now appearing in Africa. He made a decision on the spot and sought the approval of those in attendance: "Let's form a chapter in Africa," he said. "We'll call it Africa Chapter and have Mrs. James be its leader. What do you think?"

Fujie was startled by this sudden proposal, but with a look of determination, she nodded in acceptance. The next moment a wave of excited applause swept through the room.

To commemorate the occasion, Shin'ichi presented her with some prayer beads and said: "I believe the twenty-first century will be the century of Africa. We are striving to open and forge the way toward that future. That is because as human beings we have the power and noble mission to create the future."

"I'LL DO my best!" Fujie replied energetically. A Japanese woman in the audience applauded with enthusiasm as she happily took in the scene. Shin'ichi noticed this and asked her name.

"Eiko Rich," she replied. "I'm from London."

This was Shin'ichi's first encounter with Eiko, but he had heard a great deal about her from Eiji Kawasaki. She had also traveled from afar to be at that meeting.

"I understand that you are working hard in the United Kingdom," he said to her. "I have brought with me gifts of handwritten calligraphy as well as square pieces of cloth for wrapping prayer beads for our members in the United Kingdom. Would you please distribute them for me?"

Flushed with excitement, Eiko replied: "Thank you so much! I know our members will be very happy."

Eiko was a kind and considerate leader who was always thinking of the members. She joined the Soka Gakkai in 1958 in Yokohama at the introduction of her older sister. It was a time when she was suffering from an unhappy relationship and was extremely depressed. Touched by her sister's concern for her and the sincere way she encouraged her to take up faith, Eiko began practicing.

Before long, Eiko met an Englishman who was working on an international cruise ship. They decided to get married and Eiko moved to England in 1961. It was there that she developed strong conviction in the Daishonin's Buddhism.

Eiko soon became pregnant. When she started experiencing morning sickness, the doctor prescribed a drug to help her relax and sleep. The first time she took the drug, however, she suffered an attack of nausea and vomited it up. She also developed pains in her lower abdomen and began to hemorrhage.

She went to see a doctor who told her there was a chance that she would miscarry and he hospitalized her immediately. She chanted earnestly from her hospital bed to give birth to a healthy child. When the doctor examined her again and said that she and the baby were going to be all right, Eiko wept tears of gratitude.

To her great joy, she eventually gave birth to a healthy baby boy. She was in awe of the power of the Gohonzon.

This feeling was driven home to her further when, several years later, the adverse side effects of the drug thalidomide—the very drug that the doctor had prescribed for her morning sickness—became a widespread social problem.

AS SHE WATCHED her baby grow strong and healthy, Eiko thought about what might have happened if she hadn't vomited up the thalidomide and had kept taking it throughout her pregnancy. Filled with deep appreciation, she solidified her resolve to work for kosen-rufu in the United Kingdom.

In August 1963, Shizuko Grant, who had been the main contact person for the Soka Gakkai in London until then, had to leave the country because her husband was transferred. Eiko then replaced her. At that time there were only five member-households in the United Kingdom, but Eiko burned with great hope and was determined to spread the Daishonin's Buddhism. Reminding herself that "A thousand mile journey begins with a single step," she started holding discussion meetings in her home and writing letters of encouragement to members on a daily basis.

She didn't have a lot of money but she cut back on purchasing such things as lipstick so that she could save enough to travel around the country to encourage members and introduce Buddhism to others. As a result, soon the membership grew to more than thirty member families.

Eiko and Fujie, as well as members like them who spread Nichiren Buddhism in America and Southeast

Asia, were not professional missionaries such as one finds in Christianity. The task of realizing worldwide kosen-rufu has been shouldered by ordinary lay Soka Gakkai members, not clergy draped in robes of authority. And most of them have been women.

Living in a foreign land without any support, these women cultivated people's trust and friendship and shared the Mystic Law as they struggled to overcome differences of language, customs and culture in their daily lives. No doubt they were criticized because of misunderstanding and prejudice. It has indeed been an endeavor requiring tremendous perseverance.

In the history of religion, there have been many cases in which propagation was carried out by the use of military force, political power or economic might. But that directly contradicts the spirit of Nichiren Daishonin, whose life was devoted to transmitting his teaching through dialogue aimed at inspiring and empathizing with others. The greatest characteristic of Nichiren Buddhism is that its teachings have spread not through force but through the dedicated propagation efforts of ordinary men and women. This itself is testimony to the fact that it is a religion *for* the people.

In Shin'ichi's eyes, each of these sincere members who was working so hard for kosen-rufu in distant lands was a Buddha. After he had finished speaking, he fielded questions from those present, encouraging them wholeheartedly with a sense of respect and admiration.

WHILE in Paris, in addition to looking at buildings that might serve as a new community center,

Shin'ichi Yamamoto also shopped for materials and furnishings for the Grand Main Temple. At the same time, Soka Gakkai youth division leader Eisuke Akizuki, who was also the executive vice president of the Min-On Concert Association, met with René Nicoly, the director of the French young people's musical organization Jeunesses Musicales de France. Seeking to further promote cultural and musical activities rooted in the lives of ordinary people, Akizuki wanted to learn as much as he could from other cultural organizations and deepen ties with them.

From five o'clock on the evening of October 21, a study exam and a guidance session were held in a room in the foreign students' center at the University of Paris, Sorbonne. Nineteen members sat for the exam and fifty participated in the guidance session that took place in the same room afterward. At the meeting, Eiko Rich was appointed the leader of London District and a new district was formed in Belgium.

Around noon the following day, October 22, Shin'ichi and his party left Paris for their next destination, West Germany. When Shin'ichi saw that Koichiro and Michiya, who worked at a coal mine there, had come to greet him at the Frankfurt Airport, he called out to them: "Hello there! It's been a while, hasn't it? How are you?"

Koichiro's cheeks flushed with excitement as he replied: "We're fine. The other ten members who came from Japan to work here in West Germany are all in high spirits and doing their best as well."

Shin'ichi smiled. "That's wonderful," he said. "These young men devoting their lives to kosen-rufu here are the treasures of the Soka Gakkai. Please take good care of them."

"We will!" they replied immediately in energetic voices.

With a slight nod, Shin'ichi said: "Let's go to the hotel and you can tell me how everyone is doing. I'd also like to discuss with you what new steps we can take in order to develop our organization here in West Germany."

Koichiro felt deeply moved by President Yamamoto's great expectations and concern for the ten young men who recently had come from Japan. He had met with Shin'ichi in Paris in October of the previous year and discussed with him his wish to bring youth of strong faith to West Germany to work for kosen-rufu. At that time, Shin'ichi encouraged him, saying how important it was for those with longer experience in faith to set the stage upon which younger members who wished to be active outside Japan could succeed them.

KOICHIRO returned to Japan in early November, the month following his meeting with Shin'ichi in Paris. While taking care of the necessary paperwork for extending his stay in West Germany, he began to look for members who wanted to return with him to West Germany.

At the introduction of friends, he visited one young men's member after another in Hokkaido and asked if they wanted to come to West Germany to work in a coal mine and join him in the struggle for kosen-rufu there. Meanwhile, in West Germany, Michiya was laying the groundwork so that any members Koichiro brought back from Japan would have a job in the coal mine where they worked in the German city of Castrop-Rauxel. German coal mines were short of laborers and anyone who wanted a job was welcomed with open arms. In March 1965, Michiya also returned to Japan.

Though initially a dozen or so young men's members had shown interest in Koichiro's proposal, in the end the number came to ten. The oldest of them was Hisazo Ogachi, who was thirty-two and worked as an auto mechanic in Sapporo, Hokkaido. Three years earlier, he had been preparing for his wedding, but just before the ceremony, his fiancée experienced an attack of severe stomach pain. When she was examined at the hospital, it was discovered that she had a malignant tumor in her abdomen. It was quite large and she was in extremely weak condition, so surgery was ruled out.

While in the hospital, she met a Soka Gakkai member and decided that she wanted to practice. Ogachi had no interest in religion but since it was for the sake of the person he loved most in the world, he decided to join the Soka Gakkai, too, in January 1963.

From that day, a young men's member began visiting Ogachi at home to teach him gongyo. Ogachi was touched by the firm commitment demonstrated by this young man, who traveled 2.5 miles day after day over icy winter roads on his bicycle to see him.

But Ogachi's fiancée died soon after. It was a peaceful death, and she was surrounded by her family. Ogachi's grief overwhelmed him. Having lost the reason for his faith, he started to distance himself from the Soka Gakkai. Concerned about him, his fellow members visited him frequently to offer support and encouragement but Ogachi just couldn't summon the desire to practice.

Then one day he had a car accident. He walked away unscathed but his car had flipped over and he could very well have lost his life. Filled with a sense that he had been miraculously protected, he concluded this was a sign that he must not give up his faith.

FROM THAT time on, Ogachi participated wholeheartedly in Soka Gakkai activities. As he learned about the Buddhist view of the eternity of life, a firm determination began to well up inside him—a resolve, partly in memory of his deceased fiancée, to practice strongly and devote himself to kosen-rufu throughout his life. Whenever he read about the activities and experiences of members overseas in the *Seikyo Shimbun* and other Gakkai publications, he also felt that he would like to work for kosen-rufu in a similar manner.

Then, in the spring of 1965, a young men's leader from his area came to see him and said: "A member named Koichiro Sada, who works in a coal mine in West Germany, is currently visiting the Hokkaido Headquarters. He says he wants to take about ten young men's members back with him to promote kosen-rufu in West Germany. Have you any interest in going?"

It was a sudden proposal and Ogachi didn't know how to reply. He was interested in meeting Koichiro and hearing his plan, however, so he made his way to the headquarters building.

As he was driving there, Ogachi's head was spinning. "This is the age of worldwide kosen-rufu," he thought to himself. "President Yamamoto has said that it is time for young people to make their way out into the world and spread the Daishonin's teachings. My efforts until now also have been motivated by that vision."

Before meeting Koichiro, his mind was almost already made up: "Alright, then—I will devote my life to propagating Buddhism in West Germany!"

Koichiro, meanwhile, had received word that Ogachi was on his way, and he was waiting for him at the Hokkaido Headquarters. When Ogachi arrived, Koichiro greeted him with a smile: "Thanks for coming. I hope you'll join me in advancing kosen-rufu in West Germany!"

In a resounding voice, Koichiro spoke enthusiastically about the mission of young people to go out into the world. Koichiro was brimming with great passion to spread Buddhism in West Germany.

When Ogachi asked him about the work available, Koichiro replied: "There is plenty of work in the coal mines, so you don't have to worry about supporting yourself. I would recommend that you start out working at the mine and then once you've established yourself you can look for another job—perhaps related to what you're doing now in auto repair.

"The most important thing, however, is whether you are prepared to spend the rest of your life in West Germany working for kosen-rufu."

Ogachi replied decisively: "I understand, and I'm ready to do just that. Please let me go with you!" Thus the decision was made.

THE YOUNGEST volunteer was Daigo Aoyama, a twenty-year-old chef working at a restaurant in Kushiro, Hokkaido. He learned about Buddhism from Shinji Tamaru, another chef about his age with whom he worked, and began practicing in December 1963. Both young men threw themselves into Soka Gakkai activities, and after reading President Yamamoto's essay in the Gakkai study journal *The Daibyakurenge,* "Youth, Become World Leaders!" they often talked about their determination to go out into the world to spread the Daishonin's teachings.

Koichiro had once worked in a coal mine in Kushiro, so the members in that area were well aware of his story. They were proud that a fellow Kushiro member was a pioneer of kosen-rufu in West Germany and both Aoyama and Tamaru had heard much about him. It was from one of their leaders that they learned Koichiro was looking for members to go back to West Germany with him to work for kosen-rufu.

The young men were eager to go; neither of them hesitated for a moment. When they met Koichiro, they begged him to take them to West Germany, conveying to him their strong determination to contribute to worldwide kosen-rufu. But Koichiro warned them about how hard life could be there and asked them if they were prepared to devote themselves completely to the effort. Without a pause, they replied earnestly that they were indeed prepared to do so and that they had already resolved to dedicate their lives to spreading Buddhism.

Koichiro was moved by their determination and agreed to take them.

A young man from Sapporo named Kosaku Osanai also read President Yamamoto's essay in *The Daibyakurenge* and was profoundly moved. He, too, made an instant decision to go overseas to propagate Buddhism. From that day, he began chanting sincerely to the Gohonzon with the prayer that within three years he would achieve that dream. It was just a year later that he heard about Koichiro's search for members to go to West Germany with him.

Osanai had studied German as one of the two languages he was required to study at his university's night school, so he felt a strong connection with that country. Certain that his prayer to the Gohonzon had been answered and that this was his chance to realize his dream, he was overjoyed. He went to see Koichiro and asked him if he could go to West Germany with him.

THE MEMBERS going to West Germany were firmly determined to do their best to advance kosen-rufu there. They cared nothing for property, wealth, social status or recognition, and had not the slightest desire to live easy lives or to be better than others. Having pondered the best way for human beings to live in light of the unchanging teachings of Buddhism, they each concluded that spreading those teachings, which would lead to the realization of peace and happiness for all humanity, was the supreme and ultimate way of life. They were thus resolved to give themselves completely to this cause.

This was the feeling of many of the young people in the Soka Gakkai. Those caught up solely in the pursuit of their own immediate personal desires do not understand the nobility of this spirit.

Nichiren Daishonin writes: "Fish want to survive; they deplore their pond's shallowness and dig holes in the bottom to hide in, yet tricked by bait, they take the hook" (WND, 301). This is a passage from the famous "Letter from Sado." In order to protect themselves, fish live in holes dug at the bottom of the pond but they foolishly come out and take the bait when it is dangled before them. The Daishonin continues: "Human beings are equally vulnerable. They give their lives for shallow, worldly matters but rarely for the Buddha's precious teachings. Small wonder they do not attain Buddhahood" (WND, 301).

Life is infinitely valuable; there is no greater treasure. The most important challenge we therefore face is how and to what purpose we should dedicate our precious lives.

The Daishonin tells us to use our lives to spread Buddhism—in other words, to use our lives for kosen-rufu. For that is the direct path to attaining Buddhahood, the state of absolute happiness, in this life.

The young men going to Germany firmly believed this.

The spirit of the Soka Gakkai youth division is to spare no effort to actualize kosen-rufu and to go anywhere necessary in order to do so. Sharing this spirit, most of their families happily saw them off into the world.

When Eiji Onoda, a young men's group leader in Sapporo, decided to go to West Germany, he discussed it with his mother who lived nearby. He was the third of six children. His father and eldest brother had passed away and his mother lived with his second-eldest brother and his wife.

EIJI'S MOTHER was the first in her family to start practicing the Daishonin's Buddhism, persisting in her faith despite the opposition of other family members. It was from her that Eiji learned about the practice.

Eiji sat up straight as he announced to his mother his wish to devote himself to kosen-rufu in West Germany.

"Mother, may I go to West Germany?" he asked.

"How many years do you plan to stay there?" she inquired. Her voice was calm, without a hint of surprise.

Though Eiji was determined to spend the rest of his life there, he didn't want to worry her, so he said: "Just two years."

His mother's response was quite unexpected. "If you're going to go," she replied, "you should spend your entire life working for kosen-rufu there. Whatever happens, always embrace the Gohonzon, never abandon your faith and always do your very best. I hope you will build a happy life there."

Tears of appreciation filled Eiji's eyes as he listened to his mother's words.

The members going to West Germany immediately began preparations for the journey. One of their biggest challenges was raising the money for their fares. None had any savings and even if they were to receive severance pay from their companies it would not be enough to cover the cost. They had to find extra part-time jobs in order to come up with the money.

Their departure date was set for August 12. When a

leader of the Sapporo young men's division learned that five members from his area were going to West Germany, he organized a series of special study sessions so that the young men would correctly share the true spirit of Buddhism with people there. The leader made time in his busy schedule to give them lectures on such things as the Daishonin's writings and the history of the Soka Gakkai. Deeply appreciative of this special effort on their behalf, the young men listened intently to his lectures, wanting to remember every word.

The leader also presented the five young men with fountain pens as parting gifts. Each pen was inscribed with one of the five Chinese characters from the passage in the "Parable of the Phantom City" chapter of the Lotus Sutra that reads: "Constantly reborn in company with their teachers" (LS7, 140). He gave them this gift in order to convey to them the importance of advancing together in unity, never forgetting that wherever they went, they were working for kosen-rufu alongside their mentor in life, President Yamamoto.

In addition, the young men's division threw a splendid going-away party for the young men at the Hokkaido Headquarters.

AT THE END of June, as the ten young men continued to make preparations for their departure, Michiya, who was also visiting Japan from West Germany, received a letter from a friend there. The letter said that the country's economy had suddenly taken a turn for the worse and an increasing number of foreign laborers were being let go. Unsettled by this news, Michiya consulted with Koichiro. They decided that Michiya and one of the ten new recruits, a student named Teruo Sunayama, would go to West Germany in advance to survey the situation.

Michiya had come home to Japan to get married to Michiyo Anzai, a young women's member whom he had known since junior high school. Michiyo's younger brother Akito, incidentally, was among the young men scheduled to go to Germany. After the wedding on July 9, Michiya left for Germany with Sunayama, leaving Michiyo behind in Japan for the time being. Michiyo was not altogether pleased that her husband was leaving for West Germany before they even had a chance to go on a honeymoon but she was also reassured by his sincere dedication to kosen-rufu.

At about the same time, Koichiro was introduced to a prospective marriage partner by a leader of the Hokkaido men's division. Her name was Yukiko Kawada and she was a young women's division member. Yukiko's father had passed away when she was in her second year in high school.

As they spoke, Koichiro said: "My father died when I was young and I wasn't able to finish elementary school. My mother died when I was eighteen.

"I don't have an impressive academic background or money. My only treasure is my faith. I am confident that no one can surpass my firm faith in the Gohonzon and my determination to put President Yamamoto's guidance into practice.

"I'm sorry that what I am about to say is so sudden but in a month, on August 12, I am going to West Germany.

A simple yes or no will do, but could you please let me know by tomorrow morning whether you would agree to marry me?"

They had only known each other for an hour.

Yukiko was considerably taken aback, but at the same time she felt an attraction to this young man who was so forthright and warmhearted. That night she chanted straight through to morning. She prayed earnestly to the Gohonzon to have the wisdom of the Buddha that pervades past, present and future in order to see if this was the person with whom she could work for kosen-rufu and find true happiness.

As the eastern sky began to grow light, Yukiko suddenly knew that he was the right person for her. She thus made her decision.

But when she told her mother about it, the entire family rose up in opposition.

IT WAS only natural that Yukiko's family would oppose her marriage to Koichiro. She had only just met him the day before, and then only for an hour. Even though she knew nothing about him, she was already talking about marrying him. What's more, after the wedding, she would be going to live in a coal-mining town in West Germany where she didn't even understand the language.

Her mother pleaded with her, tears in her eyes: "You lost your father and have spent the best years of your youth working to help support your younger brother and sister, unable to buy yourself nice clothes or enjoy being a young girl. That's why I want you to be happier than anyone else. I have always prayed for that.

"But I can see how difficult things will be for you if you marry someone you hardly know and go to live in a distant foreign country. When I think about how much suffering you are going to have to endure, I feel so bad that I just cannot bring myself to agree to this marriage."

Yukiko could understand her mother's feelings of concern only too well, and she was profoundly moved. But her decision remained unchanged.

"Your concern is perfectly reasonable and I am very grateful to you," she said. "But my mind is made up. I want to work for kosen-rufu in Germany with this person. I feel like this is my mission. I promise that I will become happy and fulfill my duty as your daughter. Please give me your permission to get married."

Sitting in a kneeling position, she placed her hands together on the *tatami* matting and deeply bowed her head in a gesture of formal entreaty.

Her mother watched her intently for a time and then said firmly: "If you are so certain you want to do this, there is nothing I can say. But I hope that if you are going to go, it will be with the determination not to come back to this house for at least five years, no matter what may happen. You can't accomplish anything if you are half-hearted."

Tears flowed from Yukiko's eyes. She agreed completely with what her mother said.

"Thank you, thank you mother! I will do my very best. You just watch!" She squeezed her mother's hand tightly.

Koichiro and Yukiko got married just ten days after their meeting, on July 21.

IN LATE JULY 1965, Shin'ichi received a letter from Koichiro announcing that the ten new members who would go to West Germany had been decided and that their departure date was set for August 12. It also related that one of the ten members had already gone on ahead to Germany with Michiya, and that both Koichiro and Michiya had gotten married.

After reading through the letter, Shin'ichi said to a leader who was with him: "The summer training course at the head temple will start soon. Let's invite the youth going to West Germany to the young men's session. Introducing them to their fellow members from all over Japan will send them off in high spirits, don't you think?"

Of the ten youth who would be making a new life in West Germany, eight were from Hokkaido and two were from Kanagawa Prefecture, near Tokyo. At the beginning of August, the remaining seven members still in Hokkaido—Sunayama having already gone to Germany—said farewell to that northern land, sent off with the best wishes of their friends.

On August 4, Koichiro and the Hokkaido youth joined up with the two Kanagawa members at the head temple and participated in the second session of the training course. This was the first time that the young men all met in one place.

On August 5, the second day of the training session, Shin'ichi joined Koichiro and the others in a commemorative photograph.

"I've been looking forward to meeting you," Shin'ichi said with a smile. He understood well the young men's wholehearted determination and feelings as they prepared to set out on their journey.

"I deeply appreciate your commitment," he continued. "You are all pioneers of kosen-rufu and treasures of the Soka Gakkai. Someone must lay the foundation. Someone must blaze the trail. I am counting on you to realize kosen-rufu—together with me and as my representatives."

Shin'ichi's words had profound impact on the members.

That evening, young men's leaders from across Japan gathered in the head temple's Grand Reception Hall and conducted a guidance session with President Yamamoto. It was here that the departure of the ten young men was announced.

"Tonight I would like to introduce some young men's division members who will be traveling to West Germany soon," Shin'ichi said.

Youth Division Leader Akizuki then read the members' names aloud, one by one. As their names were announced, each energetically responded. Their voices rang out like the stirring cries of young warriors heading into battle and their eyes shone with strong determination.

AS THE NAMES of each were read out, Shin'ichi shook their hands and offered them words of encouragement. To Toshiyuki Osawa of Yokohama he said, "Work together in solid unity!" and to Katsuzo Asada of Sapporo, "Do your best and take care of your health."

Thunderous applause filled the hall in celebration of the group's departure. The summer training course became their farewell party. Holding back tears, the young men burned with fierce resolve as they reaffirmed their commitment to propagate Buddhism in Germany.

The next morning, the group climbed Mount Fuji together with other young men attending the course. Gazing up at the peak and thinking that they would be unable to look on this gallant sight again for many years to come, they were deeply moved. They silently vowed to the majestic mountain towering into the heavens: "I will live a bold and courageous life dedicated to kosen-rufu that is as indomitable as Mount Fuji!"

The group stayed briefly in Tokyo before returning to the head temple to attend the fourth session of the summer training course from August 8. This session was for young women's members including those from overseas. Koichiro's wife, Yukiko, and Michiya's wife, Michiyo, were also invited to attend.

During that session, the members headed for West Germany took another commemorative photograph with Shin'ichi, and once more they were introduced to the training course participants at a guidance meeting. Shin'ichi also made time to offer encouragement to Yukiko and Michiyo, who were traveling to Germany with the group so soon after their weddings.

In a warm voice, he said: "Your life abroad is probably going to be more challenging than you can imagine. But you mustn't be defeated. You will definitely become happy. The only way to do so is to carry out sincere faith and chant Nam-myoho-renge-kyo abundantly.

"Husbands are supported by their wives. As long as you aren't defeated, your husbands can do their best. Never lose heart, no matter what happens. I hope you will cheerfully and joyfully play your roles in the grand drama of life, as the champions of your respective missions. I will visit Germany in the near future and we shall meet again then." With these words from Shin'ichi, the two young women solidified their determination. Bathed in sunlight, Mount Fuji seemed to smile down upon them.

AROUND NOON on a scorching hot August 12, Koichiro and the others, twelve in all, set sail for West Germany from the port of Yokohama aboard the *Baikal*. Some thirty or forty members sent them off. In order to save as much as possible on traveling expenses, they were traveling by ship to the Soviet port of Nakhodka. From there they would cross the continent by train and airplane.

Each member brought only a single trunk of personal belongings. Aside from the Gohonzon, they carried little more than clothes for the journey, a copy of the Gosho and other Soka Gakkai publications. But their hearts were filled with great hope for kosen-rufu and passionate commitment coursed through their veins.

Meanwhile, Michiya, looked desperately for places for the young men to work. When he arrived in Germany he found that, just as his friend had warned him, economic conditions had worsened. The coal mine in Castrop-Rauxel that originally had job openings could no longer provide jobs to foreign workers, and the employment that they had been counting on evaporated.

Michiya was deeply shaken by this turn of events. He knew that the members had already quit their jobs in

Japan and couldn't very well cancel their plans to come to West Germany. He also knew he had to do something. He spent days looking everywhere for jobs for the arriving members, but to no avail. And then the members departed from Japan.

They arrived at Dortmund Station in West Germany on the morning of August 18. Michiya, Sunayama and women's members living in various parts of Germany—some of them having traveled from places one hundred or two hundred miles away—were there to welcome them.

When the young men shook hands with those who had come to greet them, all the weariness of their journey disappeared. "Thank you for coming to meet us!" they gratefully exclaimed. Smiles filled everyone's faces, except for Michiya, whose expression was grim.

THE EUROPE General Meeting and First Europe Culture Festival would be held in Frankfurt, Germany on August 29. It was arranged that the young men who had arrived from Japan would temporarily lodge in members' homes until the general meeting so that they could help out with preparations for the event.

After seeing them all off to their lodgings, Michiya said to Koichiro: "Mr. Sada, the coal mine at Castrop-Rauxel says that they don't have enough work right now to hire foreign workers, and though I contacted a number of other mines, I haven't had any luck."

"I see . . ." Koichiro replied before lapsing into silence. Though he had intended to be prepared for news of this sort, the severity of the situation still shocked him. Unless something was done, the young men who had trusted him and come all the way to West Germany would find themselves turned out on the streets. It had all been his idea from the start.

"I was the one who told President Yamamoto that there would be no problem finding employment for the young men," he thought to himself. "How angry President Yamamoto would be if he learned what has happened! It's all my fault. I should have prepared more thoroughly before asking anyone to come. Now I've done something that can't be undone." He blamed himself. No matter how hard he was on himself, he felt it wasn't enough.

"What are we going to do now?" Michiya's voice brought Koichiro back to reality. Realizing that simply regretting what had happened wouldn't solve the problem, he concluded that he must do whatever it took to keep President Yamamoto's precious disciples from being put out on the street. All he could do was chant. He knew that if he chanted with all his heart, a way out of this situation would open.

Rousing his spirits, Koichiro said: "Let's chant. Let's chant Nam-myoho-renge-kyo in earnest. And let's keep contacting every coal mine we can think of. We have the Gohonzon on our side, so things are sure to be all right."

The morale of the young men who had newly arrived in Germany was high, and they were determined to make both the general meeting and culture festival a great success. It was decided that they would perform a play about Shijo Kingo, the Daishonin's disciple who was characterized by his indomitable faith, and they were avidly devoting themselves to preparations and rehearsals. They also accompanied the local district leaders on their visits to members' homes to offer encouragement and invite them to participate in the general meeting.

WHILE CARRYING out preparations for the general meeting, Koichiro and Michiya continued to search diligently for employment. So far, however, they didn't have any prospects.

On August 29, the Europe General Meeting and First Culture Festival took place high-spiritedly at a hall in Frankfurt. Some five hundred members from West Germany, England, France, Italy and other countries attended, and the auditorium overflowed with the dynamic spirit of fresh departure.

The youth from Japan were a driving force behind the events, assuming a crucial role in their organization and preparation. The play about Shijo Kingo that the Japanese youth put on for the culture festival was also very well received. But Koichiro and Michiya remained gloomy, still unable to find work for their colleagues.

Then, on that very day, after the events were completed, Michiya at last received word that the Hamborn coal mine in Duisburg, which he had contacted earlier, would employ all ten of the young men. The mine also had jobs for Koichiro and Michiya, as both were also in need of work.

The two were overjoyed. But this meant that they would have to live for some time in a dormitory run by the coal mine and thus apart from their wives. The two young women would temporarily stay with the families of women's members.

For the new brides, it was a very lonely and sad start to married life. But they both sent their husbands off with a smile, telling them not to worry and to do their best. Even so, when the men were gone, they felt like crying their eyes out. They struggled to control their feelings and told themselves not to be defeated by the situation and to keep their chins up. When they thought of their husbands, they sighed; when they thought of Japan, they wept.

The only thing to do was look ahead. Dreaming of the hope-filled future of kosen-rufu in Germany, they thought of President Yamamoto, their mentor in life.

Three days after the Europe General Meeting, the young men's life at the coal mine began. The first month was spent learning the minimal amount of German they would need to do their jobs, how to operate the machinery and equipment, and safety training. From October 1, they started work in the mine. Aside from Koichiro and Michiya, it was the first time any of them had done such work.

WORKING 3,280 feet below ground was harder labor than any of the young men had imagined. It was extremely hot, more than eighty-six degrees, and rivers of sweat poured off their bodies. The half-gallon water bottles they carried were soon empty. At the start they were so exhausted by the work that they couldn't even eat. Even though they wore gloves, their hands were soon covered with blisters, and they were constantly being cut by flying chips of stone and coal. Cave-ins were also a frequent occurrence.

Almost unable to bear the hard physical labor, there were times when they felt like throwing in the towel and returning to Japan. But then they reminded themselves that they had come to Germany of their own free will to spread Buddhism, telling themselves not to lose heart.

Each day when their work in the mines was done and they returned to the surface, they joyfully thought, "I won again today!" And with their teeth gleaming against their faces pitch black from the coal dust, they would laugh heartily and joke, "We really are Bodhisattvas emerging from the Earth!" slapping each other on the back.

At the dormitory they pooled their earnings and used the money to buy necessities. The first thing they purchased was a car to use for Soka Gakkai activities. Driving their car along the Autobahn, Germany's high-speed expressway, they began their proud advance of kosen-rufu. They also poured their energies into studying both German and Buddhism, spurring each other on in friendly rivalry. Theirs was the only room in the dormitory where the electricity burned late into the night.

Koichiro and Michiya, who looked after the young men and spent their days and nights working and doing Gakkai activities, rarely had an opportunity to see their wives.

One night, Koichiro finally had a chance to get together with Yukiko. A beautiful full moon shone in the sky. Koichiro pointed to the moon and said: "Your mother in Japan is looking at the same moon as we are, so remember, you're not alone."

Gazing at Yukiko, he then added: "Everyone is doing their best, striving hard to become accustomed to their jobs at the mine. They all depend on me and look to me for support. Even though we can't see each other very often, I know you understand my feelings."

Yukiko nodded silently. Tears filled her eyes, and she began to cry.

She wept out of joy at the warm consideration of her husband, who was devoting his life to kosen-rufu.

OUR INNERMOST determination can move the universe. Because cause and effect are simultaneous, all results are encompassed in our present resolve. Determination is not just words. True determination contains earnest prayer and brims with concentrated energy. It gives rise to wholehearted action and leads without fail to splendid victory.

The moment that the young men made their decision to spread the Mystic Law regardless of whatever hardships they might face and actually arrived in West Germany, the remarkable advance of kosen-rufu in that country was already decided.

At long last, the good news the young miners had been anticipating arrived. On October 11, Eiji Kawasaki, the leader of Europe Headquarters, came to West Germany and told them that President Yamamoto and other leaders from Japan would visit Europe from the 20th of that month, arriving in West Germany on October 22.

The thought that President Yamamoto was coming to Germany, just as he had promised, filled everyone with delight, and their weariness from the strenuous labor in the mines evaporated.

"Though there's not much time before President Yamamoto's arrival," one of them suggested, "let's try to produce some results that we can proudly show him as a demonstration of our work so far."

Everyone felt the same way, and they agreed on the spot. They were all keenly aware of the importance of the present moment. By rising up now, they could attain future victory. By opening the way forward today, they would ensure future success.

They decided to hold a study examination and guidance session in Frankfurt on October 23. The young men stepped up their Gakkai activities and, resolved to pass the study exam, put great effort into studying the Daishonin's writings. Finally, to the members' great joy, the day of Shin'ichi's arrival came.

As they walked through the airport in Frankfurt, Shin'ichi said to Koichiro: "I am so happy to hear that our young eagles have taken flight. A vision of them soaring boldly toward the summit of kosen-rufu in the twenty-first century unfolds in my heart like a beautiful painting. But once they have taken flight, they cannot rest their wings. If they stop, they will fall. That mustn't happen. This year in particular will decide everything. The present moment is what matters. Now is the time to initiate a new current of kosen-rufu in Germany."

WHEN he arrived at the hotel, Shin'ichi and the leaders who had accompanied him from Japan began to discuss the reorganization of Germany Chapter together with Koichiro and Michiya.

Shin'ichi told Koichiro: "We've decided to split Europe Headquarters into two. Europe No. 1 Headquarters will be based in France and Europe No. 2 Headquarters in Germany.

"I know I'm asking you this after the fact, but we already announced in Paris that you, Mr. Koichiro, would be the Europe No. 2 Headquarters leader. We would also like to appoint you, Mr. Moro'oka, to the position of vice headquarters leader. Will you accept?"

They both nodded and said yes but they couldn't hide their surprise. After a moment, Koichiro said with an apologetic expression: "I am prepared to do anything I can but I really don't have any abilities. To be honest, I don't feel confident about fulfilling such a big responsibility."

With a smile, Shin'ichi began to speak: "No one is confident that they will succeed before they try—unless they are taking the responsibility lightly or they're just arrogant. Take Shigeo Nagashima of the Yomiuri Giants, for example. He is considered the best baseball player in Japan. But though everyone calls him a brilliant hitter now, at first he probably didn't have any confidence, either.

"I'm sure that he gave great thought to how he could increase his batting average and what his weak points were, then sought ways to improve his swing. Gradually, he acquired a sense that a certain way of batting would produce good results and allow him to bat successfully. But things didn't always go the way he expected, so he studied some more, tried new techniques and practiced some more. In the process, his batting results actually improved, and that in turn gave him self-confidence.

"Self-confidence isn't something you acquire overnight. You don't need it at the start. The important thing is the spirit of challenge, the courage to keep trying. It is the strength to persevere through all without becoming discouraged, without giving up and without packing it in, no matter what happens.

"Mr. Sada, I hope you will look on this appointment as your mission, and start by just doing your best for one year."

"I will. I may not have the necessary ability, but I will try my hardest," Koichiro replied enthusiastically.

A discussion of the organizational changes thus began. Two new chapters—one in Frankfurt and one in Nuremberg—would be formed, giving Germany a total of three chapters.

THE NEXT morning, Shin'ichi went out looking for materials for the construction of the Grand Main Temple, while Akizuki, Ittetsu Okada and Bunji Nishimiya visited a girls high school in Frankfurt. They requested permission to do so in preparation for the establishment of Soka University and Soka High School.

Akizuki and the others were surprised to see that class size ranged from twelve to twenty-five students—less than half the size of most Japanese high school classes at the time. They also noticed that classes were centered on students' questions and great importance was placed on the individual in the educational process.

From half past three that afternoon, Akizuki and the other leaders from Japan supervised a study examination held at a rented public hall in the suburbs of Frankfurt. A little after six o'clock that evening, Shin'ichi and representative members of the German organization dined at a Chinese restaurant in Frankfurt. When Shin'ichi arrived at the restaurant, the members were already gathered.

"I'm sorry to keep you waiting," he said. "Looking for materials for the Grand Main Temple took more time than expected. In fact, there's still more to be done after this meeting."

A round table and a long rectangular table were set up in the restaurant for the occasion. Shin'ichi and the leaders accompanying him were supposed to be seated together at the round table. Instead of going to his assigned seat, however, Shin'ichi went directly to the table where the members were seated and asked, "Are the young men who came here from Japan all doing well?"

"Yes!" said the youth who were there representing the group.

"I'm happy to hear that, really happy to hear that," Shin'ichi said. "You are very important people who have taken on the mission of forging a new course for kosen-rufu. It wasn't work or other personal reasons that brought you to West Germany. Rather, you chose to come here for the sake of the happiness of the German people. You are volunteers for kosen-rufu.

"Without a doubt, Nichiren Daishonin is wholeheartedly praising your valiant spirit. I also have the greatest respect for you. I hope you will never be defeated, whatever difficulties you may face. Not being defeated is victory.

"Because of space limitations, we couldn't invite everyone today, but please know that I am chanting for each of you every day."

Shin'ichi then announced the formation of Europe General Headquarters, explaining that it would consist of two headquarters, with Europe No. 2 Headquarters being based in Germany. Next, he introduced the new leaders.

CONTINUING his announcement, Shin'ichi said: "In addition to the current Germany Chapter, two new chapters will be established. These will be the Frankfurt and Nuremberg chapters. I hope that the new leaders I am about to announce will do their best in their respective roles as chapter leaders, women's leaders and as leaders of the young men's and young women's divisions. If you have any thoughts you'd like to share in connection with these appointments, please feel free to speak up now. If not, I'd like to make them final and then place a call to Japan and have them published in the *Seikyo Shimbun*."

Shin'ichi then proceeded to read out the appointments. Koichiro Sada, the new Europe No. 2 Headquarters leader, was appointed leader of Germany Chapter. Michiya Moro'oka, the new Europe No. 2 Headquarters vice leader, became Frankfurt Chapter leader. Kosaku Osanai, who had just come to Germany from Japan, was appointed Nuremberg Chapter leader.

In addition to Osanai, several of other recent arrivals from Japan were assigned important posts. Toshiyuki Osawa, Teruo Sunayama and Akito Anzai were appointed the young men's leaders of Germany, Frankfurt and Nuremberg chapters, respectively.

Koichiro's wife, Yukiko, became Germany Chapter women's leader and Michiya's wife, Michiyo, was appointed the young women's leader for Germany Chapter.

After making these personnel announcements, Shin'ichi asked: "Do you agree to these appointments?" Everyone replied energetically in the affirmative.

The young men who had recently come to Germany lived in Duisburg, which was about 13 or 19 miles from Düsseldorf and more than 155 miles from Frankfurt. Nuremberg was an additional 125 miles from Frankfurt.

Taking care of such a widely spread-out organization would certainly require a great deal of the leaders' time, not to mention a considerable financial burden in terms of the cost of gasoline and travel expenses. Yet not a single person voiced a complaint or reservation.

To champions of faith who have determined to open the way for a new course of kosen-rufu, the waves of hardship are by no means an impediment. In fact, the higher those waves, the brighter the fighting spirit of such champions burns.

After taking his seat, Shin'ichi gazed intently at those present and said: "Let's eat! Today we are celebrating a fresh departure."

SHIN'ICHI noticed that the young miners' looked thinner than before, and he was concerned about their well-being. They were no doubt becoming fit from the hard labor in the mines, but he thought that they might also be having difficulty adjusting to the local fare.

In fact, many of Japanese miners were having a hard time with the food served at their dormitory. They had all found German sausages to their liking, but after being served them a couple of times, the sausages disappeared from the menu. It turned out that many of the miners they worked with were Turkish and followers of Islam, and since eating pork was prohibited in that religion, it hadn't been on the dormitory menu for some time. But the cook, out of consideration for the Japanese workers, served them sausages as a favor. Some miners complained, however, that this was special treatment and that everyone should eat the same meals, so the sausages were taken off the menu altogether.

Smiles spread across the faces of the Japanese youth as they began eating. "You're young, so please eat your fill. Here, finish this, too," Shin'ichi remarked, passing the serving plate on his own table to theirs. For the young men, this sincere affection expressed by their mentor was the most delicious treat of all.

After a while, Michiya approached Shin'ichi's table and said: "Sensei, I have a favor to ask of you. We are planning to publish a newspaper here in Germany, and we would like you to name it for us."

"All right," Shin'ichi replied. "Have you thought of any names yourselves?"

"Actually, we were thinking of *Seikyo Zeitung*. *Zeitung* means 'newspaper' in German."

"*Seikyo Zeitung?* That's catchy, isn't it? Let's go with that. Simple names are good for newspapers because they're easy to remember."

"That's very true. Thank you," Michiya responded.

"You're planning to start a newspaper, but do you have a camera?" Shin'ichi inquired.

Hearing that they didn't, Shin'ichi chuckled and said: "I guess I have no choice, then, but to give you the one I brought from Japan! I want to support your efforts."

THE DINNER became a warm, family-like discussion between Shin'ichi and the members.

When everyone finished eating, Shin'ichi said: "I still have work to finish, so I must say farewell now. Please give my best regards to the members who couldn't be here today. Take care of yourselves!"

The members regretfully said good-bye.

Afterward, Akizuki led a guidance session in the hall where the study examination had been held. Some sixty members gathered for this session. When Akizuki announced the new changes and leadership appointments for the German organization, loud applause rang out.

Continuing, Akizuki said: "When President Yamamoto heard about this meeting, he asked me to convey a message to you on his behalf. It reads:

> I am sorry that I could not join you this evening, but my heart is always with you. I am praying and praying for your good health and happiness each day.

At the time, there were more than two hundred member-households in West Germany, the majority of which were families of Japanese women who had married American military personnel and then gone to Germany when their husbands had been posted there. Shin'ichi's message was thus aimed mainly at encouraging those women.

Akizuki continued reading Shin'ichi's message:

> I hope that you will not become caught up in vanities and outward appearances, but instead become people who shine with the brilliance of faith and who are trusted by all. The purpose of faith lies in creating a life in which we enjoy ourselves and are at ease[3]; it is to live a life that is enjoyable beyond imagination. The place that we do so does not exist in some other realm; it is where we are right now.
>
> Buddhism teaches that the place we reside is transformed into a Buddha land, a land of Eternally Tranquil Light. To make that happen, we need to decide that our present location is itself the grand

stage upon which we will carry out our mission and then take courageous action to advance kosen-rufu. Those who strive courageously are filled with youthful vigor. Their lives abound with hope and joy. And the great path toward a state of absolute happiness will open before them without fail.

I hope that you will work together in harmony and unity and build the best Soka Gakkai organization possible here in Germany.

When Akizuki finished reading Shin'ichi's message, enthusiastic applause reverberated throughout the room.

"I WOULD now like to present to you a poem that President Yamamoto composed just before this meeting for all of the members in Germany. Congratulations! The poem reads:

> *The vow we made*
> *At Eagle Peak is far-reaching,*
> *You— to the West,*
> *We— to the East,*
> *Advancing gallantly astride white steeds.*

Once again the room erupted in applause. Some of the members were moved to tears.

Next, the newly appointed leaders stood up one after another to introduce themselves. Each of their greetings resounded with their vigorous determinations for the future.

The guidance meeting came to a joyous close, with

each participant receiving a cardboard plaque with Shin'ichi's calligraphy and a cloth for their prayer beads.

Akizuki left the building. The stars were shining beautifully in the night sky. In contrast to the warmth inside the hall, outside the air was cold, a sign that winter was on the way. Suddenly, a voice rang out behind him.

"Mr. Akizuki!" When he turned, he saw Koichiro and several other youth come running toward him.

Short of breath, Koichiro said: "We have composed a song for the young men's division of Germany and we wanted to sing it for you."

"That's great, but what a pity that you didn't sing it for President Yamamoto earlier. Anyway, let me hear it, and I'll tell him about it."

The young men formed a circle in the courtyard in front of the meeting hall. Their excited faces were illuminated by the dim light of the street lamps. The high-spirited voices of the youthful lions echoed through the night.

> *Dispelling the mist*
> *As we make our way on the Autobahn,*
> *Youthful passion burning brightly,*
> *We, the Young Men's Division of Germany,*
> *Will usher in the dawn*
> *Of a new age in Europe.*
>
> *No matter how challenging*
> *The path of pioneers may be,*
> *As ardent champions of our cause,*
> *We will continue to struggle to the very end,*
> *Embracing the spirit of our mentor in our hearts.*

Cherishing lofty ideals,
We of the Soka Gakkai in Germany
Call the youth to rally to our banner.
Upholding an eternal philosophy,
We will create the Third Civilization.

When they finished singing, other members standing nearby applauded them.

"That's a very stirring song," Akizuki said.

HEARING Akizuki speak so highly of their song brought smiles to the young men's faces.

Akizuki continued: "I don't think there's any song as powerfully stirring as yours among the ones recently composed by the young men's and young women's divisions in various chapters in Japan."

The creation of such songs had been decided at the youth division summer training course that year, and now they were appearing in chapters across the country.

"It's a great song, so I'd like to share it with everyone at the next young men's leaders meeting when I get back to Japan. May I have a copy of the sheet music?"

Koichiro replied with some hesitation: "Um, actually, we don't have any, because none of us can read music."

The young miners wrote the song on September 10. Meeting in their dormitory at the coal mine, they started with the lyrics. This process basically consisted of everyone sharing the words or phrases they wanted to be included. When they had come to a rough consensus of what to put in the song, two or three volunteers arranged the lyrics, and then the whole group gathered again to make revisions. Once the lyrics were finished, however, they were faced with another challenge—setting them to music. None of them had any experience in music composition.

They each thought of bits of melody and sang them to each other, but when someone came up with a tune that the others liked and he was asked to sing it again, he usually couldn't reproduce it. Even so, they managed to tie the snatches of melody together into a song, which they then made changes to and polished. It took a full week before the song was finished.

The young men wrote the lyrics down on paper and then drew rising and falling marks above words to indicate rising and falling pitch so they wouldn't forget the melody. They also sang the song whenever they could during their Soka Gakkai activities and while at work. They were very proud of their creation which was an expression of their firm resolve.

Deeply moved by the passion for kosen-rufu that resounded in the song and made up for any deficiency in musical technique there may have been, Akizuki said to the youth: "Since you don't have any sheet music, would you mind making a tape of the song and sending it to me in time for the young men's leaders meeting on the 28th of this month?" He then continued: "Now, I'd really like to hear you sing the song one more time before I go."

"All right!" they exclaimed, and once again their youthful voices reverberated in the night sky.

THE FOLLOWING day, Shin'ichi was scheduled to depart. At eight o'clock in the morning, several members gathered at the hotel to see him off.

Wanting to express his gratitude, Shin'ichi used the limited time remaining to speak with them in the hotel lobby. He asked how their work was going and shook hands with them as he offered encouragement.

Among those gathered were three young men who, while they were in high spirits, were visibly exhausted. They were Toshiyuki Osawa, Teruo Sunayama and Katsuzo Asada.

Shin'ichi remarked to them: "You don't look very well. Are you getting enough sleep?"

Osawa replied: "Actually, we drove quite a distance last night to enshrine a friend's Gohonzon, and we just got back this morning."

Inspired by their encounter with President Yamamoto, the young men drove to the house of a German friend after the meetings the previous night. This friend, whom they had been talking to about Buddhism for some time, had expressed a desire to join the Soka Gakkai, so they went to his home to enshrine a Gohonzon.

It was a three-hour drive one way but they didn't let that stop them. Having renewed their determination to realize kosen-rufu in Germany, they were filled with a powerful urge to introduce as many people as they could to Buddhism as quickly as possible, so they jumped at this chance to take action.

After enshrining the Gohonzon, they did gongyo and chanted together. Then they made their way back to Frankfurt, arriving after dawn. They parked their car in the underground parking lot of the hotel where Shin'ichi was staying and took a nap there before going to the lobby to see him off.

On hearing this, Shin'ichi said in a stern tone: "You mustn't overexert yourself or engage in actions that lack common sense. All your efforts would be for naught if you were to have an accident or do something that invited censure from the general public. Buddhism is reason. Actions that fly in the face of reason and common sense are just self-serving, no matter how good your intentions.

"In the long run, such actions will only arouse unnecessary opposition to the Soka Gakkai in society and end up impeding our movement to spread the Daishonin's teachings. Therefore, I hope you will get plenty of sleep, eat properly, chant earnestly and vigorously engage in activities in accord with common sense.

"The path of kosen-rufu is long. To walk that eternal road, you must take care of yourselves and stay strong and healthy. Do you understand?"

Shin'ichi was first and foremost concerned about the health of these precious disciples living in Germany.

THE THREE young men said they understood, but they were obviously crestfallen. Noticing this, Shin'ichi smiled and added: "But your enthusiasm in immediately going to enshrine your friend's Gohonzon after the meeting last night is impressive. You are truly people of action. That's the way youth should be." When Shin'ichi said this, smiles returned to the young men's faces.

Kosaku Osanai, the newly appointed Nuremburg Chapter leader, then asked Shin'ichi: "The Daishonin writes, 'My disciples, form your ranks and follow me, and surpass even Mahakashyapa or Ananda, T'ien-t'ai or

Dengyō!" (WND, 765). Could we say that our having come to Germany is an action that accords with this passage?"

Immediately before these words, the Daishonin states: "Now, at the beginning of the Latter Day of the Law, I, Nichiren, am the first to embark on propagating, throughout Jambudvipa, the five characters of Myoho-renge-kyo, which are the heart of the Lotus Sutra and the eye of all the Buddhas" (WND, 764–65). He then goes on to describe the behavior he expects from his disciples. In other words, he encourages his disciples to spread the Mystic Law in the same way he did, and thus surpass other outstanding practitioners of the Lotus Sutra.

Shin'ichi nodded. "That's right. You who have stood up with the mission to realize the propagation of the Daishonin's teachings are the Daishonin's successors and the pioneers of kosen-rufu. Because you are spreading the supreme Law, each of you will be a person who surpasses even Mahakashyapa, Ananda, T'ien-t'ai and Dengyō.

"In light of the Gosho and from the perspective of the Buddhist Law, it is clear just how wonderful are the lives of those who dedicate themselves to kosen-rufu. Even if you don't realize this now, it will become evident in the next thirty or forty years. Please do your best!"

"We will!" everyone present replied.

Shin'ichi looked at his watch. It was time to go. "Thank you for everything," he said. "Let's meet again." He then bowed to the members and got into the car.

Nearly pressing their faces against the car's windows, the young men called out: "Sensei! Please take care of yourself!" "Please come to Germany again!" "We'll do our best!"

As the car pulled away, several of the members ran after it, waving. Tears shone in their eyes. Shin'ichi turned around and continued waving back until they had disappeared from sight.

SHIN'ICHI and his party departed from Frankfurt at 9:35 AM on October 24. Flying over the Alps, about an hour later they reached their next stop, Milan, the flourishing industrial and commercial center of northern Italy. There were many buildings in the city—including the famous marble Duomo cathedral, with its 135 spires—that Shin'ichi wanted to visit in reference to the construction of the Grand Main Temple.

After arriving at their hotel, Shin'ichi met with the others to discuss their schedule in Milan. When everyone had gathered, Shin'ichi said: "Mr. Akizuki, at last you're going to visit La Scala."

"Yes," Akizuki replied. "Mr. Okada, Mr. Nishimiya and I have an appointment at half past four this afternoon, but we're not sure yet whether we'll be able to see the superintendent."

Founded in 1778, La Scala is the most celebrated opera house in Italy, with its own orchestra and opera company. It was there that such great works as Giuseppe Verdi's *Otello* and *Falstaff,* and Giacomo Puccini's *Madame Butterfly,* as well as numerous other masterpieces debuted. Many highly acclaimed musicians had been invited by the theater to work as art and music directors—among them the renowned conductor Arturo Toscanini[4].

Shin'ichi, as founder of the Min-On Concert Association, and the other Min-On executives hoped to sponsor a performance by the La Scala Opera Company in Japan to promote international cultural exchange. One of the reasons for Min-On's establishment was to provide ordinary citizens with opportunities to come into contact with the finest in art and culture the world has to offer.

On this trip, Akizuki, the executive vice president of Min-On, had arranged a visit to La Scala to begin negotiations for such a tour. He looked extremely tense. He was nervous about the upcoming meeting and not without good reason.

Up to then, several singers from La Scala had come to perform in Japan, but the La Scala Opera Company as a whole had never performed there, or indeed, anywhere in Asia. When people affiliated with the arts in Japan heard that Min-On wished to invite La Scala to perform, some of them snickered, saying it was little more than a fanciful dream and that a world-famous company such as La Scala would never accept an invitation from Min-On or the Soka Gakkai. The fact that Shin'ichi was only thirty-seven at the time seemed to have led many to underestimate both organizations.

OBSERVING Akizuki's expression, Shin'ichi Yamamoto smiled and said: "There is nothing to worry about, Mr. Akizuki. It will be just fine. La Scala has a proud heritage of dedication to promoting musical culture. I am certain that the heirs to that tradition cannot fail to be interested in Min-On, an organization that is advancing a great new musical movement for and by the people.

"All you have to do is sincerely and earnestly convey Min-On's ideals and spirit. If I could, I would like to meet the superintendent with you, but while I am Min-On's founder, I am not in a position to represent the organization in an official manner. Besides, during our stay here, I have to take care of various matters, such as purchasing construction materials. So I leave the negotiations this time entirely to you, Min-On's executive vice president. Please take full responsibility, proceeding with confidence and assurance."

Akizuki was deeply encouraged by Shin'ichi's words. That evening, he and his colleagues left for La Scala. They were immediately struck by the solemn dignity of the building's stone façade. Inside, they beheld the theater with its some 3,600 seats, beginning at ground level and rising in six curved tiers along the theater walls. A sparkling chandelier hung from the ceiling.

A short time after being shown into a private room, Akizuki and his companions were greeted by a distinguished, silver-haired gentleman, Antonio Ghiringhelli, La Scala's superintendent. Since Akizuki was not expecting to meet the superintendent on his first visit, he was very happy.

After they had introduced themselves, Akizuki began to talk about Min-On's goals and activities, explaining that it was a people's music movement that sought to promote international cultural exchange. At this, Mr. Ghiringhelli's eyes sparkled and a smile spread across his face.

Sensing that his message was getting across, Akizuki continued: "We want to invite La Scala to perform in Japan, both for the sake of cultural exchange and to inspire and educate young Japanese musicians. I hope you will accept our invitation."

Nodding at Akizuki's request, Mr. Ghiringhelli said: "I understand your intent perfectly, and in principle, I am in complete agreement. We of La Scala believe we have a mission as ambassadors of music, and are always eager to engage in such exchange. But we already have concert dates scheduled for next year and the year after, in the Soviet Union, Canada and the United States. A performance in Japan in 1968 or anytime after would certainly be possible, however." Akizuki's face lit up with delight.

"The details of the actual program, performance dates and other practical issues can be discussed at a later time between our respective staffs."

AFTER RETURNING to the hotel, Akizuki immediately reported to Shin'ichi, who said: "That's great news. It's all due to your strong determination."

Akizuki chanted and prayed wholeheartedly that Min-On could realize a Japan tour by La Scala so that it could fulfill its purpose of encouraging cultural exchange.

Shin'ichi added: "Music and art have the power to transcend national and ethnic differences, deepen mutual understanding and forge solid ties between people. It is my wish to see the hearts of people everywhere linked through these endeavors.

"To start off this undertaking, Min-On has invited Frank Pelleg to Japan this December, right?"

"Yes, that's correct," Akizuki replied. "He is scheduled to arrive on December 15."

Pelleg was an Israeli pianist, and he was the first foreign artist that Min-On had invited to perform in Japan. It had chosen an Israeli musician rather than one from the United States or Europe as a means of fostering understanding between Japan and Israel, which at that time had very little contact with each other.

Smiling at Akizuki, Shin'ichi continued: "A Min-On–sponsored Japan tour by the La Scala Opera Company will form the centerpiece of the music association's fledgling movement to conduct international cultural exchange. La Scala is the pride of Milan—indeed, of the Italian people as a whole—and a symbol of peace. The famous opera house was destroyed during World War II, but as soon as the fires of war were extinguished, the Milanese set about rebuilding it before anything else. This is well known. Bringing the Italian company to Japan will be a major achievement. Let's proceed with the arrangements patiently. You have my full support."

Akizuki left Shin'ichi's room with a renewed sense of resolve to see the project through to fruition.

The next day, Akizuki visited La Scala again to discuss the general outlines for an envisioned tour. In April of the following year, he returned once more, accompanied by a ballet company executive who was familiar with arranging such tours in Japan. On this occasion, Akizuki and Superintendent Ghiringhelli went over the performance schedule in detail and signed a preliminary agreement for a 1968 tour.

But it would be many years before La Scala's Japan tour was actualized. Later, the tour was postponed to 1970, but that, too, eventually fell through because of financial difficulties La Scala was undergoing at that time.

ALSO, Superintendent Ghiringhelli, with whom negotiations for the event had begun, passed away, and his successor, Paolo Grassi, also retired due to illness after only a few years in his post. Shin'ichi, as Min-On's founder, worked behind the scenes to make the tour a reality, using every opportunity he could to rally the support of anyone who might be in a position to help.

At last, the first performance by La Scala in Japan was slated for the fall of 1981 and was promoted by the La Scala Japan Tour Committee and cosponsored by the Min-On Concert Association and the Asahi Newspaper Company. Nearly sixteen years had passed since Akizuki had first visited the Italian opera company and begun negotiations for the tour.

In June that year, 1981, Shin'ichi visited Milan once again and paid a courtesy call on the city's mayor, who was also the chairperson of La Scala's board of directors. The mayor expressed his joy at La Scala's upcoming Japan tour and presented Shin'ichi with a silver medal from the city.

Shin'ichi also visited La Scala on that occasion and met with Superintendent Carlo Maria Badini and other executives. During their discussion, Mr. Badini conveyed his respect for Shin'ichi as the founder of Min-On, saying that their two organizations were joined by a deep bond of friendship. Voicing his resolve that the tour would be a success, he thanked Shin'ichi for his efforts toward its realization. The superintendent seemed to be well aware of Shin'ichi's activities behind the scenes. Shin'ichi was pleased that La Scala understood and agreed with his goal of bringing people around the world together through art and music.

And so it was that this epochal event, a magnificent full-scale La Scala performance involving some five hundred performers, crew and staff members, opened in Japan. It was truly a spectacular showcase of art and beauty.

Expressing appreciation for Min-On's role in realizing the event, one opera critic said: "The performance was perfect. Bringing a production of such scale to Japan is an incredible feat." Another cultural figure exclaimed similarly: "The wave you set in motion has given rise to ten thousand waves."

Shin'ichi had believed all along that his dream of bringing La Scala to perform in Japan would be realized. That is why he thought nothing of the criticism he and Min-On had been subject to in the process.

The brilliant laurels of victory lie in striving tenaciously to achieve our goals in accord with our conviction.

ON the afternoon of October 25, Shin'ichi and his party flew from Milan, Italy, to their next stop, Nice, in the south of France. During the next two days, he met with and encouraged the local members who came to see him, and busily attended to a number of other commitments. On October 27, he and the others headed for Lisbon, Portugal, by way of Barcelona, Spain. They arrived in Lisbon just before one o'clock in the afternoon and immediately set out to see the city.

Portugal was the first European country that Japan had come in contact with many centuries ago. This encounter brought firearms and many new cultural innovations to Japan. Shin'ichi thus had a special interest in Portugal.

Standing at the ruins of Saint George's Castle atop the highest hill in Lisbon, Shin'ichi could see over the rows of red-tiled roofs to the Tejo River and the Salazar Bridge (now the April 25 Bridge), which was under construction. There were numerous buildings in and around Lisbon—including the Tower of Belem and the Queluz Palace, the latter of which was modeled after France's Versailles Palace—that might provide ideas for the construction of the Grand Main Temple.

Driving along the Tejo River on their tour of the city, Shin'ichi and his companions came upon a white marble monument in the shape of a ship. They got out of the car and went for a closer look. The Monument to the Discoveries, built five years earlier, stood before them and commemorated the 500th anniversary of the death of Prince Henry the Navigator.[5] Some 170 feet in height, the monument was carved with the figures of great scholars and explorers who had contributed to the establishment of new sea routes during the fifteenth and sixteenth centuries. Prince Henry stood in the lead.

Shin'ichi had learned of Henry the Navigator from his mentor Josei Toda, and he had also read several books about the prince and was deeply impressed by the story of his life.

He said to the others: "I remember Mr. Toda commenting to me on the courage of the Portuguese and saying how he wished he could visit their country. In the fourteenth century, the rise of the Timur Empire[6] obstructed the Silk Road, cutting off trade routes between East and West. The Portuguese decided that if they could not go to Asia by land, they would go by sea.

"Though Portugal was just a small country of scarce resources on the western edge of the Iberian Peninsula, it blazed the way in the Great Age of Discovery of the fifteenth century and became a major empire with possessions around the globe. How was this possible?"

"IT WAS THE EFFORTS of Henry the Navigator," Shin'ichi continued, "that enabled Portugal to become a dominant power in that age."

Prince Henry was the third son of King John I. During his youth, filled with a burning desire to contribute to the advancement of his country, he founded a school of navigation in Sagres, at the southwestern tip of the Iberian Peninsula. It was a barren region whose shores were pounded by the rough waves of the Atlantic Ocean. But the prince took up residence there and invited leading scholars from various countries and with diverse specialties—including navigation, mapmaking, shipbuilding, geography, astronomy, mathematics and other subjects—to join him.

Prince Henry believed that the discovery of a sea route to the East would usher in a new era for Portugal. Realizing that this enterprise would require the efforts of talented young people, he devoted himself painstakingly to the task of raising such youth. Because he remained single, dedicating all his energies to laying the groundwork for his vision, he became commonly known as "the prince married to the sea."

Henry invested all his personal wealth in the endeavor. He collected the latest information, learning and knowledge about the field and brought together top experts. Then, he formed a society that would allow them to collaborate and make the most effective use of their abilities toward the achievement of their goal. They improved upon the shipbuilding technology of the day and succeeded in developing a type of ship that could sail into the wind.

But no matter how many attempts the navigators trained by Prince Henry made to explore the west coast of Africa, they could not open a new course to Asia. This was because they refused to go beyond Cape Bojador, some 150 miles south of the Canary Islands. Everyone still believed the myths and legends about the area that had persisted since the Middle Ages—in other words, that it was a "Sea of Darkness" of boiling waters and monsters from which no ship ever returned.

Prince Henry called on the explorers to sail past the cape, to be courageous and cast aside baseless superstitions. One of his attendants, Gil Eannes, rose to that call. He, too, had once turned back in fear on a voyage of exploration, but when Prince Henry convinced him to set sail again, he vowed that he would not return until he was successful.

In 1434, Eannes came back to Prince Henry with the news that he had sailed past Cape Bojador.

THE SUCCESS of Eannes' voyage was just a small step. Having merely sailed a short distance past the cape, he was far from discovering a route leading to the East. But the significance of his achievement was immeasurably vast. He had revealed that the much-feared Sea of Darkness beyond Cape Bojador was actually no different than the rest of the ocean, thus dispelling the dark cloud of superstition obscuring people's minds. Indeed, the Sea of Darkness existed only in the mind. With the rudder of courage, Eannes succeeded in sailing beyond his own personal "cape of fears."

Portuguese explorers continued to push farther and farther south along the coast of Africa, but Prince Henry the Navigator died in 1460, before his goal had been reached. Those whom he had trained, however, formed a crucial foundation for exploration that led to the discovery of the Cape of Good Hope and a route to India. They also succeeded in opening sea routes extending around the African Continent that linked Europe and Asia, giving Portugal unsurpassed power in the world for a time.

Shin'ichi spoke with great feeling: "The history of Portugal teaches us that without courage there can be no progress or victory. As Nichiren Daishonin implies when he says: 'Nichiren's disciples cannot accomplish anything if they are cowardly' (WND, 481), kosen-rufu cannot be accomplished if we are fainthearted. A new course of kosen-rufu will be forged through courage. We must sail beyond our own personal 'cape of fears.'"

Looking across the Tejo River, Shin'ichi continued: "Building the future requires fostering people. The only way to do that is through education. We need to make the twenty-first century a 'Great Age of Discovery for Peace'—an age of spiritual exchange in which people are joined as fellow human beings, transcending ethnic and national barriers.

"Toward that end, I am at last going to begin preparations for the establishment of a Soka High School and a Soka University. I regard education as my final undertaking. Laying the foundation is crucial. Let us create a brilliant, golden future."

THE MONUMENT to the Discoveries began to take on the color of the blazing sun. His face flushed with excitement, Shin'ichi said as if speaking to himself: "The time has come. Let's start on our journey! Let us embark on a great voyage of kosen-rufu that will open a new course to peace."

To Shin'ichi, it seemed as if the crimson setting sun was smiling at them.

Notes

1 See GZ, 1600.

2 Words of Twenty-sixth high priest Nichikan, in *Fujishugaku Yoshu* (Selected Works of the Fuji School), edited by Hori Nichiko (Tokyo: Seikyo Shimbunsha, 1977), vol. 3, p. 273.

3 See LS16, 230.

4 Arturo Toscanini (1867–1957).

5 Prince Henry the Navigator (1394–1460).

6 The Timur Empire (1369–1501): A Turkish empire founded by Timur (1336–1405) bordering the Balkans in the West, the Volga in the North, Indian Ocean in the South and Central Asia in the East.

Crown Champions

THE TIME had finally come for Shin'ichi Yamamoto to embark on the task of realizing the vision of his mentors, first and second Soka Gakkai presidents Tsunesaburo Makiguchi and Josei Toda.

The headline on the front page of the November 8, 1965 edition of the *Seikyo Shimbun* read: "Soka University Establishment Steering Committee Formed." The wheels had at last been set in motion for the long-anticipated creation of Soka University.

Shin'ichi had returned from Europe on October 31 and immediately called a meeting to discuss the university's establishment and organize a steering committee to look into the necessary procedures. Shin'ichi was named the chairperson of the committee, while Soka Gakkai general director Kiyoshi Jujo was appointed the secretary. In total, the committee was comprised of thirty-six members, including vice general directors and members of the Soka Gakkai's education and academic departments. Its mission was to oversee the establishment of both a Soka University and a Soka High School.

The steering committee's first meeting was held on November 26 at the Soka Gakkai Headquarters. Here, Shin'ichi proposed that they aim to open Soka High School around 1968, and then focus on the university from around 1970. Toward that end, he suggested the formation of three subcommittees: an Establishment Preparatory Subcommittee, which would oversee the legal matters involved in establishing the academic institutions, as well as a Soka University Subcommittee and a Soka High School Subcommittee to specifically deal with each separate project. The steering committee members unanimously agreed to these proposals. Thus it was that this momentous undertaking began.

Shin'ichi felt a surge of emotion rise in his heart. "Mr. Toda!" he called out silently. "It is happening at last. I am going to create the great institution of humanistic education that you dreamed of!"

Shin'ichi never for a moment forgot the occasion when his mentor had spoken to him about establishing a university. It was November 16, 1950. Toda's Toko Construction Credit Union had been forced to suspend its business operations due to financial difficulties, and the Daito Commerce Company, which he had founded in hopes of making a comeback, had just started up on a very modest scale.

When Toda fell behind in paying his employees' salaries, they began to complain bitterly and quit one after another. Things were so tough that Shin'ichi had to do without an overcoat as winter approached.

On that November day, Shin'ichi and Toda ate lunch at the student cafeteria of Nihon University, which was near Toda's company in West Kanda, Tokyo.

TODA'S financial situation was so tight that the only place they could afford to eat was a cheap student cafeteria. It was the harshest life-or-death struggle Toda had faced since the end of World War II. But he remained perfectly calm and composed. As they made their way to the cafeteria, Toda shared his grand vision for kosen-rufu with Shin'ichi.

The cafeteria was alive with youthful chatter. Looking around at the students, Toda smiled at Shin'ichi and said: "Shin'ichi, let's build a university. A Soka University."

Shin'ichi nodded silently. Gazing into the distance, Toda then began to speak nostalgically of President Makiguchi: "The seventh memorial of Mr. Makiguchi's death is fast approaching," he remarked. "I remember how he used to say to me, 'In the future, we must found a school based on the theory of value-creating (*soka*) education I have been formulating. If we can't do it during my lifetime, you do it during yours. Let's build a school system of value-creating education from elementary school and all the way through to university level.'"

Toda's expression turned solemn as he continued: "But Mr. Makiguchi's life came to an end in prison. I can only imagine the bitter disappointment and regret he must have felt at not realizing his dream. As the disciple to whom he entrusted this vision, I made a vow to establish the schools in his stead. I cannot allow Mr. Makiguchi's wonderful educational philosophy to fall into obscurity. That would be the loss of an unparalleled spiritual legacy for humanity. For the sake of humanity's future, I must create a Soka University. But this may not be possible for me to achieve during my lifetime. If that's the case, I am counting on you, Shin'ichi. Let's make it the best university in the world!"

Shin'ichi never forgot these words. But now his mentor was gone, too. The task of establishing a school based on value-creating education had been passed from President Makiguchi to President Toda, and from President Toda to Shin'ichi. Now, the full weight of it rested on his shoulders.

Shin'ichi was overjoyed that he was at last taking this first step toward actualizing the dream of his predecessors. True disciples are those who realize their mentor's ideals for the sake of kosen-rufu. The noble and great Buddhist path of the oneness of mentor and disciple is found only in such resolute action and victory. It is a path sparkling with the brilliant light of joint struggle.

IN NOVEMBER and December, Shin'ichi poured his energies into traveling around Japan to encourage members, taking commemorative photos with them, among other activities. For Shin'ichi, the photo sessions were more than an opportunity to sit for a group picture. Determined to make these encounters serve as a fresh source of inspiration for the members in their advance toward happiness, he threw himself wholeheartedly into giving guidance and encouraging as many of them as he could in the limited amount of time available.

For example, on November 4, he took commemorative photos with men's and women's group leaders from Nara Headquarters in the Kansai Headquarters Annex. The event turned into a friendly conversation between Shin'ichi and the members and a chance for him to offer personal guidance.

He asked a number of the men their ages and inquired about their health. When an elderly gentleman responded that he was not well, Shin'ichi encouraged him sincerely, saying: "The 'Life Span of the Thus Come One' chapter of the Lotus Sutra teaches the principle of prolonging one's life through faith. In other words, through our faith in Buddhism, we can extend even our original life span. This means that if we continue to strive with strong faith, there is no illness that we cannot surmount. Please chant abundantly and live a long, healthy life!"

After presenting the man with a set of prayer beads, Shin'ichi inquired if anyone else in the room was suffering from poor health. Several members hesitantly raised their hands. Shin'ichi asked them to stay behind, and then spent the break before the next session encouraging them and speaking about the causes of illness.

Shinichi said: "In talking about the origins of illness,

the Daishonin quotes T'ien-t'ai's *Great Concentration and Insight*: 'There are six causes of illness: first, disharmony of the four elements; second, improper eating or drinking; third, inappropriate practice of seated meditation; fourth, attack by demons; fifth, the work of devils; and sixth, the effects of karma' (WND, 631)."

Closer examination of these points reveals the following. The four elements are earth, water, fire and wind. According to traditional Eastern thought, nature and all things in the universe, including the human body, are made up of these four elements. "Disharmony of the four elements" refers to unseasonable weather and other conditions of discord in the natural world, which have a powerful influence on the human body and can cause various illnesses.

THE SECOND and third causes of illness—"improper eating or drinking" and "inappropriate practice of seated meditation"—refer to a lack of control in one's dietary habits and other aspects of day-to-day living. When our daily lives fall out of rhythm, our diet may suffer. Also, insufficient sleep and exercise may cause disorders in our internal organs, muscles or nervous system.

The demons in number four—"attack by demons"—refer to external causes. These include microorganisms, such as bacteria and viruses, as well as the stress we experience in our daily lives. Number five, "the work of devils," indicates the various inner impulses and desires that disrupt the healthy functioning of our minds and bodies. Afflictions that prevent us from practicing Buddhism also arise from the workings of such devils.

Number six, "the work of karma," refers to causes that derive from the inner depths of our life. This indicates sickness that stems from the distortions or deeply rooted tendencies in our life. Buddhism views such distortions as karma.

The origins of illness are divided into these six different categories, but in actuality many illnesses have overlapping causes. In the case of influenza, for example, the cause is a virus. This could be looked at as an "attack by demons." Infection can, however, be triggered by changeable weather—in other words, by "disharmony of the four elements." In addition, a poor physical condition brought about by an unhealthy lifestyle—"improper eating or drinking"—can be a contributing factor. Negative functions may also be at work in the depths of one's life to keep one from engaging in Buddhist practice, and there are also cases when karma may be an important consideration.

"In short," Shinichi continued, "one of the first steps in avoiding illness is taking such precautions as dressing according to the changes in our environment. Leading a well-balanced life, not overindulging in food or drink, and getting enough sleep and exercise are all vital, too. In this way, we can avoid the first three causes of illness. Faith means employing the wisdom to do so. And with the help of medical science, we can control illness caused by germs and viruses, the fourth cause of illness.

"BUT NO matter what the sickness, the speed with which we recover depends upon our life force. And faith is the wellspring of that life force. At the same time, if the root cause of an illness is the work of demons or the effect of karma, then even the best efforts of medical science alone cannot bring about a cure.

"It is only through strong faith in the Gohonzon that we can defeat such negative workings in our life and transform our karma. And among the illnesses caused by karma, the most severe are those resulting from having slandered the Lotus Sutra in a previous existence."

At this point, a man of small build in his mid-fifties sitting directly in front of Shin'ichi said in an anxious voice: "Sensei! I recently went to see the doctor for a checkup because I was experiencing stomach pains. I was told that I have cancer and will have to undergo surgery. And, about six months ago, the car I was driving was hit by another car and I had to be hospitalized for two weeks. I have also suffered with various illnesses during the past three years.

"My wife became a member before I did, and for about five years I was adamantly opposed to her faith. Could my health problems be karmic retribution for that? And is it possible for someone like me to really overcome such karma?"

Shin'ichi's response overflowed with conviction: "Nichiren Daishonin's Buddhism enables us to overcome any karma, no matter how heavy or deep-rooted. You may ask yourself, 'Why do I have to endure such misfortune?' However, while we may be aware of our slander of the Law in this life, we do not know what causes we made in previous existences. We may have committed great slander of the Law and have a heavy karmic burden as a result.

"Originally, our karma would only manifest itself a

little at a time, and we would have to suffer over many lifetimes. But by devoting ourselves to faith, we bring all of our karma to the fore at once. And what we would have experienced as heavy suffering comes to us in a lighter form, enabling us to transform our karma. This is the principle of lessening one's karmic retribution.

"To overcome the suffering of illness caused by karma, we need to sincerely self-reflect in front of the Gohonzon for our slander of the correct teaching and chant Nam-myoho-renge-kyo.

"King Ajatashatru, who at Devadatta's instigation killed disciples of the Buddha and persecuted Shakyamuni, was afflicted by a karmic illness. But in his writings, Nichiren Daishonin tells us that even King Ajatashatru, who had committed such heinous acts, was immediately cured when he sought out Shakyamuni and sincerely expressed remorse for his actions.

"NICHIREN DAISHONIN says, 'Our worldly misdeeds and evil karma may have piled up as high as Mount Sumeru, but when we take faith in this sutra, they will vanish like frost or dew under the sun of the Lotus Sutra' (WND, 1026). Such is the great power of the Gohonzon.

"When we sincerely reflect upon the negative acts we have committed in the past, incredible appreciation toward the Gohonzon is bound to well up in our lives at the realization that we, too, have a chance at genuine happiness. Such deep gratitude to the Gohonzon arouses great joy within our hearts, which then translates into great life force.

"Though we may be chanting Nam-myoho-renge-kyo,

if our prayer is unfocused or we harbor doubts about the Gohonzon, we won't be able to overcome illness. It is crucial to pray with the strong conviction that we will absolutely conquer whatever ails us. And we must pray sincerely to reflect upon and eradicate our past offenses with a deep sense of gratitude to the Gohonzon for enabling us to expiate our negative karma.

"If you have stomach cancer, please continue chanting, sending it directly to the affected area. It is also important for you to determine to dedicate your life to kosen-rufu, and then pray that you will be restored to a state of health that will allow you to do so to your heart's content. Those who are committed to working for kosen-rufu are Bodhisattvas of the Earth. They are practitioners of the Lotus Sutra. When we live for that noble cause, the incredible life force of the Bodhisattvas of the Earth fills our beings. That dynamic life force will triumph over illness."

The man nodded vigorously and remarked: "I understand. Your words have given me courage. I will do my best with renewed determination." His whole expression had brightened, and his eyes had begun to regain their life.

Smiling warmly, Shin'ichi added: "From a Buddhist perspective, your diagnosis of cancer has deep meaning. The Daishonin also says, 'Illness gives rise to the resolve to attain the way' (WND, 937). It can be said that your sickness is a working of the Buddha's wisdom to motivate you to arouse strong faith.

"Practitioners of Buddhism use illness as a means for developing and strengthening their faith. Now is the time for you to stand up based on faith and make a fresh resolve to dedicate your life to kosen-rufu."

"THE FACT that you suffer from a serious illness means that you have a profound mission. The deeper your suffering, the more you can demonstrate the tremendous power of Buddhism when you surmount that suffering and the more you can contribute to kosen-rufu. In order to do that, you have created various kinds of karma, taken on this illness and appeared in this world as a Bodhisattva of the Earth. You cannot fail to overcome this!"

Next, a thin, pale man in his forties spoke up. Haltingly, he said: "I have diabetes and need regular insulin injections. My doctor tells me that if I continue with the injections and follow his instructions about diet and exercise, I can live a normal life, but at the same time, it's a chronic condition that will never be cured. Hearing that I will have to endure this for the rest of my life has made me lose hope, and I haven't the energy for anything."

Shin'ichi responded: "If you exert yourself wholeheartedly in faith, your life will be filled with hope, supreme happiness and fulfillment even if you have a chronic illness. The Daishonin writes, 'Nam-myoho-renge-kyo is like the roar of a lion. What sickness can therefore be an obstacle?' (WND, 412). Nam-myoho-renge-kyo is a lion's roar. A lion's roar will send even the fiercest of animals running. In the same way, when faced with chanting Nam-myoho-renge-kyo, there is no ailment that can be an obstacle to one's happiness or to kosen-rufu.

"People in modern society have been described as being only half-healthy, meaning that we are all afflicted with some kind of illness and that our physical health will decline as we age. But is sickness necessarily the cause of unhappiness? Absolutely not. It is being defeated by illness and losing hope that makes us unhappy. We become unhappy when we forget our mission to strive for kosen-rufu.

"There are many people with perfectly healthy bodies who are unhappy because they are ailing spiritually. On the other hand, there are many Soka Gakkai members who, while struggling with illness or disability, are not only genuinely happy themselves but also work for the happiness of others.

"At life's most fundamental level, health and sickness are one. There are times when our life manifests a healthy condition and times when it manifests illness. The two conditions are interconnected. Thus, by making earnest efforts in faith and fighting against illness, we can establish a state of genuine health both mentally and physically."

SHIN'ICHI placed his hands on the man's shoulders and said: "There are many people who must take insulin injections regularly for the rest of their lives. But if you think about it, eating and sleeping is something we must do every day, too, to live. Try to view your injections as just one more thing that's been added to your daily routine. It won't do any good to let it get you down.

"I hope you will live in such a way that others struggling with the same condition will marvel and say: 'Look how energetic he is, despite his diabetes!' 'Look at what a long life he is enjoying!' 'Look how happy he is!' If you are able to do that, you will be a brilliant example of the power of Buddhism. That is your mission in life. Don't allow yourself to be defeated. Keep going! Never give up!"

Shin'ichi gave the man's shoulders a reassuring shake.

With tears in his eyes, the man replied: "I won't. I won't be defeated. Ever!"

Shin'ichi then addressed all of the members present, saying: "The Daishonin will not fail to protect those who dedicate their lives to kosen-rufu. When his disciple Nanjo Tokimitsu was ill, the Daishonin sent him a letter in which he wrote: 'You demons, by making this man suffer, are you trying to swallow a sword point first, or embrace a raging fire, or become the archenemy of the Buddhas of the ten directions in the three existences?' (WND, 1109). In sternly rebuking the devilish functions causing his disciple to suffer, the Daishonin protected him. We are all embraced by this same great conviction and compassion.

"I hope all of you will also be filled with certainty and indomitable resolve not to be defeated by those negative forces. Muster your courage. I also used to suffer from poor health and a doctor said I probably wouldn't make it to age thirty. But I'm strong and healthy now and able to handle the most demanding of schedules. You can all become healthy, too!"

Smiles lit the faces of the men who had stayed behind to talk with Shin'ichi between photo sessions. Shining, their expressions were completely different than when they first sat down with him. Shin'ichi's guidance, into which he had poured his entire being, had been powerful and inspiring.

ON NOVEMBER 7, a photo session was held for Chiba and Saitama prefecture district leaders, including those of the young men's and young women's divisions, at the Soka Gakkai Headquarters in Shinanomachi, Tokyo. Once again Shin'ichi put his heart and soul into speaking with the members and giving personal guidance. He even used the time in between sessions to offer marriage advice to one of the young women's members.

Shin'ichi always made an effort to find and encourage those members who were working hard behind the scenes or doing their best amid adverse circumstances. He prayed earnestly each day to encounter such people. Through such effort and determination, he developed and honed the ability to read and understand people's situations.

On this day, he devoted every moment to listening to the members' reports, sometimes encouraging them warmly and gently and at other times rousing their spirits with the sternness of a strict father. He also presented them with cloths for wrapping their prayer beads and other items, which he had prepared in advance.

During the session for the young women of Chiba, he stressed the importance of training and polishing oneself. "Life is a struggle with various challenges," he said. "It is by overcoming numerous hardships that we can experience true happiness. Therefore, hardships and difficulties are our treasures. They provide the means by which we polish our lives.

"I hope that whatever challenges you face during your youth, you will never be defeated. Confront them boldly and move forward to victory."

When Shin'ichi had finished speaking, a voice called out to him: "Sensei! My father died in August of this year and my mother and I are on our own now."

"I'm very sorry to hear that. But don't give up! None of your hard work will ever be wasted. I want you to become happy without fail!"

Next, two young women sitting toward the top of the bleachers raised their hands and called out "Sensei!" in unison. The member in the top row spoke up: "My name is Toshie Soda." Then the young woman sitting one step down said: "I'm Mutsumi Soda."

Mutsumi, the elder of the two, began to speak: "Our mother died in October of last year. Our father was originally opposed to our faith, and although he is starting to show more understanding now, he still won't become a member. But all six of us children are determined to work together to create a happy family. Our younger sister Chika is going to share her experience at an upcoming high school division meeting."

TEARS filled Mutsumi eyes as she told Shin'ichi about her family situation. Her sister, Toshie, was also overcome with emotion.

Family discord and economic hardship led the Soda family to join the Soka Gakkai and begin practicing the Daishonin's Buddhism eight years earlier. Of the six children in the family, the five eldest were all girls and the youngest was a boy. Mutsumi was the second eldest and Toshie was third. When they became Soka Gakkai members, the eldest daughter, Sachiyo, was sixteen and the youngest child, the boy, was just two.

Their father worked in a steel plant but he didn't earn enough money to support his wife, Kiku, and their six children. Perhaps exhausted and frustrated because their lives never improved no matter how hard he worked, he began to go out drinking almost nightly and spending most of his salary. When Kiku asked her husband for a little more money to run the household, he exploded in anger and struck her. The sight of their mother weeping with her face swollen was etched in the children's minds.

When Sachiyo entered high school, she got a job at a

local diner and contributed her earnings to the family budget. She chose that particular job because it offered staff meals when on duty.

Their father grew more depressed and angry and their mother became gloomy and embittered. The sound of laughter disappeared from the house. Then, one day, Kiku went to visit her parents' home in Kobe, Hyogo Prefecture. While there, a relative told her about the Soka Gakkai. She decided that if it would really bring her happiness, she would give it a try.

After returning home, Kiku told her husband that she wanted to join the Soka Gakkai and asked him if he would join with her. But he rejected her suggestion out of hand. She decided to become a member without him, but she didn't know where to go to do so. She made a trip to the municipal government offices in her area to try to find out. When she asked the clerk where she could go to join the Soka Gakkai, he was visibly taken aback. Another employee, however, having overheard her question, piped in and told her that he believed his neighbors were members and suggested that she go see them about it.

The neighbors turned out to be the family of a classmate of Toshie. After hearing more about Buddhism from them, Kiku enthusiastically joined the Soka Gakkai in March 1957. As she began doing gongyo and participating in Gakkai activities, Kiku grew more positive and cheerful each day. Seeing this dramatic change in their mother, who had once been in constant tears, the children followed her example and began practicing in quick succession.

WHEN his entire family joined the Soka Gakkai, Mr. Soda began to feel left out and lonely. He reacted by vehemently opposing their faith. He also began drinking more heavily. But Kiku would not be defeated. She had come to strongly believe that practicing the Daishonin's Buddhism was the only way for her to find happiness.

As her husband's opposition intensified, Kiku hid the Gohonzon in the closet. After he had fallen asleep, she would take it out and chant desperately in a low voice. When he found the Gohonzon and destroyed it, Kiku and the children chanted Nam-myoho-renge-kyo through their tears.

On the way home from a meeting one day, Kiku said to her daughters: "Your father is against the practice now, but I think this is actually the Gohonzon testing the strength of our faith through him. In light of the principles of Buddhism, we must have slandered the Mystic Law in a past life and persecuted practitioners of the Lotus Sutra. That's why we're faced with this opposition now. By continuing to do our best under these circumstances, however, we can expiate the negative causes we made in the past. This is the principle of transforming poison into medicine. If we look at it this way, I really think we should be grateful for father and take good care of him. He's the one who's feeling alone, after all. If he really knew about the Soka Gakkai, I'm sure he would want to become a member. Whether or not that happens is up to us."

Hearing their mother's perspective on the situation, the girls, who had hated their father for the way he was behaving, experienced a change of heart. Mr. Soda nevertheless began to withhold even more of his paycheck. But the girls joined forces and found part-time jobs to support the family.

For the first three or four years after they started practicing, all the family had to eat every day was noodles. When the clam season came around, they would gather clams at the nearby seashore and add them to their noodles. Their life was hard, but together Kiku and her children were cheerful and positive. They had great hope for the future.

And slowly but surely, their father's opposition to their faith lessened and he began to show signs of understanding toward the Soka Gakkai.

KIKU became a women's group leader, while Sachiyo, Mutsumi and Toshie became young women's district leaders. Shouldering the mission to spread the Daishonin's Buddhism, Kiku and her elder daughters devoted themselves sincerely to practicing the Mystic Law and supporting their fellow members.

Two years later, in May 1964, Sachiyo was appointed a young women's chapter leader. No one was more delighted by this news than Kiku. Poor as they were, she made the traditional celebratory dish of steamed rice with adzuki beans and congratulated her daughter from the depths of her heart. With tears in her eyes, she said: "Nothing could make me happier than to see my children developing into leaders of kosen-rufu. The struggle has been worth it. I truly feel my life has been rewarded. I want all of you to become happy."

The Sodas eventually fulfilled their long-cherished dream of building a new home. It appeared as if the harsh winter endured by the family had ended and spring had finally come. But then Kiku, who had been her family's rock and mainstay, developed liver trouble and died suddenly in October.

Kiku's death came as a tremendous shock to the children. But her beautiful countenance on passing away drove home to them the greatness of faith. As she drew her last breath, the jaundiced tint of her skin caused by her illness disappeared and her natural color returned. A faint touch of pink tinged her cheeks and her expression was serene, as if she were smiling gently. Kiku's husband was also moved by his wife's countenance, and from that time on he never complained to his children about their faith.

The Soda children pledged together that they would

work hard enough to do their mother's part as well. They looked after the house and threw themselves into activities for kosen-rufu, believing that their development in faith was the best way to show their appreciation to their mother.

They grew into fine, self-reliant youth, and Chika, the second youngest daughter, also grew in faith to become a high school division leader at the general chapter level.

When Mutsumi and Toshie learned that a commemorative photo session with President Yamamoto would be held for Chiba district leaders at the Soka Gakkai Headquarters, the two decided they wanted to take the opportunity to report to him about their family situation. They hoped to tell him how they were all working together to do their best since their mother's death, as well as make a new start with fresh resolve. The Soda sisters chanted sincerely toward that day.

AFTER HEARING Mutsumi's story, Shin'ichi gazed intently at her and her younger sister, Toshie. "I'm sure it has been difficult for you," he said. "But you have really done your best. I'm confident that your mother is delighted to know how well you are doing."

Praying deeply in his heart for the happiness of the Soda family, he added: "There are certain to be many more tough times ahead, but you mustn't be defeated. I hope you will stay with the Soka Gakkai for the rest of your lives and become absolutely happy. Please give my best to the other members of your family."

"We will!" the girls called out in unison.

Shin'ichi then handed them a small gift and asked

them to give it to their sister in the high school division. It was a brief exchange, but for Mutsumi and Toshie—indeed for all six of the Soda children—Shin'ichi's words became a spiritual beacon that illuminated their futures.

On January 6, 1966, Chika Soda shared her experience at a high school division meeting held at the Taito Ward Gymnasium in Tokyo, which was attended by Shin'ichi. She spoke about overcoming her grief at her mother's death and how, determined to fulfill her mission as a high school division member, she challenged herself to study hard and chant Nam-myoho-renge-kyo and as a result achieved high marks in school. Her story had a powerful impact on the other students.

As Shin'ichi listened to her speak, he silently applauded her and prayed that she would continue to do her best. After the meeting ended, he asked a high school division leader to present Chika with a set of prayer beads from him. Shin'ichi determined to watch over these praiseworthy Soda children for the rest of his life.

Sachiyo, the eldest, married that year, and Mutsumi, the following year. Their father also remarried. Shortly after this, it fell to Toshie, who was working at a kindergarten, to look after her younger brother and sisters. She rented an apartment and they moved in together. By the time she finished paying the rent, buying food and paying her siblings' school fees, most of her salary was gone. Their daily diet consisted of little more than rice and fried cabbage. But basing themselves on President Yamamoto's encouragement that they strive to become happy no matter what obstacles they face, they continued to support each other and advance along the path of kosen-rufu.

NOW, some thirty-five years after that commemorative photo session, the members of the Soda family remain active on the front lines of kosen-rufu and are leading happy lives.

Adversity does not cause unhappiness, nor does hardship. A defeated, apathetic and bitter spirit, an impoverished spirit filled with envy and resentment toward others, is what causes unhappiness.

Shin'ichi used every possible occasion, no matter how brief, to go among his fellow members who were facing hardships and to encourage them to be strong and never give in.

Even in a momentary encounter, words spoken from the heart that are filled with a powerful wish for the other person's happiness can deeply touch that person's life and revive his or her spirit; they can become a source of inspiration for an entire lifetime.

On November 28, the Soka Gakkai Study Department held separate evaluation exams for its professors and associate professors, with the exam for the former also serving as the first part of a promotional exam for those wishing to advance to the level of professor. Shin'ichi went to encourage the examinees at the venue—a building in the law department of Nihon University in Tokyo's Kanda area—before the noon exams began.

A total of 1,175 associate professors and 121 professors from around the country were scheduled to sit for the three-hour exams, each of which required examinees to select and answer ten questions from a total of fifteen given.

The questions were not restricted to interpreting passages from the Lotus Sutra or the Daishonin's writings. Several required examining the relationship between Buddhism and various social phenomena—for example, "Discuss the limitations of science" or "Explain the significance of dispelling attachment to the five vehicles and establishing the one ultimate principle in terms of contemporary society."

When Shin'ichi arrived at the building, he visited each classroom and encouraged the examinees. While doing so, the young man escorting him mentioned that a men's division member named Taikyu Kawase, who was blind, was taking the examination in a separate room.

Shin'ichi recognized the name. "He's in his fifties and from Okinawa, isn't he?" he asked.

"Yes," the young man replied.

"I'd really like to see him," Shin'ichi said, and they straightaway headed for the room.

Shin'ichi met Kawase several times before and had encouraged him to study hard and become a professor of the Study Department despite his disability. Kawase's wife was with him in the examination room to record his oral answers to the questions. Shin'ichi called out: "Hello there! May I come in?"

KAWASE must have recognized Shin'ichi's voice because when Shin'ichi entered the room, he rose from his chair and said: "Sensei!" He directed his unseeing eyes toward Shin'ichi and gazed at him as if etching Shin'ichi's image into his very being. Tears streamed down his cheeks.

Kawase was born with retinitis pigmentosa, an inherited degenerative disease of the retina that is characterized by slowly deteriorating sight. As he grew older, his vision declined year by year. Fighting against his condition, he earned a license as an administrative notary and, with the help of his wife, Sumi, continued working.

Kawase joined the Soka Gakkai in 1957. By that time, he could no longer clearly see the large print of a newspaper headline. In July 1960, when Shin'ichi made his first trip to Okinawa and a chapter was established there, he joyfully accepted an appointment as district leader. He felt it was the mission of the members in Okinawa to make their island the most peaceful and happy place in the entire world and was resolved to give his all to achieving that goal. Relying on what little sight he had left, he shared Buddhism in high spirits with others. He even traveled by boat to other islands, determined not to return home until he had succeeded in helping someone embrace the Gohonzon. His example was an inspiration to fellow members.

Kawase eventually lost almost all of his vision. His single-minded devotion to faith, however, kept him from feeling worried or afraid. He had already prepared himself for this to happen. He thought to himself: "This is my karma, but I will not be defeated by it! I will open the eye of my heart. Though I may be losing my sight, I still have a fine mouth with which I can talk about Buddhism and chant. I still have legs on which I can get around to introduce Buddhism to others. As long as I am alive, I will dedicate myself to kosen-rufu and bring courage to others."

From that time on, his wife, Sumi, became his eyes. He continued to visit all of the members living in his area, led by Sumi. Losing his sight brought difficulties, of course, but he also developed a sight he never had before. More than anything, he could now see the kindness and consideration of others. His feeling of gratitude toward his wife and others around him grew, and the light of joy filled his heart.

He also learned to sense fine distinctions in people's emotional states by the tone and timber of their voices, and he rediscovered the beauty of the songs of birds and insects.

TAIKYU KAWASE regarded Soka Gakkai activities as a right bestowed equally on all people so that they could attain Buddhahood in this lifetime. That is why he continued to exert himself in faith even with the challenge of his disability. There were times when he went alone, using his cane to guide him, to visit and encourage members in their homes.

Kawase also maintained a strong seeking spirit toward Buddhist study. His wife, Sumi, read to him from the Daishonin's writings every day, and he knew almost by heart the page numbers for each writing. When he met with other members in his district, he would have them read to him from *The Daibyakurenge* and the *Seikyo Shimbun*. He also asked anyone who came to his home, whether they were Soka Gakkai members or not, to read to him from various Gakkai publications. On those occasions, Kawase listened intently, his entire being given to the task of absorbing every word. Being unable to read a passage again and again like a sighted person could, he earnestly strove to memorize what he heard at that moment.

He had also secretly chosen a friendly rival to spur him on in his studies. This person was a certain student division leader who was the first university student to become a professor of the Study Department. When Kawase read about the young man in a Gakkai publication, he resolved that he, too, would achieve the rank of professor as quickly as possible and started to apply himself more diligently to his studies. As a result, he had reached the level of associate professor.

Now, with Shin'ichi suddenly standing before him in the room as he was about to take the promotional exam for professor, Kawase was speechless with astonishment and delight. Smiling, Shin'ichi said: "Please sit down. Thank you for coming all the way to take the exam. You have my full support, so please do your best to become a professor."

Shin'ichi shook Kawase's hand and Kawase grasped his firmly in return.

The Soka Gakkai is filled with noble children of the Buddha, who shine with the golden light of mission; it is filled with great heroes of the people. Shin'ichi wished to sincerely praise each and every one of them and crown them as champions of life.

For Kawase and Sumi, this encounter served as a springboard to further personal advancement. A few days later, Kawase composed a poem expressing the joy and determination he felt from meeting President Yamamoto:

> *What joy to be born*
> *Together with my mentor*
> *And to share*
> *The journey of kosen-rufu*
> *Across the three existences.*

SHIN'ICHI always strove to reach out to and illuminate his fellow members with the light of hope. He wanted to encourage the suffering, to give courage to the sorrowful and to praise those making valiant efforts.

To treasure each person, to share their sufferings and to protect them is the spirit of Nichiren Daishonin, the Buddha of the Latter Day of the Law, and the spirit of the Soka Gakkai. It is also the starting point of humanism.

As long as all of its leaders embrace this commitment, the Soka Gakkai is certain to grow and develop forever. But if they lose sight of people as individuals and start thinking of them as just numbers, or as defined by their positions in the organization or society, the Soka Gakkai, like many other organizations, will degenerate into a cold, heartless, mechanical bureaucracy. If that were to happen, the Gakkai's ruin would begin from within—more specifically, from the core—just as the Daishonin implies when he writes, "Only worms born of the lion's body feed on the lion" (WND, 302).

What, then, would be the fundamental cause for the Soka Gakkai growing bureaucratic? It would be when leaders forget the organization's original purpose—that is, of working for kosen-rufu and serving the members, who are the children of the Buddha—and instead lapse into self-interest. It would happen when leaders no longer focus on kosen-rufu but on themselves.

During the past year, Shin'ichi had devoted great attention to conveying the Soka Gakkai spirit as well as his own spirit to the Gakkai Headquarters staff, who comprised the core of the leadership. He wanted to foster people of the highest caliber. "People are the walls; people are the fortress." Citing these words, his mentor Josei Toda had stressed that the Soka Gakkai must build a stronghold of capable people.

At the time, because of the dramatic increase in the organization's membership, the number of employees in both the main Headquarters and in various regional offices was also expanding rapidly to meet the needs of the organization. When Shin'ichi became the president in 1960, for example, there were only 130 Headquarters staff members, but by early 1965 there were more than 1,100 across Japan. In addition, with the *Seikyo Shimbun*'s shift to daily publication in July 1965, that number continued to grow.

Also, because the Headquarters was hiring talented youth who could shoulder the next generation, the average age of the staff was quite young—twenty-nine in the general administration office and twenty-seven in the editorial and publications offices.

Within youth resides infinite potential. But even the most magnificent rough gem will not sparkle unless it is buffed and polished.

SHIN'ICHI did his utmost to train each Headquarters staff member. He took every opportunity to speak with them and get to know them, trying to acquaint himself with their personalities, their family circumstances and other aspects of their lives. Whenever he had a moment, he listened to their questions and opinions.

When the staff didn't ask him questions, Shin'ichi would quiz them on a wide range of topics that included Buddhist doctrine, literature, philosophy and international affairs, including the nuclear issue. The staff members therefore had to make a constant effort to be aware of current events and important issues and maintain an interest in various subjects. They had to study so that they could respond when he asked them something. Shin'ichi also continued to encourage them to acquire the habit of reading good books, asking them what they had read recently and what they thought of it.

For some time, Shin'ichi awarded gold and silver prizes to those who did well at their jobs or who wrote an impressive article for a Soka Gakkai publication, and wishing to further encourage staff members, he decided to put more energy into such efforts. He would have to carefully read through the *Seikyo Shimbun, The Daibyakurenge* and other Gakkai publications in order to do so but this was not a problem. He pored over them all, thrilled with the joy of discovering new young talent.

On occasion, he also wrote guidelines on the office bulletin board to encourage the staff to energetically and confidently go about their work. These included:

- Live each day in a good rhythm.
- Never put off to tomorrow what you can do today.
- Take care of the business at hand with confidence.
- Coolheaded judgment and prompt action.
- Return to the Soka Gakkai spirit.
- Put the chanting of Nam-myoho-renge-kyo, work and propagation of the teachings first.
- Think of your work as a privilege, not a chore.
- Employ your creativity and produce good work.
- Start the morning energetically to set things off right for the day.

Most important to Shin'ichi, however, was conveying to the Headquarters staff through his own actions the spirit of devoting one's life to kosen-rufu and of protecting and serving the members.

This spirit is the exact opposite of a bureaucratic or organizational mentality.

ONE DAY in late November, Shin'ichi sat at a desk in the administrative office on the first floor of the Soka Gakkai Headquarters. A pile of books and note cards lay before him in which he was writing dedications, autographs and words of encouragement for members. When he lifted his head to dip his writing brush in the ink, he noticed a woman standing in the lobby. She seemed to be a Gakkai member. A few minutes later, he looked toward the lobby again and saw that she was still there.

Shin'ichi put his brush down and walked over to her. "Sorry to keep you waiting," he said. "Do you have an appointment with someone?"

"President Yamamoto!" the woman exclaimed in surprise, her cheeks reddening. Then she explained why she had come to the Headquarters. She was a women's group leader and was having difficulty solving some human relations problems within the organization, so she had called a leader from her area who worked at the Headquarters and asked to receive guidance. The leader told her to come to the Headquarters.

She had arrived at the appointed time but the leader was away from his desk, so she had been waiting for him. Shin'ichi didn't want to keep her waiting further, so he decided to offer her guidance in the leader's place. He listened warmly as she explained her situation and then gave her sincere advice. He then retrieved a book from his desk, wrote her name and some words of encouragement and presented it to her. At that moment, the leader with whom the woman was originally supposed to meet returned. He was nearly an hour late.

When he saw Shin'ichi, the leader blanched and said, "Sensei, I am so sorry," bowing deeply.

"You shouldn't be apologizing to me," Shin'ichi said. "You should apologize to this lady who has been waiting so long."

"Of course. I am very late. Please accept my apologies," the leader said to the member.

The woman smiled and replied, "Oh, not at all. Actually, I'm the one who should apologize for insisting that you meet me despite your busy schedule. And now I have been able to receive guidance directly from President Yamamoto, making this a day I will treasure all my life. It's like a dream. If you hadn't told me to come to the

Headquarters, I wouldn't have met President Yamamoto. Thank you so much!"

The woman departed with a happy smile.

WHEN Shin'ichi Yamamoto returned to the office, he asked the staff member why he was late.

"I was in a business meeting, and it took longer than anticipated," he responded.

"When that happens," Shin'ichi said, "the proper thing to do of course is to make a phone call and ask someone here to convey a message to your guest that you are going to be late for the appointment."

Though it may have seemed a minor problem, Shin'ichi realized it was just such incidents that gave rise to a bureaucratic mentality and he couldn't overlook it. Rather, he thought it better to nip the problem in the bud before it was too late.

Shin'ichi continued: "If your appointment had been with the president of a large company that had dealings with the Soka Gakkai, would you have been more than an hour late without even calling?"

"No, I don't think I would have done that," the staff member replied.

"I didn't think so. That's a sign that you have a lax attitude toward Gakkai members; you feel it's all right to keep them waiting. It also suggests arrogance on your part—the idea that since you're a leader you will be forgiven for being late. Such an attitude shows contempt toward people and it is proof that bureaucratism has already set in.

"All leaders, especially Headquarters staff, exist to

protect and serve the members. But some leaders take advantage of the members' trust and respect, growing arrogant because they think their position makes them important. There is nothing more dangerous than this."

Shin'ichi then turned to everyone in the room and said: "I am not just talking about this individual. Another problem is when, for example, the reception desk calls up to the office to say that a visitor is here to see a certain person, and the person taking the call simply says, 'He's not here,' and does nothing else. What that staff member should actually do is find out where his colleague has gone and when he'll be back and give that information to the reception desk. Depending on the circumstances, he might even volunteer to fill in for the person who's not in, meet with the visitor and see what he can do to help.

"I've also noticed that recently staff members don't even make an effort to answer the phones of colleagues who are away from their desks, or if they do, they speak in a cold, curt manner. This is the selfish and lazy attitude of those who try to shun as much as possible anything that doesn't directly involve them or that requires them to take responsibility. Soka Gakkai staff must always be ready to take full responsibility for everything.

"A RUDE or inconsiderate telephone manner can cause a member to lose faith in the Soka Gakkai Headquarters. And a non-member calling might think that we are a dreadful organization and become critical of or hostile toward the Gakkai. Each such incident may seem of small importance, but their accumulation can actually result in the destruction of the Soka Gakkai, a citadel built of solid trust.

"That is why even small matters must be taken seriously. Major problems and accidents all arise from minor lapses. The recent disaster of the burning of the passenger liner *Yarmouth Castle* off the coast of Miami, Florida, is just such an example of many small oversights resulting in a terrible tragedy."

Shin'ichi was referring to the loss of some ninety lives in a fire on the *Yarmouth Castle,* a 5,002-ton passenger liner registered in Panama, on November 13. The ship carrying 552 passengers and crew had set sail from Miami at five o'clock in the evening on November 12 for Nassau in the Bahamas. It was a night voyage scheduled to take about twelve hours.

The causes and progress of the fire were reported on later by the U.S. Coast Guard. The *Yarmouth Castle* had been built some thirty-eight years earlier and signs of its aging were becoming apparent, including the ship's failure to meet its schedule on a few journeys. Much of the ship was covered in wood paneling and fire prevention measures on board were inadequate.

The fire started at about 12:05 AM on November 13 in a storeroom on the main deck, though the cause still remains unclear. The storeroom had been converted from a bathroom and lacked a sprinkler outlet. It was packed with unused furnishings and other easily flammable items.

At half past twelve, twenty-five minutes after the fire started, a crew member went on security patrol, but he only made a cursory inspection and did not check every room adequately. If there had been a careful room-by-room inspection at this point, the fire would have surely been discovered.

Only at 1:10 AM was the officer on the ship's bridge informed of the fire. By that time, more than an hour had passed since its start and it had grown so strong that it was impossible to put out.

THE CREW began to fight the fire but the pumps did not deliver enough water. The blaze was out of control. Flames engulfed the entire ship as it reverberated with the screams of passengers trying to find their way to safety. Because the regular safety inspections of the ship had not been properly performed, many cabin windows could not be opened and passengers, died trapped inside the ship.

A stampede of passengers rushed to the lifeboats at the rear deck, which was not yet in flames. There they witnessed an unbelievable sight: the captain and other officers were in a lifeboat, making their escape ahead of everyone else. Later, the captain came under fierce attack for this behavior.

But though the captain and his officers abandoned their responsibilities and fled, there were crew members who stayed behind to aid the passengers. One of them was the ship's twenty-three-year-old third purser Terry Wise, who risked his life in the rescue effort. He helped people trying to escape through their cabin windows by pulling them up onto the deck above, and he threw chairs, mattresses and other items that would float into the water so that those who had jumped overboard without life jackets would have something to hold onto.

When the flames grew closer, he gave his own life jacket to an air force officer, who had been assisting him and urged him to jump overboard. He stayed on the burning ship until the very last moment encouraging and helping passengers, including a woman who was lying semiconscious with a broken leg. In the end, he managed to save some thirty lives in all.

A nearby Finnish ship and another passenger liner, the *Bahama Star,* which was about 12.5 miles behind the *Yarmouth Castle,* also rushed to the scene to help. The *Bahama Star* got as close at 330 feet to the burning ship and, under the direction of its captain Carl Brown, saved many of the passengers who had jumped into the water.

Six hours after the fire had started, at 6:05 AM, the *Yarmouth Castle* sunk. The story was covered in depth by Japanese newspapers, and Soka Gakkai members in the United States had also made detailed reports to Shin'ichi. He did not regard this as something that had happened to others; for him it offered an important lesson for the Soka Gakkai as an organization.

SHIN'ICHI continued speaking to the staff members. His tone was severe.

"Before a big accident occurs there is always some kind of warning. The attitude that it is all right to keep our visitors waiting is just such a warning. Another example is tardiness. In the past, no one was late for work but recently this has changed. This is another sign of an impending problem. If we let these signs go unchecked without correcting them right away, we are creating the cause for later trouble. That's why I'm so strict about these things, though it may seem like I'm belaboring the point.

"On the *Yarmouth Castle,* the fire should have been detected at the very beginning through the crew's regular safety inspections, but it wasn't. That's because the crew neglected to follow proper procedures. In other words, they were lax. To think that everything will be OK even if a few corners are cut is a perfect example of carelessness and apathy. It was this mind-set on the part of the ship's crew that led to an irrevocable tragedy.

"Where does such a careless and negligent attitude come from? It comes from a lack of a sense of responsibility. Therefore, Headquarters staff, who shoulder the responsibility to advance kosen-rufu, must never think of themselves as mere hired help who need only to do their assigned job and ignore everything else.

"I want all Headquarters staff to share my same resolve and awareness to take full responsibility for the entire Soka Gakkai. I want all of you to look at yourselves as my representatives. And I want us all to devote ourselves wholeheartedly to protecting the Gakkai and our place of work."

It was because of his earnest desire to realize kosen-rufu and his firm determination to protect the Soka Gakkai that Shin'ichi was strict with the Headquarters staff—but he was the strictest with himself. For that reason, no matter how tough he was, everyone trusted him and followed his lead.

Fostering others requires more than just empty words. It can only be done by working together with others and showing them through one's own example.

Every morning when Shin'ichi arrived at the Headquarters, he looked closely at the staff members' faces. He was concerned about whether they were tired, whether they were maintaining a balanced life and how their health was. He also showed great consideration toward their parents and families, sometimes going as far as to help the parents of some staff find work. Shin'ichi was determined to make the Soka Gakkai Headquarters the best workplace in every regard, so that all the staff could utilize their abilities to the fullest extent without any unnecessary worries or distractions.

ONE DAY toward the end of the year, Shin'ichi made a detailed inspection of every department of the Soka Gakkai Headquarters and the *Seikyo Shimbun* offices. He even visited the boiler room in the basement of the *Seikyo Shimbun* building. There he found an employee dressed in soot-stained work clothes who was diligently cleaning the pipes.

"Thank you for all your hard work!" Shin'ichi said, startling the man.

"President Yamamoto!" he exclaimed, turning toward Shin'ichi. As he removed the towel from around his neck, he then said in a more formal tone: "Thank you so much for everything you've done this year. Under your leadership, I have made this a meaningful and victorious year with no regrets. I will continue to do my best next year with renewed determination. Thank you for your support!"

The man's face was beaming and his workplace was clean and tidy. Though it was an inconspicuous and modest job, Shin'ichi could see that he took great pride in it and felt a strong sense of responsibility. Shin'ichi bowed deeply to the man, as if crowning him a champion of victory.

While some Headquarters staff are in conspicuous positions that often place them in the limelight, others have positions that support the organization from behind the scenes. People tend to do their jobs enthusiastically when their work is seen and appreciated. But what really matters is how seriously and diligently one exerts oneself when away from the limelight. Whether or not one can do one's best in a job that is inconspicuous and challenging, or that is different from what one really wishes to be doing is also an issue of extreme importance. Such times are the true test of one's mettle both as a human being and as a Buddhist.

Shin'ichi keenly understood this through his own experience. In January 1947, he began working at Josei Toda's publishing company, Nihon Shogakkan, as the editor of a boys' magazine. But the business ran into trouble and Shin'ichi had to transfer to the Toko Construction Credit Union, another company run by Toda, who was its managing director. There he was involved in sales and other duties requiring him to have direct contact with customers.

Before long, the credit union also hit hard times and folded. Shin'ichi then became a sales manager for the Daito Commerce Company for which Toda was a consultant. As a young man whose inclinations lay more to writing and literature, there was nothing he was more ill-suited to than sales.

WHEN Shin'ichi began working for Josei Toda, he had already decided to devote his life to kosen-rufu. He had concluded that the concrete way to do this was to embrace Toda, an unparalleled leader of kosen-rufu, as his mentor and to serve and protect him as a disciple. That is why Shin'ichi did not waver in the slightest when his mentor's business hit difficult times and his salary fell into arrears for several months. It is also why he readily accepted any job he was given. He believed that this was the way to protect the Soka Gakkai and advance kosen-rufu.

Though ill-suited for sales at the Daito Commerce, Shin'ichi nonetheless turned it into an opportunity to train and develop himself, vowing to do his very best. Through challenging himself, he became a model for other employees, achieving record sales and contributing greatly to the company's development.

In contrast, many of Toda's other employees, rattled by the sudden change of fortunes in his business undertakings, quit their jobs filled with hostility and venom toward their boss. They had been people who had constantly gone around saying they would do anything for Toda and kosen-rufu, and who had encouraged others to do the same. Toda made no attempt to stop them leaving. Rather, he said to Shin'ichi with a grim look in his eyes: "They're showing their true colors at last!"

One invariably finds that when placed in disadvantageous circumstances, self-centered, power-hungry, fame-seeking individuals reveal their true nature. They grow despondent and go around sulking and complaining. This weakness derives from a basic disbelief in the Buddhist law of cause and effect, and in the invisible observance of our actions by the Buddhas and bodhisattvas throughout the universe.

Shin'ichi felt that the Soka Gakkai Headquarters staff should be a gathering of courageous individuals who have volunteered to devote their lives to the supreme goal of realizing kosen-rufu. No matter how the times might change, that prime point must never be forgotten. Shin'ichi knew that as long as this spirit pulsed in the hearts of all Headquarters staff, the Soka Gakkai would never become tainted by a bureaucratic or organizational mentality. Instead, it would flourish eternally as an organization of shining humanism.

After he finished his inspection of the *Seikyo Shimbun* offices, Shin'ichi went up to the roof of the building, inviting staff members he met on the way to join him.

"Look!" he said to the others. In the distance stood Mount Fuji in its imposing magnificence, seeming to hold its arms out to all humanity, ablaze in the crimson sunset. The December wind was crisp.

"I want you to become like Mount Fuji—people of true conviction who are unperturbed in the face of any challenge and who serve as beacons of hope for the members."

Everybody nodded, their faces aglow with the sun's brilliant light.

> *Dawn*
> *Is a child's heart.*
> *It is the hope of youth.*
>
> *Beyond the horizon,*
> *In the darkened sky,*
> *A single ray of light shines forth.*
> *The sun rises,*
> *Painting a masterpiece*
> *Of sublime beauty.*
>
> *A perfect sphere*
> *In deep crimson,*
> *The dawning sun*
> *Soars majestically into the sky,*
> *Burning with joy and passion.*
>
> *Undaunted*
> *By falling rain*
> *Or the gusting wind,*

The sun always rises,
Piercing through the darkness—
The unchanging rhythm of the universe.

Its brilliant light
Gives people courage and strength,
Bringing happiness to all equally
In every corner of the earth.
With great pride and a sense of mission,
The sun shines.

Shin'ichi wrote this poem titled "Dawn" to celebrate the start of 1966, which the Soka Gakkai had designated the Year of the Dawn. It appeared under the pen name "Shin'ichiro" in the January issue of the children's magazine *Friends of Hope,* published by the Soka Gakkai-affiliated Ushio Publishing Company.

Just as the sun *Gives people courage and strength, / Bringing happiness to all equally / In every corner of the earth,* Shin'ichi was determined to spend his life illuminating the world with the light of happiness, the light of peace. With such resolve he departed for Hawaii on January 14.

The first time the Soka Gakkai had used the theme "Year of the Dawn" was 1959, the year after second president Josei Toda passed away. Shin'ichi, the general administrator and de facto leader of the Gakkai at the time, had proposed the theme for that year, which arrived as members still grieved for President Toda. He chose it with the conviction that Toda's disciples would rise up after their mentor's passing and carry on the struggle he had initiated, ushering in a new dawn of victory.

Dawn is a time of departure, the beginning of the drama of a new day. It is hope. When the sun rises and blazes through the darkness, the seas, the mountains, the earth and all humanity are bathed in its golden light. Indeed, dawn symbolizes the infinite possibilities of the future.

Shin'ichi staunchly vowed to make this second "Year of the Dawn" a fresh start in the movement for worldwide kosen-rufu.

THE MAJOR purpose of Shin'ichi's trip to Hawaii was to attend the opening of the new Soka Gakkai community center there. The establishment of the center had been decided in August the previous year, when Shin'ichi stopped in Hawaii on his way back to Japan from a visit to the United States and Mexico. It would be the Soka Gakkai's fifth community center overseas.

Located in a hilly section of central Honolulu, the new center was a white, modern, two-story wooden building situated on a lot less than one acre. Once the building's purchase had been confirmed, Shin'ichi sent Tadayoshi Miné, a young men's leader and Soka Gakkai director, to Hawaii to assist with preparations for the center's opening and to support the development of the youth division.

Miné arrived in Hawaii in September 1965 and was immediately struck by the Hawaiian members' passionate enthusiasm for kosen-rufu and their strong seeking spirit toward Buddhism. He was particularly impressed by the determination of the young men's members, who called themselves the Pineapple Corps and whose motto was "Go for broke!" This had been the slogan of the U.S.

Army 442nd Unit during World War II. The 442nd Unit, comprised of Japanese-American volunteers from the United States mainland and Hawaii and known for its valiant fighting spirit, was the most highly decorated unit in the U.S. Army.

Adopting the unit's slogan in their activities for peace, the Hawaii young men advanced kosen-rufu in high spirits. They made a conscious decision to wear white short-sleeved dress shirts and ties instead of the more traditional Hawaiian aloha shirts when introducing others to Buddhism and encouraging their fellow members. This unofficial uniform symbolized their firm resolve to strive as champions of kosen-rufu amid the relaxed atmosphere of Hawaii.

The Pineapple Corps members worked very hard. Whenever there was a meeting, they took care of all the planning and organizing. On the day of the actual event, they would direct the parking. Also, when they learned of a new member in a district, the young men's members went out to meet them and teach them gongyo. They would visit them on a daily basis until they were able to pronounce gongyo correctly and perform it on their own.

The men's and women's members jokingly complained that they had nothing to do when Pineapple Corps members came to the discussion meetings because the youth did everything from emceeing to leading Soka Gakkai songs to sharing their personal experiences. The fact, however, was that the members felt reassured, inspired and encouraged by the presence of these fine young men.

WHEN their activities finished, many of the young men would go to the new community center and pose questions regarding faith to Miné, who stayed there while preparing for the opening. Their questions covered a wide spectrum of topics, ranging from Soka Gakkai activities to Buddhist doctrine, such as "What kind of activities are the Tokyo young men's members engaging in?" "Why did the five senior priests at the time of the Daishonin abandon their faith?" and "What does the principle of the oneness of life and its environment mean?" Because these impromptu question-and-answer sessions were extended due to interpretation between Japanese and English, they often went late into the night.

All of the local members pitched in to help renovate and spruce up the new center. Since the building originally had been a private residence, the interior needed remodelling and the exterior, a fresh coat of paint. Everyone joyfully worked together. And when they learned in November that President Yamamoto would visit Hawaii in mid-January the following year, they applied themselves with even greater energy and enthusiasm.

The center's garden was a beautiful, lush expanse of green, planted with many of the fruit-bearing trees indigenous to Hawaii, including banana, guava, papaya and coconut. The members took pride in their new community center as a symbol of Hawaii, and they wished to make it known throughout the islands. They were also determined to have everything perfect to welcome President Yamamoto.

During discussions related to his Hawaii visit, Shin'-ichi suggested having a delegation of about one hundred representative leaders from the various divisions in Japan join him on the trip.

"As leaders," he said, "it's important that we know about the world. Also, for the sake of the future advancement of kosen-rufu, I would like to open the way for international exchange."

After careful consideration of Shin'ichi's proposal, the Soka Gakkai Headquarters decided to send an exchange delegation comprised of about 120 representative leaders and more than ten Nichiren Shoshu priests to Hawaii.

At ten o'clock in the evening on January 13, the delegation, led by Vice General Director Hiroshi Izumida, departed from Haneda Airport ahead of Shin'ichi and the leaders who would be accompanying him. They arrived in Honolulu shortly after nine o'clock in the morning on January 13, Hawaii time. Several dozens of members were waiting at the airport to greet them, along with reporters and photographers from local newspapers.

When Izumida appeared in the airport lobby, the journalists fired a barrage of questions at him about the purpose of the group's visit, the history of the Soka Gakkai and the organization's relationship to the Clean Government Party. It seemed that the media in Hawaii had a strong interest in the Soka Gakkai.

A GOHONZON-conferral ceremony was held for 264 new members at an elementary school in Honolulu rented for that purpose. Following this, exchange discussion meetings with the delegation members from Japan were held in seventeen locations.

When Shin'ichi first visited Hawaii about five years

earlier, there were only about thirty members at the discussion meeting he attended. Now such meetings were being held simultaneously in seventeen locations with dozens of people packed into each one. In addition, the Hawaiian organization had grown from the one district that had been established on that first visit into a general chapter with two chapters and twenty districts.

As the discussion meetings took place, Shin'ichi arrived at Honolulu Airport along with General Director Kiyoshi Jujo and several other top leaders.

The following day, January 14, the opening for the new Hawaii Community Center began at half past ten in the morning amid great jubilation. From daybreak, clear blue skies stretched out overhead, and the azure ocean and lush green trees all glimmered in the brilliant sun, as if joining in the celebration.

Shin'ichi called out "Congratulations!" as he made his entrance. The faces of the members who filled the room lit up and they began applauding vigorously.

Gongyo soon commenced. Though many of the participants didn't speak Japanese, their voices harmonized vibrantly as they recited the sutra and chanted together. After gongyo, Miné delivered a report on the center's establishment, from the purchase of the building to the opening that day. This was followed by greetings from America Headquarters Leader Masaki, Soka Gakkai Young Women's Division Planning Department Leader Yumie Fujiya and others.

Fujiya was overcome with emotion as she spoke.

"I heard that President Yamamoto showed his consideration for the Hawaii young women's division by composing a poem for us while flying over the Pacific during his flight from Japan," she said. "I would like to share it with you now:

Young women
Soaring into the skies
Of the Mystic Law,
Strong and noble,
Filled with happiness."

AT THE TIME, there were about one thousand member-households in Hawaii, but the young women's division numbered only sixty or seventy members. Perhaps because there were so few of them, they were relatively inactive and lacked enthusiasm. Having learned of this, Shin'ichi composed a poem for them, wishing wholeheartedly to encourage them and instill them with hope.

After introducing President Yamamoto's poem, Yumie Fujiya said: "President Yamamoto has given us, the Hawaii young women's division, fresh courage. Though we are small in number, I hope that each one of us will begin to shine from today like a beautiful blossom.

"Flowers bring hope and comfort to people. People gather where flowers bloom. It is by developing ourselves into bright young women and becoming flowers of Soka that we will attract many other young women to our cause and inspire them. Flowers bloom because they have deep roots and continue to draw sustenance from the soil.

"People also need sustenance to grow. That sustenance

comes from a philosophy, a faith, that serves as the foundation for one's way of life. If we allow ourselves to be distracted by fleeting excitement and pleasures, if we forget the importance of self-improvement and instead lead empty, rootless lives, we will never truly shine as individuals or realize genuine happiness.

"Let us send our roots deeply and firmly into the earth of faith and bring forth wonderful blossoms of hope and happiness!"

Fujiya's remarks were followed by greetings from the Soka Gakkai's vice general director and general director.

Shin'ichi spoke next, discussing the significance of establishing a community center in Hawaii. He said: "Hawaii is a place of memories for me—a place where, more than five years ago, I took the first step toward realizing worldwide kosen-rufu.

"The world today is filled with bleak news, as exemplified by the war in Vietnam. However, from the perspective of the Buddhist principle of the simultaneity of cause and effect, I am certain that the opening of this community center, a citadel of peace, will lead to fresh development in the movement to achieve world peace. Buddhism is a philosophy that links the hearts of people everywhere and creates peace, transcending national, ethnic and ideological differences. That is our mission as well. In fact, without the wisdom of Buddhism, there can be no world peace."

THE TREES in the center's garden swayed in the breeze, bathed in tropical sunlight.

"My wish is that the members here in Hawaii will

develop strong faith and attain both material and spiritual fulfillment. I hope you will all become pioneers in this endeavor and dedicate your lives to striving for the well-being of your fellow citizens, rather than seeking happiness in some distant place.

"I also hope you will demonstrate the validity and greatness of Buddhism in your lives, savoring tremendous joy as you make your way in high spirits. The world of faith is not some extraordinary realm, nor is it a realm steeped in formality. No matter what, please never forget the importance of maintaining faith in the Gohonzon and staying with the Soka Gakkai.

"I am sure that all of you have received many benefits through your practice, but the benefits conferred by the Gohonzon are unlimited and boundless. I want you to enjoy even more benefit and deepen your understanding and conviction in the magnificent power of the Gohonzon. The way to do so is to practice courageously and accumulate various experiences in faith. Experience strengthens your conviction and makes your faith unshakable.

"Please be aware, however, that while you may throw yourself wholeheartedly into Gakkai activities, your efforts to share Buddhism with others may not always bear fruit. But that's no reason to become discouraged or to be hard on yourself. The Gohonzon's great compassion is bestowed equally on all who earnestly pray and work for kosen-rufu.

"I would like you to joyfully advance in your activities, making friends wherever you go and becoming people who are respected and loved by all. That is the way to spread kosen-rufu. Please know that I am always praying for you and I will continue to do so. Let's meet again."

The members were deeply moved by Shin'ichi's warm wishes for their happiness. Applause echoed throughout the room as many of the members nodded their heads in agreement, tears filling their eyes. The opening came to a close with a joyful chorus of "Song of Worldwide Kosen-rufu."

Following this, General Director Jujo announced the new personnel appointments for Hawaii General Chapter. Mitsuru Kawakami, who had been general chapter leader, was appointed general chapter advisor, while Hiroto Hirata, who had been Honolulu Chapter leader, was appointed general chapter leader.

IN ADDITION, two new chapters, Waikiki and Oahu, were established within Hawaii General Chapter, giving it a total of four chapters. The position of general chapter young women's leader was also created, to which Yoshie Harada was appointed. She was the wife of Tony Harada, who had been the only person to welcome Shin'ichi at the airport on his first trip to Hawaii five years earlier.

Yoshie joined the Soka Gakkai together with her mother in Japan when she was in high school. At the university she studied English literature, and after graduating she became a teacher. Being active as a member of the young women's division, she developed a strong desire to go overseas and dedicate herself to working for worldwide kosen-rufu.

At about that time, a leader of the young women's

division told her about Tony Harada, who was living in Hawaii, suggesting him as a possible marriage partner. Yoshie met with Harada when he traveled to Japan to meet her in May 1965. They married, and Yoshie accompanied her husband to Hawaii.

After the personnel announcements, chapter flags were returned by the previous leaders and then bestowed upon the new ones. Shin'ichi then rose to speak one more time. He introduced a number of projects in the works for Hawaii, including the construction of a temple there.

One important responsibility of a leader is to constantly offer fresh and inspiring goals.

After the meeting came to an end, Shin'ichi joined the members for commemorative photographs in the garden of the community center. The members were divided into five groups. Each was a gathering of people with diverse backgrounds that included Japanese-Americans, African-Americans and Hawaiians. Hawaii was truly an ethnically diverse place. While different in appearance, there was no difference in the broad smiles that lit each member's face.

Shin'ichi was to stay in Hawaii for four days and three nights. He determined to use that limited time to solidify the foundation for the future growth of the Hawaiian organization. Thus, after each group's photo, he would stand among the members, addressing them individually, shaking their hands and presenting them with gifts such as prayer beads.

To one elderly woman, he said: "Please live long into the twenty-first century."

And to a child, he remarked: "When you get older, please come to Japan. I'll be waiting for you at Soka University."

He put his utmost into each moment, offering encouragement and guidance with his entire being.

Realizing that the photographs would become a treasured memento for the members, Shin'ichi wore a suit for the occasion. In the warm Hawaiian weather, he was soaked to the skin in perspiration.

WHEN THE DAY'S events had finished, Shin'ichi sat down to inscribe books and note cards with words of encouragement and calligraphy to present to members as gifts in commemoration of the center's opening.

The young men of the Pineapple Corps, working as

support staff during Shin'ichi's visit, witnessed firsthand his ceaseless devotion to the members from the moment he arrived in Hawaii. Deeply moved by this, they renewed their vow to dedicate their lives to advancing kosen-rufu together with him.

Late that night, two *Seikyo Shimbun* journalists, who had come to Hawaii with the exchange delegation, went to the community center to call in their articles to the home office in Japan. Because they didn't wish to wake President Yamamoto, who was staying there, they avoided the main entrance and made their way quietly around to the back door. Just then, a tall figure jumped out of the shadows.

"Who is it?" shouted one of the reporters.

At the same time, the dark figure demanded, "Who's there?"

In the dim moonlight, the reporters saw that it was a leader of the Hawaii young men's division and that standing behind him was another young man.

It was evident that the youth were firmly determined to prevent the trespassers from moving any closer to the center. But when they learned that the two men were *Seikyo Shimbun* reporters, they relaxed, and one of them said in English: "We are patrolling the premises to ensure President Yamamoto's safety. I apologize for mistaking you as trespassers."

The Hawaii young men had decided of their own accord to guard the center, arranging shifts throughout the night and stationing themselves in the garage.

The reporters were astonished. They could see that the young men were examples of dedicated disciples who were striving to serve and protect their mentor in life with a strong seeking spirit toward him. Having assumed that the mentor-disciple relationship was something that could only be understood within the context of Japanese cultural customs and traditions, the journalists now realized that their assumption was based on arrogance.

No matter what path we are on, if we wish to pursue it in depth, we need someone to teach and guide us and who serves as a model. This is the role of a mentor. The path of the disciple comes into being, when we determine to live up to our mentor's expectations. This is the inevitable conclusion reached by those who devote their lives to seeking the Way.

HAWAII youth members hoped to receive guidance from President Yamamoto in person. But when they thought of how exhausted he must be after his strenuous efforts to encourage everyone during his stay, they didn't feel they could give voice to that desire.

Even so, their wish kept intensifying. After thinking about it for some time, they discussed the matter with a leader who had come from Japan. "Chant Nam-myoho-renge-kyo," the leader told them. "When you don't know what to do, just sit in front of the Gohonzon and chant wholeheartedly."

Agreeing completely with this advice, the youth members began to chant in earnest.

In the afternoon on the day following the opening, Shin'ichi did gongyo at the new community center with the exchange delegation members who were scheduled to return to Japan that evening. It took quite a while before their chanting fell into rhythm.

When they finished gongyo, Shin'ichi said: "I hope you will return to Japan remembering that you came to Hawaii to work for kosen-rufu and that you never grow complacent or negligent."

He said this because he sensed a certain laxness in their attitude. He had also been disappointed at the way a women's leader in the group responded when he asked the previous night about her impressions of the visit.

She had enthused: "This trip has been full of wonderful memories. Perhaps because it was the first time for any of us to travel overseas, the entire delegation was so excited from the moment we boarded the plane. One of the priests even got a little tipsy during the flight and we wondered if he'd be all right when we saw him staggering to the restroom.

"Everything we've experienced here has been new and interesting, and we stayed up late into the night at our hotel talking about it."

Unfortunately, her reply conveyed no earnest spirit to help advance kosen-rufu in Hawaii.

The members of the exchange delegation were all leaders of various divisions. However, there was a significant difference between their attitude and that of Shin'ichi, who had struggled with all his might during his limited time in Hawaii to open the way for the future development of kosen-rufu there.

Shin'ichi rose from his seat and looked out into the garden. On the lawn, he saw a group of local young men's members sitting attentively, waiting on standby until they were needed. Waving to them, Shin'ichi walked out to say hello. The young men smiled, their eyes sparkling with delight.

Shin'ichi had been looking for an opportunity to meet with them and encourage them.

SHIN'ICHI said to the young men: "Thank you for all your efforts! Please sit comfortably."

But no one moved. It seemed they wished to remain seated on their knees wishing to show their great respect for Shin'ichi.

"Please, relax," Shin'ichi urged. "Both Buddhism and the Soka Gakkai are open and free. There's no need for unnecessary formality, nor should it be forced upon anyone. Behaving in an overly formal or rigid manner may lead others to misunderstand Buddhism."

When Shin'ichi said this, the young men finally sat in a more comfortable position. A discussion ensued between Shin'ichi and the youth, most of whom were Americans not of Japanese descent.

"I have received detailed reports about all of you. The great activities of the 'Pineapple Corps of the Mystic Law,' working for the peace and the happiness of all humanity, are well known in Japan and are the focus of attention from members around the world. I am so glad to meet with you." Shin'ichi smiled, looking at each of the young men happily as he spoke.

"If you have any questions, please don't hesitate to ask."

Several hands shot up immediately as if the youth had been waiting precisely for such an opportunity.

One person asked, "How does Nichiren Daishonin's Buddhism differ from that of Shakyamuni and T'ien-t'ai?" It was a question that showed just how earnestly the member had been studying Buddhism. There were also questions that revealed the members' passion and commitment toward realizing kosen-rufu, such as "How can we deepen our conviction in faith?"

His heart filled with joy and hope, Shin'ichi poured all his energy into answering each question. The young men were a picture of sincerity. They were all ears as they tried to absorb Shin'ichi's every word, their eyes shining with seeking spirit. He was delighted to discover these young successors developing solidly in Hawaii.

"I hope you will work together to make these islands a model of kosen-rufu," Shin'ichi said. "Hawaii's mission as a pioneer of worldwide kosen-rufu is to build a humanistic organization whose members trust and respect one another and who savor genuine happiness as they strive to create a peaceful society. I have great hopes that you can achieve this! Please stay well!"

Moved by Shin'ichi's impassioned words, the young men solidified their determination. Tears filled their eyes as they pledged with fierce resolve to fulfill their mission. The trees in the garden rustled in the wind, as if applauding these young lions of Hawaii.

THE MEMBERS of the exchange delegation returning to Japan that evening stood behind the young men and listened as Shin'ichi spoke.

Gazing in their direction, Shin'ichi said sternly: "The youth of Hawaii are striving in earnest. Such dedication is crucial. Kosen-rufu is a struggle against obstacles, so if we are halfhearted or lax, we will be defeated by devilish functions. I hope you will never forget this." But almost none of the delegation members took Shin'ichi's words as being directed at them.

Soon afterward, the delegation left the Hawaii Community Center and headed for Honolulu Airport. Later, Shin'ichi, Kiyoshi Jujo and other Japanese and local leaders drove to a spot near the airport to watch the departure of the charter plane carrying the members back to Japan. Stepping out of the car, Shin'ichi looked toward the airport. The sun was beginning to set. One after another, passenger and cargo planes took off.

Gazing up at the sky, Shin'ichi murmured, "I wonder which plane is theirs?"

One of the leaders pointed upward to a plane taking off and said: "Sensei! I think it's that one. That's the logo of the company they were flying with."

"You're right. That must be the one," Shin'ichi said.

The next moment, those standing around Shin'ichi heard him chanting quietly. He prayed earnestly that the members would reach home safe and sound, his chanting continuing until the plane was long out of sight.

Meanwhile, the members on board were peering down wistfully at the beautiful shoreline of the island below, commenting variously: "The warm weather was so wonderful. Hawaii is truly a paradise," "I wish I could have stayed there forever!" Some members relaxed and chatted with their neighbors and others started to doze off.

When the aircraft started to level off, one of the cabin attendants rushed up to Hiroshi Izumida, the delegation leader, and announced with a tense expression: "After takeoff, we discovered a crack in the window of the cockpit. While this doesn't affect our ability to fly, for safety's sake we are turning back. I hope you understand."

A chill ran down Izumida's spine. He now understood what Shin'ichi meant when he warned against having a lax attitude.

SO THAT the members wouldn't be alarmed, Izumida asked the cabin attendant to make an announcement explaining the reason the plane was returning to Hawaii. Far from being concerned, however, the members cheered when they heard the news.

After watching the delegation's plane depart, Shin'ichi Yamamoto had dinner and then went back to the Hawaii Community Center. When he arrived, he was greeted by members of the group he had just seen off to Japan.

"What happened?" he asked.

Appearing somewhat embarrassed, Izumida explained the situation. Shin'ichi was relieved to learn that at least the members were safe.

"I'm glad that everyone is all right," he said. "Does that mean you'll be returning tomorrow?"

When Izumida nodded, Shin'ichi said to everyone: "No matter how wonderful Hawaii is, you must really go back to Japan this time, OK?" Cheerful laughter filled the room. Shin'ichi said nothing else.

Later, when the delegation members learned from Kiyoshi Jujo that Shin'ichi had chanted while watching their takeoff, they began to reflect on their attitude.

They thought: "After participating in the scheduled

events here, we behaved as if we were students on a school field trip, just having a good time without a care in the world. That's why we were so excited and even cheered when we heard that our plane was heading back to Honolulu. We had absolutely no awareness that we had come to Hawaii to work for kosen-rufu.

"Yet President Yamamoto chanted for our safe trip home. Without a doubt, he prayed wholeheartedly, thinking what a horrible tragedy it would be if we met with an accident. We should have been the ones who were praying for our safety. The devilish function of inattentiveness almost got the better of us."

They were all ashamed of their frivolous attitude. At the same time, through Shin'ichi's example, they were keenly reminded of their heavy responsibility as leaders of kosen-rufu never to be negligent for even a moment.

The exchange delegation finally left Hawaii at 10:50 AM the following day, January 16. Shin'ichi departed later that afternoon, arriving at Tokyo's Haneda Airport at half past eight in the evening on January 17, Japan time.

IN THE SECOND half of January and in February, 1966, Shin'ichi poured his energies once again into encouraging members across the nation—traveling to Osaka, Kagawa and Gifu prefectures—and taking commemorative photos with members from throughout the Tokyo Metropolitan Area at the Soka Gakkai Headquarters. At the same time, anticipating the Soka Gakkai's further development in accord with the changing times, Shin'ichi had been considering new appointments at the Soka Gakkai's executive level toward strengthening the organization's overall leadership. He was also thinking of a completely new leadership lineup for the youth division as well.

After careful deliberation at vice general director meetings and other executive conferences, new leadership appointments were announced at the monthly Headquarters leaders meeting held on February 27 at the Nihon University Auditorium in Tokyo. This was the most comprehensive leadership reshuffle to take place since Shin'ichi's inauguration as president.

The changes were originally scheduled to be announced at the annual Headquarters general meeting in May. The Soka Gakkai's activities and membership, however, were increasing at such a rapid pace that the organization was now accomplishing in one month what in the past had taken it three months to an entire year to accomplish, and it had therefore been decided to make the announcement two months earlier than planned, at the February meeting.

The key changes in the new lineup were Izumida replacing Jujo in the position of general director and the establishment of a board of general administrators. Jujo had become general director in December 1964 at the age of forty-one, following the sudden death of his predecessor, Koichi Harayama. He had worked very hard in the fourteen months since taking on that responsibility, but with kosen-rufu entering a new phase, it became an increasingly important issue for the Soka Gakkai to foster a wide range of capable leaders.

In order to meet such demands, the decision had been made to appoint someone older and more experienced to the post of general director, and to establish a board of general administrators that would have the same authority and responsibility as the general director and would take care of the internal operation and guidance of the organization. Consequently, the fifty-four-year-old Izumida, who had been the senior director of the board of directors (the equivalent of the current post of general director) during the Soka Gakkai's postwar period of reconstruction under President Toda, was appointed general director. Jujo, Hisao Seki, Kazumasa Morikawa and three others were named general administrators.

The post of general administrator originally had been established by then general director, Takeo Konishi, in consultation with other top leaders in June 1958, after President Toda's death. They created it for Shin'ichi, then youth division chief of the general staff, out of their desire for him to take de facto leadership for the entire Soka Gakkai. In the following two years, up to the time of his inauguration as the third president in May 1960, Shin'ichi served as the sole general administrator of the organization, bearing full responsibility for all aspects of the movement while supporting the general director behind the scenes.

Shin'ichi was certain that if the six new general administrators actively dedicated themselves with the same spirit, determination and awareness that he had as general administrator, the Soka Gakkai would experience greater growth and development.

IT WAS ALSO out of Shin'ichi's profound consideration for Jujo's health that the latter was moved from the position of general director. Serving as general director of the Soka Gakkai and its more than five million member-households, without anyone to share the responsibility, was an extremely demanding job.

Jujo, who was a naval academy graduate, was proud of his strong constitution, but if he were to carry on at the pace he was going, it would only be a matter of time before his health would be compromised. Shin'ichi wanted to give Jujo some breathing space so that he could continue carrying out his mission in the future.

The formation of the men's division was also announced at the February Headquarters leaders meeting, along with the appointment of the new general director Izumida as its leader. Seven vice leaders, including Jujo and Hisao Seki, were appointed as well.

From the perspective of the advancement of kosen-rufu, the establishment of the men's division was an event of great significance. Until then, the women's and youth divisions had taken the lead in organizational activities, with the men supporting each division as leaders in the line organization. For this reason, a conscious decision had been made not to organize the men into a separate group. But from about a year earlier, the call had begun to rise for the men to take a more active role at the forefront of activities, thereby allowing them to give fuller play to their abilities and lead the way for the other divisions. It was believed that this would enable the organization to gain further the trust of society. Thus, feeling that the time had come for the men of the Soka Gakkai to stand up, Shin'ichi decided to establish a men's division.

New leaders were appointed to each youth division

group as well. Akizuki, who had been the youth leader, was appointed youth advisor, and Shoichi Tanida, a former young men's leader, took Akizuki's place as youth leader. Goro Watari, head of the student division, replaced Kenshiro Ishikawa as young men's leader, and Akihiro Tatematsu, who was a central figure in the young men's division, became head of the student division. Yumie Fujiya, head of the young women's division Planning Department, succeeded Michiyo Watari as young women's leader.

The position of vice youth leader was also created, along with vice leaders in the young men's and young women's divisions. Many capable members were appointed to these positions, allowing the youth to make a fresh start with a strong, multilayered leadership lineup.

The new student division leader Akihiro Tatematsu was a youth of thirty-four, distinguished by his thick eyebrows and dauntless expression. He had studied medicine in order to follow in the footsteps of his grandfather, great-grandfather and great-great-grandfather, who had all been doctors, but he had been forced to quit college when his father's business hit hard times.

Initially, he took a leave of absence from school and started doing various jobs to support his family, including as a factory worker, popsicle vendor and tutor. But his father's business kept falling deeper into debt.

IN THE END, Tatematsu had no choice but to make the agonizing decision to drop out of college altogether and find a full-time job. It was at this point that he heard about the Soka Gakkai from his aunt. She had suffered from tuberculosis in the past and had overcome her illness after starting to practice Buddhism. She gave Tatematsu a copy of Josei Toda's "The Philosophy of Life" and urged him to read it.

Tatematsu's grandfather died of cancer. When Tatematsu thought of this, he felt that life was incomprehensible: Though a doctor, his grandfather had been powerless to save his own life. Wanting to understand the mystery of human existence, he made time during his packed daily routine to read any book on philosophy he could lay his hands on, but he could not find a philosophy that answered his questions. Toda's "The Philosophy of Life," however, clearly addressed all of them, covering such topics as the three existences of life and the law of cause and effect. Reading it changed Tatematsu's life.

Tatematsu joined the Soka Gakkai in 1954. Three months later, he participated in a Tokyo University Lotus Sutra Study Group lecture with President Toda. He found the content of the lecture somewhat difficult to grasp, but moved by Toda's great conviction, he strengthened his resolve to devote his life to Buddhist practice. He later also suffered from tuberculosis but overcame it through faith and eventually became active as a young men's leader in the Yokohama and Yokosuka areas of Kanagawa Prefecture.

Tatematsu was a diligent young man who loved to learn and always had a book in hand. In spite of his busy schedule, he submitted many articles on economics, literature and politics to the *Seikyo Shimbun* and other Soka Gakkai publications. His articles were well received and highly praised. He was also a considerate leader who looked after the members and was known for always making time to offer personal guidance and encouragement.

Shin'ichi had observed the young man for a long time. Though Tatematsu had not graduated from the university, his desire to learn was stronger than most and he worked hard and had forged himself through Gakkai activities. It could be said that he had studied and developed himself in the Soka Gakkai, a university without a campus. Shin'ichi believed that Tatematsu would be a fine older brother figure for the members of the student division and make full use of his talents in fostering them into future leaders.

YUMIE FUJIYA, the new young women's leader, was a bright and active young woman. Married with one child, her maiden name was Kaga, and she had joined the Soka Gakkai in her third year of junior high school.

In her social studies class in junior high, she had been assigned a project on the influence of religion on society, but when she went to the library to do research she could find no useful sources. She decided to ask at some of the temples in her neighborhood, starting with one near her home dedicated to the Mother of Demon Children.[1] The chief priest of the temple was out and his wife seemed a bit perplexed by Fujiya's inquiry. "If that's what you're interested in," she said, "there's a young man who often comes here to argue that the Mother of Demon Children doesn't have the power to save people. He might be able to help you. He seems to know a lot."

The woman gave Fujiya the young man's address and she went to his home, but he wasn't there. It took her four attempts before she finally managed to meet him. His name was Takeshi Arimura, and he later became the head of the Soka Gakkai Brass Band. Fujiya was shown into a room where several young people were gathered. Arimura was patiently talking to a pale, thin, bespectacled university student who was apparently suffering from tuberculosis. Explaining that religion is the very foundation of human existence and that there are correct and erroneous teachings, he declared that the Soka Gakkai was the only religion that could truly bring happiness to people. His words were logical, well organized and convincing.

He then said to the student: "If you take faith in this religion, you will overcome your illness and realize all of your dreams without fail. How about it?"

But the student just looked at Arimura without responding.

"What has he got to lose?" Fujiya thought to herself.

The student, however, remained silent.

When Fujiya returned home that day and mentioned the Soka Gakkai to her father, he flatly forbade her to have anything to do with it. But deeply moved by the sincerity and earnestness of the people she had met and by their absolute conviction in the power of their faith she desperately wanted to give it a try.

Yumie asked Arimura to come to her house and talk to her father about Buddhism and he gladly agreed. Impressed by Arimura's wholehearted appeal, her father also decided to join, and father and daughter began to practice together. Soon afterward, the student with tuberculosis also took faith. His name was Eisuke Akizuki.

AFTER graduating from high school, Fujiya started working at a bank in Tokyo. The bank kept long business hours, and once Fujiya became a teller she was required to work the late shift every other week. This made it difficult for her to participate in Soka Gakkai activities as often as she would have liked. This was hard for Fujiya, who had always made activities her top priority since becoming a member.

Because of work, she also couldn't attend the lectures necessary for becoming a Soka Gakkai Study Department member. Instead, she had to sit by and watch as other members she had practiced with join the Study Department one after another. Feeling as though she was being left behind, she was sad and frustrated. But she read again and again the Gosho passage, "Regard your service to your lord as the practice of the Lotus Sutra" (WND, 905) and threw herself into her work, determined to become the best employee. At the same time, she prayed earnestly that someday she would be able to engage in Soka Gakkai activities freely to her heart's content.

Two years later her prayer was answered and she was assigned to the day shift full time. Soon after, she sat for a Study Department examination and did so well that she was promoted directly to the position of teacher rather than that of assistant teacher. Then, at the May 3 Headquarters General Meeting in 1958, the year that President Toda passed away, she was appointed a young women's chapter leader. At twenty-one, she was the youngest person in Japan to hold such a position.

Chapters at the time were very large, and she was responsible for more than 1,400 young women covering an area that reached from Tohoku in the north of Japan to Shikoku in the south. Shin'ichi, then youth division chief of the general staff, did his utmost to support the young Fujiya in fulfilling this heavy responsibility.

He immediately sent her a letter of encouragement: "My most heartfelt congratulations on your appointment. I hope you will take your place as a youthful leader of the Bodhisattvas of the Earth with optimism, strength and courage. Those with faith always triumph. I pray that you will create a great organization dedicated to faith."

When she received Shin'ichi's letter, Fujiya renewed her vow to make the best organization possible.

But her supporting leaders were all older than she was. At first, she was reserved and held back her opinions, taking a rather passive approach to her responsibility. Consequently, her chapter activities didn't smoothly progress.

After two months, Shin'ichi spoke to her strictly: "You are the most timid of all the young women's leaders! What are you doing? A person who lacks courage cannot lead kosen-rufu activities!"

His words hit home and pierced through her weaknesses.

FUJIYA resolved to become stronger and keenly understood that there should be no hesitation when it comes to faith. She racked her brains and prayed about how she could encourage and guide leaders and members who were older than she was. As a result, she began sincerely reaching out to each one and praising them wholeheartedly.

She also worked harder than anyone else. She put forth utmost effort in every task she took on and produced wonderful results. Gradually, everyone came to recognize her character and ability and they applauded her, saying, "She may be young, but she's doing an amazing job."

More members began seeking her advice. At the same time, under her leadership, solid unity emerged among the members and eventually a strong organization was built.

When Shin'ichi Yamamoto became the third president of the Soka Gakkai, in May of 1960, the chapter headed by Fujiya achieved the greatest growth in membership in all Japan. That month, Yumie quit her job at the bank and became a Headquarters staff member. Soon after, however, she contracted pleurisy and took a leave of absence from work. She was terribly depressed at being bedridden just when she was embarking on the challenge of her life. But there was also a small part of her that had the defeated attitude, "I can't help it if I'm ill."

Shin'ichi knew Yumie well, and he realized that for the sake of her happiness, she had to conquer the inner weakness that would allow her to give in to illness. When she returned to work two months later, Shin'ichi suppressed the words of comfort that he wanted to say to her and instead remarked sharply: "The fact that you were defeated by illness means that your faith was defeated. That is a disgraceful example for a young women's leader to set!"

Shin'ichi's words powerfully struck Fujiya and made her think. She came to understand that she had almost forgotten the spirit of challenge.

She later married Hideo Fujiya, an architect and leader of the young men's division, and soon after had a child.

With changes in personal circumstances, one finds that even those who have exerted themselves energetically for kosen-rufu may, to a smaller or lesser extent, lose some of the passion and enthusiasm with which they devoted themselves to faith.

But even after she married, Yumie never took a single step backward. She strove vigorously for kosen-rufu and developed herself more and more as a leader. That is what led Shin'ichi to recommend her for the position of head of the young women's division at this time when the kosen-rufu movement was making a fresh start.

Ushering in this new age of Soka, the leaders of the youth division—Shoichi Tanida, Goro Watari, Akihiro

Tatematsu and Yumie Fujiya—were gallantly setting forth into the future together.

MARCH 5 was a beautiful, clear spring day in Tokyo. Shin'ichi Yamamoto looked forward to this day with great anticipation. In the evening, a ceremony marking the establishment of the men's division, which had been announced at the February 27 Headquarters Leaders Meeting, would be held at the Soka Gakkai Headquarters. During the day, whenever Shin'ichi saw one of the Headquarters staff who would be joining the new division, he would joyfully remark: "The time for men of the Soka Gakkai to stand up is here at last. The curtain will now rise on an age of full-fledged activities for kosen-rufu."

Shin'ichi firmly believed that the members of the men's division were the pillars supporting the grand structure of kosen-rufu. During the time of Nichiren Daishonin, it was his middle-aged male disciples who played central roles among the laity.

For example, Shijo Kingo, one of the Daishonin's leading disciples in Kamakura, was about forty years old when he accompanied the Daishonin during the Tatsunokuchi Persecution, prepared to give his own life to protect his mentor. It was also from his mid-forties that he tried to persuade his lord Ema to take faith in the Daishonin's Buddhism and bravely endured personal attacks and persecution that arose as a result, including the confiscation of some of his lands.

Despite this, Shijo Kingo is often thought of as a youthful follower of the Daishonin. This impression is partly due to the fact that he was twenty-seven when he began practicing. More than anything, however, it can be attributed to his single-minded devotion to kosen-rufu, his sincerity and his incredible passion.

The Japanese name for the men's division is *sonen-bu*—with *bu* meaning "division" and *sonen* literally meaning "men in the prime of life." It is important therefore that the men's division members, while on the one hand being self-possessed and levelheaded, also demonstrate courage, energy and action as people who burn with a passionate commitment to kosen-rufu.

In addition to Shijo Kingo in Kamakura, the core followers of the Daishonin in the Shimosa region were Toki Jonin, Ota Jomyo and Soya Kyoshin, all men in their prime.

Toki Jonin gave the Daishonin refuge in his own home following the Matsubagayatsu Persecution, where Pure Land school believers made an attempt on the Daishonin's life. Several years the Daishonin's senior, he joined in the struggle to spread the Mystic Law when he was in his mid-forties. Ota Jomyo, who was introduced to the Daishonin's teachings by Toki Jonin, is thought to have been around the same age as the Daishonin. Soya Kyoshin was two years younger than Jomyo. Thus, at the time of the Tatsunokuchi Persecution in 1271, Toki Jonin was around fifty-six years old, Ota Jomyo was about fifty and Soya Kyoshin was about forty-eight.

Because these men rose up to valiantly strive and encouraged their fellow practitioners to do the same, they served as pillars of strength for many followers, who were inspired to persevere in faith amid great persecution.

Where there are such men, others feel reassured. When men stand up, it gives others courage. Their presence is significant and their potential is tremendous.

AT FIVE O'CLOCK in the afternoon, the ceremony marking the establishment of the men's division began in the hall on the third floor of the Soka Gakkai Headquarters. The brilliant rays of the setting sun poured into the room.

Shin'ichi led everyone in a solemn gongyo. The participants' faces shone with joy, excited to think that the time had come for them to demonstrate their real abilities. Shin'ichi prayed wholeheartedly that the members of the men's division, the great bulwark of the Soka Gakkai, would resolutely stand up.

Afterwards, General Director Izumida addressed the gathering. He encouraged the participants to win in their workplaces and make outstanding contributions to their communities, gaining trust in society at large. Shin'ichi sat forward in his seat and applauded.

Men in their prime hold many key leadership positions in society. An important factor, therefore, in realizing a peaceful society based on Buddhist ideals lies in the men's division members playing active roles in every area of society and developing into great leaders.

The age of the essential phase of kosen-rufu is the time when each individual manifests actual proof of their practice based on the principle of faith equals daily life.

The general director's remarks were followed by greetings from the vice leaders of the new division and then guidance from President Yamamoto.

Shin'ichi smiled broadly and said: "Congratulations on the establishment of the men's division. I am truly overjoyed that this day has come and I feel even more confident about the future of kosen-rufu."

This was Shin'ichi's honest sentiment. Next he stated that for the sake of the continuous advancement of kosen-rufu, it was important to combine the strength of conservative caution with the youthful, vigorous spirit of reform, adding that it had been the exemplary efforts of maturity and youth together that had contributed to the Soka Gakkai's progress thus far. He further remarked that at this time of new beginning in the organization's movement, both the power of youth that fuels kosen-rufu's development and the experience and wisdom of the mature, well-rounded men's members were crucial.

Shin'ichi then touched upon the role of the men's division within the Soka Gakkai as a whole: "It goes without saying that our organization advances through the cooperation of its various divisions. However, just as fathers are often the backbone of their families, the members of the men's division have an important mission to ensure the success of our activities. That is why men serve as central figures in each chapter and district.

"While one of the men's division's main functions is to foster men, I hope you will not view yourselves as just one of the Gakkai's divisions but that you will promote harmony among all and shoulder responsibility for protecting the Soka Gakkai and the entire membership."

SHOUTS of affirmation and applause filled the room.

Shin'ichi said: "If the men's division sets an outstanding example, then the women's, young men's and young women's divisions will also splendidly develop. The sincere encouragement of the men's division will help to nurture truly capable people in every division.

"I would particularly like you to support the young men as they strive to reveal their potential, providing them with opportunities to actively work on the front lines and taking full responsibility for their development. I would also like you to warmly support and protect the women's and young women's members. The men's division is a model of faith for the other divisions. Everyone is watching to see how all of you, with the wide range of practical life experience you possess, will tackle your various challenges.

"If you persevere with strong faith no matter what happens, members of the other divisions will readily follow your admirable example. If, on the other hand, you are insincere and shrewdly maneuver circumstances to your own benefit, behave halfheartedly or abandon your faith, it will cause others to lose sight of their goals and perhaps even to doubt their faith. Indeed, the role of the men's division is significant."

Shin'ichi wanted to impress upon them the importance of carrying out faith throughout their lives. It is not uncommon to see men's passion wane as they get older, even though they may have been vigorously active in their youth and vowed to devote themselves to kosen-rufu. There are many reasons for this. One is that they become busier in their jobs as a result of increased responsibility; sometimes illness or declining health is the cause. There are other instances in which they allow their faith to lapse, feeling that because they have given so much energy to their Soka Gakkai activities in the past, they deserve a break.

Of course, there are times in one's life when work must take top priority. Also, when one falls ill, it is important to rest and recuperate. But Buddhist practice is something we pursue throughout our life. No matter what circumstances we may encounter, it is vital that we never regress in faith. Even the slightest inclination to do so means that our faith is slipping, even though we may not be aware of it.

Nichiren Daishonin writes: "Strengthen your faith day by day and month after month. Should you slacken in your resolve even a bit, devils will take advantage" (WND, 997). If we backslide in faith or fall victim to negligence or cowardice even a little, we create an opening by which the devilish functions can enter to try to destroy our faith and the foundation of our happiness.

IT WAS SHIN'ICHI'S hope that all the members of the men's division would dedicate themselves to pursuing the path of attaining Buddhahood in this lifetime, to achieving their human revolution and to realizing glory and victory across the three existences. To abandon faith is to betray oneself. Pointing to the pitiful end that had come to those members who had left the Soka Gakkai and slandered and attacked President Toda and the organization, he spoke to the men about the importance of carrying out faith throughout their lives.

His voice rang with the firm determination not to allow even a single member to fall by the wayside: "No one can escape the strict workings of the Buddhist law of cause and effect. That's why, no matter how you are denounced or criticized, it is vital that you remain steadfast in faith, always believing in the Gohonzon and sticking with the Soka Gakkai, certain of the great inconspicuous benefit you are accumulating.

"Quoting the Lotus Sutra, the Daishonin clearly states that those who uphold strong faith 'will enjoy peace and security in their present existence and good circumstances in future existences' (LS5, 99). There is no falsity in the words of Nichiren Daishonin."

Shin'ichi's voice grew more forceful: "You, the members of the men's division, are entering a period of securing the foundation for the final chapter of your lives. Each of you possess great ability. I hope you will apply all of your talents to the advancement of kosen-rufu.

"The Daishonin writes: 'Since death is the same in either case, you should be willing to offer your life for the Lotus Sutra. Think of this offering as a drop of dew rejoining the ocean, or a speck of dust returning to the earth' (WND, 1003). Because none of us can escape death, the Daishonin urges us to give our lives for the sake of the Lotus Sutra, the eternal Law of life. In other words, he tells us to use our lives working for kosen-rufu.

"That is the only way to become one with the Mystic Law, the great life of the universe, and to live an eternal life, just as a dew drop rejoins the ocean and a speck of dust returns to the earth. A lifetime passes quickly. And the period in that lifetime when we can be energetic and active is limited. Once people reach middle age, it all seems to go by in an instant.

"If you don't stand up now, when will you? If you

don't exert yourselves now, when will you? How many decades do you intend to wait before you take your stand? There is no telling what condition you will be in then. You are in the prime of your life. It is a precious time in this present finite existence. I say this because I want you to have no regrets!"

Shin'ichi's voice, reverberating like the roar of a lion, deeply struck the hearts of the men.

THE PARTICIPANTS listened earnestly, wanting to absorb every word.

He continued: "President Makiguchi took faith when he was fifty-seven years old. President Toda was forty-five when he stood up alone to carry out kosen-rufu following his release from prison. They were both around the same age as many of you when they aroused great faith and embarked on the challenge of advancing kosen-rufu. This is a Soka Gakkai tradition.

"I am also a member of the men's division. I hope that

you will join me and rise up valiantly with the Gakkai spirit and become golden pillars supporting the citadel of Soka."

The members' faces shone with the determination of champions of kosen-rufu.

In closing, Shin'ichi said: "I am counting on you. If the men's division develops remarkably and establishes a solid framework for kosen-rufu, our organization will remain secure forever."

Thunderous applause, infused with the members' proud and joyous vow to carry out kosen-rufu, reverberated endlessly throughout the room.

Next, Kazumasa Morikawa, one of the new general administrators, read the editorial that Shin'ichi had just completed for the April edition of *The Daibyakurenge* study journal, titled "Valiant Champions of the Mystic Law." In it, Shin'ichi set forth the attributes of such people.

The first was absolute conviction in the power of the Gohonzon; second, the ability to face and challenge difficulties; third, to be a leader well versed in all matters of society; fourth, passion to foster younger members; fifth, to be a broad-minded and humanistic leader; and sixth, a strong sense of duty and the ability to draw up a plan of action.

Approximately six years had passed since Shin'ichi had become president of the Soka Gakkai. Now, preparations for a new phase of kosen-rufu were complete.

Shin'ichi bowed to the participants and made way to leave the room. Then he stopped, raised his fist and called out: "Everyone! Let's strive together! Let's make a history of fresh achievements! If we are going to live this life, let us use it striving dynamically for the sake of the Law!"

The members raised their fists in response and shouted out in agreement. Tears shone in many an eye. Their hearts burned with fighting spirit. Filled with pride, these crown champions, great warriors of the Mystic Law, began their gallant march into the future.

Outside, the sky had grown dark, but the third floor of the Soka Gakkai Headquarters blazed with the light of joy.

Notes

1 Mother of Demon Children: A Buddhist demon revered in India as a goddess who could bestow the blessings of childbirth and easy delivery. The worship of her became popular in Japan in the twelfth century.

Index

absolute happiness, 20, 196, 221
adversity, 263
Africa, Shin'ichi Yamamoto on, 180–81
Africa Chapter, formation of, 185
African-Americans, discrimination of, 86. *See also* black Americans
Ajatashatru, karma caused illness of, 249
Akizuki, Eisuke, 4, 38–39, 46, 51, 56–57, 175, 189, 203, 215, 219, 222–24, 228; appointment of, 177, 307; basis for joining Soka Gakkai by, 310–11; Shin'ichi Yamamoto's encouragement to, 229–30
America, Yasushi Muto's assignment in, 97, 99; Shin'ichi Yamamoto on, 97
America Headquarters, development of, 96–97

American kosen-rufu, expansion of, 144
Anzai, Akito, 199; appointment of, 217
Anzai, Michiyo, 199; appointment of, 217; Shin'ichi Yamamoto's encouragement to, 204–05
Aota, Susumu, 43–44
Aoyama, Daigo, 194
appointments, leadership, 178–79
April 25 Bridge, 235
Arimura, Takeshi, 310
Army, U.S., 442nd unit of, 286
Asada, Katsuzo, 225; Shin'ichi Yamamoto on, 203
Asahi, 56, 233
authority, religious groups and, 34

Badini, Carlo Maria, 233
Bahama Star (passenger liner), 277
Baikal (ship), 205

Belem, Tower of, 235
Belgium, district formation in, 189
black Americans, voting rights of, in Mississippi, 85
Bodhisattvas of the Earth, 250
Brass Band, formation of, 100
Brazil Seikyo, 59
Brazil Soka Gakkai, development of, 114
Brown, Carl, 277
Buddha, 22
Buddhahood, 25; attaining, 12, 196
Buddhism, 91, 226; Nichiren Daishonin's, 91–92; power of, 83–84; true spirit of, 127; Shin'ichi Yamamoto on, 16, 291
Buddhist, mission of, 175
bureaucracy, cause of, in Soka Gakkai, 268–69; defeating, within Soka Gakkai, 282; example illustrating, within Soka Gakkai, 271–73

cancer, Buddhist perspective of, 250–51
Cape Bojador, 237–38
Cape of Good Hope, 238
Castrop-Rauxel (German coal mines), 191
challenge, 40–41
Civil Rights Act, of 1866, 84–85

Civil Rights Act, of 1964, 84
Clean Government Party, election results of, 62–63; opposition to, 33; role of, 70–71; threat to, 34
Clean Government Political Federation. *See* Clean Government Party
coal mines, work in, 209–10
Collected Lectures of the President, 8
Collected Works of Tsunesaburo Makiguchi, The, 34
common sense, exercising, 226
Comprehensive Dictionary of Buddhist Philosophy, A, 36
Constitution of the United States, fifteenth amendment of, 85
contribution, Shin'ichi Yamamoto on, 171–72
conviction, 12
courage, 268; Nichiren on, 238; and kosen-rufu activities, 312
culture festival, importance of holding, 109

The Daibyakurenge, 26, 119, 125, 194–95, 266, 270
dawn, 285
death, 11; accidental, 12; as obstacle, 191; Shin'ichi Yamamoto on, 19–20
determination, true, 211–12

Devadatta, 249
devilish forces, 22, 32, 301, 320; Nichiren Daishonin rebuking, 253
difficulties, overcoming, 149; Shin'ichi Yamamoto on, 254–55. *See also* hardships
disciples, path of, 297; true, 244
discrimination, causes of, 108; overcoming racial, 83; racial, 92
disease, Taikyu Kawase's attitude in handling degenerative, 265–66
district leaders, 23–24
Dominguez, Miguel (1756–1830), 131
dying, young, 11, 20

Eannes, Gil (Portuguese explorer), voyage of, 237–38
Ellick, Kazuko, 74
Ema, 315
Emancipation Proclamation, 84, 105
encouragement, 7–8, 268
enlightenment, attaining, 6–7. *See also* absolute happiness
eternal happiness. *See* enlightenment
ethnic conflict, 92
Etiwanda, culture festival in, 100, 103–07
Europe Culture Festival, first, 206, 208
Europe General Headquarters, formation of, 216; reorganization of, 177, 213
Europe General Meeting, 206, 208
Europe Headquarters, establishment of, 177–80
event staff, encouragement to, 153; Shin'ichi Yamamoto's photo session with, 153
evil ruler, 33–34
exchange delegation members, to Hawaii, 287–88; reflects on attitude for kosen-rufu, 302–03; Shin'ichi Yamamoto on, 297–98
experience, Shin'ichi Yamamoto on, 292
explorers, Portuguese, 238

faith, 12, 22, 110, 247, 251, 312; champions of, 218; Nichiren on, 320–21; Nittatsu on, 171; Shin'ichi Yamamoto on, 292
Fife and Drum Corps, formation of, 100–03
formality, Shin'ichi Yamamoto on, 299
fostering, people, 238–39, 278
Frankfurt, study exam in, 212
Friends of Hope, poem "*Dawn*" in, 283–84
Fuji, Mount. *See* Mount Fuji

Fujikawa, Tad, 91
Fujiya, Hideo, 314
Fujiya, Yumie, 289; appointment of, 307; basis for joining Soka Gakkai by, 309–11; basis of appointment of, 309–15
future, human beings and, 185

German guidance meeting, 222; Shin'ichi Yamamoto's message at, 220–21; Shin'ichi Yamamoto's poem at, 221
German members, Shin'ichi Yamamoto on, 215–16
Germany, kosen-rufu in, 217
Germany Chapter, 216; reorganization of, 213–14
Ghiringhelli, Antonio, 230–33
Gifu Community Center, 24
good fortune, accumulating, 6
Gohonzon, appreciation toward, 249–50; Nichiren on, 249; Shin'ichi Yamamoto on, 149, 292
Grand Main Temple, 74, 215; buildings referenced for, 123, 235; completion ceremony for, 173; construction committee for, 159; construction plans for, 158, 161; contribution campaign for, 157–59, 163–69; Nikken's declaration on, 173–74; Nittatsu on, 159–61, 173; Nittatsu's remarks on, contribution campaign, 169–71; overseas contribution campaign for, 169; "On the Significance of Offerings for the Construction of the Grand Main Temple," 162–63; Toda on, 158
Grant, Shizuko, 187
Grassi, Paolo, 233

happiness, realizing, 92
Harada, Tony, 293
Harada, Yoshie, appointment of, 293; finding marriage partner, 293–94
Harayama, Koichi, 8, 304
hardships, 263; Shin'ichi Yamamoto on, 254–55
Haruki, Fumiki, 116, 175
Haruki, Seiichiro, 148
Haruyama, Emiko, 115
Hawaii, purpose of visiting, 285
Hawaii Community Center, 287; Yumie Fujiya's remarks at opening ceremony of, 290–91; opening ceremony of, 289; "Song of Worldwide Kosen-rufu," 293; Shin'ichi Yamamoto's encouragement at opening ceremony of, 291–93

Hawaii General Chapter, new chapters within, 293
Hawaii organization, mission of, 300
Hawaii young women's division, Shin'ichi Yamamoto's poem to, 290
Hawaii youth members, 297; Shin'ichi Yamamoto's encouragement to, 299–301
Hawaiian members, Shin'ichi Yamamoto's photo session with, 294–95
Hawaiian organization, growth of, 288–89
Hayashida, Chikako, 98
Headquarters General Meeting, of 1958, 311
Henry the Navigator, Prince (1394–1460), 235–37; death of, 238
Hidalgo y Costilla, Miguel (1753–1811), 131–32
Hirata, Hiroto, appointment of, 293
Honolulu, visit to, 143–44
House of Councilors (Upper House), elections, 62
human revolution, 1
Human Revolution, The, 2–3, 26
humanism, 268

Ikeda, Mineko (wife of Shin'ichi Yamamoto), 175

illness, avoiding, 247; causes of, 245–47; Nichiren on, 250; dealing with chronic, 251–53; health and, 252; overcoming karma caused by, 248–50
India, 238
Inohashi, Miyuki, 101, 103
inspiration, source of, 263
Ishikawa, Kenshiro, 307
Ishizaki, Isamu, 11, 19
Ishizaki, Toshiko, Shin'ichi Yamamoto's encouragement to, 19, 22–23
Iwadate, Raul, 117, 124, 135; actual proof of, 120–21; basis of appointment of, 120–21; on Nichiren Buddhism, 120; determination of, 133; life of, 118–19; Shin'ichi Yamamoto's encouragement to, 132–33; Shin'ichi Yamamoto's support to, 129–30
Iwadate Chisako, 122, 135; appointment of, 124; Shin'ichi Yamamoto's encouragement to, 130–32
Iwadates, 128, 134; Shin'ichi Yamamoto on, 129
Izumida, Hiroshi, 13, 17, 82, 106, 288, 301, 306; basis of appointment of, 304–05

James, Fujie, 180–85; appointment of, 185; Eiji Kawasaki on, 182;

Shin'ichi Yamamoto's
encouragement to, 185
Japan, 1965 recession of,
164–65
Japan National Railways,
49–50
Japanese members who are
miners, Shin'ichi Yamamoto's care for, 218
Jeunesses Musicales de
France, 189
Jiyu Genronsha Publishing
Company, 3
job, Shin'ichi Yamamoto
recognizing inconspicuous and modest, by Headquarters staff member,
279–80
Johnson, Lyndon B. (U.S.
President), 84; on
Voting Rights Act, 85–86
Jujo, Kiyoshi, 79, 81, 98, 106,
114, 122, 124, 126–28, 145,
289, 293, 301–02, 304–06;
appointment of, 242

Kajiyama, Hisao, appointment of, 74
Kato, Yoshiko, appointment
of, 74
Kawada, Yukiko, appointment of, 217; faith experience of, 199–201;
Koichiro Sada's moment
with, 210–11; Shin'ichi
Yamamoto's encouragement to, 204–05

Kawasaki, Eiji, 75, 176, 180,
184–85, 212; appointment
of, 178
Kawase, Sumi, 265–67
Kawase, Taikyu, 264; on
Buddhist study, 266–67;
poem by, 268; on Soka
Gakkai activities, 266;
Shin'ichi Yamamoto on,
267
Kennedy, John F. (U.S. President), 84
King, Martin Luther, Jr., 88;
"I Have a Dream" speech,
105
King Joao I, 236
King John I. *See* King
Joao I
Kiyohara, Katsu, 82, 106, 114,
122
Komei Shimbun, 39
Komori, Hiroaki, 45
Konishi, Takeo, 305
kosen-rufu, 21, 36; achieving, 154, 238; advancing,
12, 24, 112, 130, 292–93;
aim of, 7; commitment
to, 97–98; firm determination for, 127; halfhearted attitude for, 301;
lives dedicated to, 227;
path to, 226; Shin'ichi
Yamamoto on, 16–17,
134; Shin'ichi Yamamoto
advances, under Josei
Toda, 281
"Kuroda Bushi," 106

Kuroki, Akira, 79–82, 137; assignment of, 99
Kyushu Headquarters, visit to, 10

La Scala Opera Company, 228–29; Eisuko Akizuki's meeting with, 229–32; goal of, 234
La Scala Tour Committee, 233
L'avenir, publication of, 59
leader(s), commitment of, 268; developing core, 142; example illustrating responsibility as, 301–02; responsibility of, 143, 294; spirit of, 41; Shin'ichi Yamamoto's action as, 107–08
lessening one's karmic retribution, principle of, 248–49
Li Ming Sheng Bao, birth of, 60; publishing difficulties of, 61
life, purpose of, 196
life force, 110, 127, 140, 249–50; wellspring of, 247
life span, extending one's, 245
"Life Span" chapter (Lotus Sutra), teaches, 245
Lincoln, Abraham (U.S. President), 84
Lisbon (Portugal), visit to, 234–40

lives, Nichiren Daishonin on using our, 320
Los Angeles, first Nichiren Shoshu temple in, 89–90; Nichiren Shoshu temple in, 80; proposed visit to, 82–84; visit to, 88–89
Los Angeles Community Center, encouragement at, 109–10; visit to, 108–09

Mahanama, 12
Mainichi, 56
Makiguchi, Tsunesaburo, 179, 241, 322; *Jinsei Chirigaku* (The Geography of Human Life), 116
Masaki, Nagayasu, 87, 99, 107, 110, 114, 122, 128, 289
Maximilian, Emperor of Mexico, (1832–1867), 122
members, Shin'ichi Yamamoto's send off to, to West Germany, 202–04
men's division, 315–17; formation of, 306, 317; Japanese name for, 316; Hiroshi Izumida's address at opening ceremony of, 317; Kozumasa Morikawa's address at opening ceremony of, 323; Shin'ichi Yamamoto outlines responsibilities of, 318–24
men's group leaders,

Shin'ichi Yamamoto's photo sessions with, 144–50, 153
mentor, role of, 297
Mexico, independence movement of, 131–32; Toda's interest in, 115–17; visit to, 114–15, 117–18, 121–23
Mexico Chapter, development of, 135–36; Kiyoshi Jujo on, 128; three districts of, 126; Shin'ichi Yamamoto's encouragement to, 127–28, 135
Mexico Soka Gakkai, establishment of, 120–21
Mexico youth division, Shin'ichi Yamamoto on, 134
Michael, Robert, 105; actual proof of, 95; discrimination faced by, 93–94; encountered Buddhism, 94–95; in Soka Gakkai activities, 95; vow of, 92–93, 96
Milan (Italy), visit to, 228
Miné, Tadayoshi, 285, 289
Min-On Concert Association, 189, 228, 233; purpose of, 229; sponsored tour of La Scala by, 232–34; Shin'ichi Yamamoto on, 176
mission, 129
Monument to the Discoveries, 235, 239
Morikawa, Kozumasa, appointment of, 305
Morinaga, Yasushi, 90, 114, 134
Moriyama, Daizo, 14
Moro'oka, Michiya, 189–91, 198–99, 205–06, 210; appointment of, 213, 217
Mother of Demon Children, 309
mothers, Shin'ichi Yamamoto on, 152
Mount Fuji, 77; Shin'ichi Yamamoto on, 283
music and art, Shin'ichi Yamamoto on, 231
Muto, Yasushi, Shin'ichi Yamamoto's encouragement to, 97–98
Mystic Law, 179; becoming one with the, 321; effects of disbelieving in the, 281–82

Nagano Headquarters district leaders meeting, 26
Nagashima, Shigeo, Shin'ichi Yamamoto on, 214
Nagoya, 24
Nakada, Tsunemitsu, 122, 125, 128, 133, 135; appointment of, 126; determination of, 134–35; struggles of, 126; Shin'ichi Yamamoto's encouragement to, 134–35
Nakhodka (Soviet port), 205

Nam-myoho-renge-kyo, Nichiren on, 91, 251
Nanjo Tokimitsu, 165, 253; Nichiren on, 12
Napoleon I, Emperor of France (1769–1821), 33–34
Nice (France), visit to, 234
Nichikan, 170
Nichiren Daishonin, 11; "Letter from Sado," 33, 196; writings of, 226–27, 268, 311; on T'ien-t'ai's *Great Concentration and Insight,* 246
Nichiren Shoshu temples, 89
Nicoly, René, 189
Nihon Shogakkan, 5
Nikken Abe, Shin'ichi Yamamoto on, 175
Nishimiya, Bunji, 175, 215, 228
Nittatsu, 80, 82, 89, 91, 114, 122, 124, 162, 168, 172
nuclear weapons, 92
Nuova Era. See Brazil Seikyo

Ogachi, Hisazo, actual proof of, 192; joins Soka Gakkai, 191; Koichiro Sada on, 193; resolve of, 193; and Soka Gakkai activities, 192
Okada, Ittetsu, 80, 87, 175, 215, 228
Okubo Hikozaemon, 14
Olympics (Mexico), 136
Opinions, 3–4
Oritiz de Dominquez, Maria Josefa, 130–31
Oritiz de Dominquez, Dona Josefa (1768–1829), 130–31
Osaka, visit to, 10
Osaka Campaign (1956), 111, 148
Osanai, Kosaku, actual proof of, 195; appointment of, 217
Osawa, Toshiyuki, 225; appointment of, 217; Shin'ichi Yamamoto on, 203
Ota Jomyo, 316
overseas members, Shin'ichi Yamamoto's encouragement to, 74, 77
Ozaki, Aiko, illness of, 137–38
Ozaki, Tad, appointment of, 142; joins Soka Gakkai, 141–42; life of, 137–38; observes Soka Gakkai, 140–41; on Soka Gakkai, 139; Shin'ichi Yamamoto on, 143

Pacific War, Shin'ichi Yamamoto on, 92
Paris, visit to, 176
Paris Chapter, 178
Paris University, guidance session at, 189; study exam at, 189

Parks, Rosa, 84
peace, building, 31; foundation for, 175–76
Pelleg, Frank, 231–32
people, Toda on, 269
Peru Seikyo, publication of, 60
Phantom City Parable, 198
photo sessions, commemorative, 154–55
Pineapple Corps members, 285–87; resolve of, 296
Pineapple Corps support staff, encounter with *Seikyo Shimbun* journalists, 296–97
pioneers, actions of, 134
poison into medicine, transforming, 258
politics, Toda on, 71–72
Portugal, Toda's desire in, 236
praise, 268
priesthood, during World War II, 178–79
propagation, 31; in America, 142–43; in Nichiren Buddhism, 188; of religions, 188; Shin'ichi Yamamoto on, 292
publications, problems of, 61–62
Puccini, Giacomo, *Madame Butterfly*, 228

Queluz Palace, 235

rain, symbol of, 28
reason, exercising, 226
"Record of the Orally Transmitted Teachings," 91
Rich, Eiko, 181, 183–84; actual proof of, 186; appointment of, 189; Shin'ichi Yamamoto on, 185–86
Ryokan, 32

Sada, Koichiro, 189, 192, 199, 210; action taken by, 207; actual proof of, 208; appointment of, 178, 213, 217; dilemma faced by, 206–07; Michiya Moro'oka on, 206; resolve of, 199; Shin'ichi Yamamoto on, 190, 213–14
Saiki, Setsuko, 110; actual proof of, 111; illness of, 111
Saiki, Yasuhiro, appointment of, 110–11; determination of, 113; encouragement to, 114; joins Soka Gakkai, 112; Shin'ichi Yamamoto on, 112–13
Saikis, appointment of, 114
Salazar Bridge. *See* April 25 Bridge
San Francisco, visit to, 137
school, Makiguchi's desire for establishing a, 243–44
Science and Religion, 34, 143

Sea of Darkness (area around Cape Bojador), 237–38
Seattle, visit to, 143–44
seeking spirit, 76
Seikyo News (film series), 165
Seikyo Shimbun, 2, 119–21, 161, 192, 217, 266, 269–70, 308; cameramen, 27; circulation of, 56; as daily publication, 52–53; deliverers, 55–56; delivery system of, 52–54; development of, 37–40, 44–51; encouragement to staff of, 40–44; first daily edition of, 50–51; news articles in, 58; "Plans for the Epochal Grand Main Temple," 167; role of, 56–57; "Soka University Establishment Steering Committee Formed," 241; Toda's encouragement to staff of, 47–48; *The Uncrowned*, 55
Seikyo Zeitung, birth of, 219; publication of, 60
Seki, Hisao, 13, 17; appointment of, 305
self, strong, 110
self-confidence, 214
Shakyamuni Buddha, 249
Shijo Kingo, devotion to kosen-rufu by, 315–16
sickness, Buddhist faith and, 140
Soda family, experiences of, 256–63

Soda, Chika, 256
Soda, Kiku, 256–58; appointment of, 259
Soda, Mutsumi, 255; appointment of, 259
Soda, Sachiyo, 256; appointment of, 259
Soda, Toshie, 255, 257; appointment of, 259
Soka Gakkai, 31, 267; cause for destruction of, 274–75; development of, 304; leadership reshuffle in, 304–07; purpose of, 269; schemes against, 32–33; spirit of, 72–73; Shin'ichi Yamamoto on, 29–30; Shin'ichi Yamamoto protects, under Toda, 281; theme of 1959 of, 284; theme of 1966 of, 284; tradition of, 322
Soka Gakkai activities, importance of, 110
Soka Gakkai Europe Office, opening of, 176
Soka Gakkai Headquarters, cost cutting by, 165
Soka Gakkai Headquarters Leaders Meeting, 168–73
Soka Gakkai Headquarters Staff, Shin'ichi Yamamoto on, 269; Shin'ichi Yamamoto's guidelines for, 270–71; Shin'ichi Yamamoto's strict training of, 270, 273–74, 277, 282–83

Soka Gakkai Study Department, evaluation exams by, 263–64

Soka High School, basis for establishing, 239

Soka University, basis for establishing, 239; steps taken towards the creation of, 241–42; steering committee, creation of subcommittees of, 242; Toda's desire for establishing, 243–44

South America Headquarters, development of, 114

Soya Kyoshin, 316

success, 127

Sudatta, 165

summer training course, French members trip to, 75–76; Shin'ichi Yamamoto's encouragement at, 73–74

Sunayama, Teruo, 199, 206, 225; appointment of, 217

Suzuki, Daisetsu, 117

Taisei Gakuin, 5

Tamaru, Shinji, 194

Tanida, Shoichi, 314; appointment of, 307

Tatematsu, Akihiro, 314; basis of appointment of, 307–09

Tateyama, Kurazo, 47, 49–50

Tejo River, 235, 238

Teotihuacán (Mexico), 124

Timur Empire, 236

Toda, Josei, 52, 169, 235, 241, 322; companies of, 280; death of, 35; financial situation of, 243; members betrayed, 280; lectures "On Establishing the Correct Teaching for the Peace of the Land," 35; lectures on "The Object of Devotion for Observing the Mind," 35; lectures on "The Opening of the Eyes," 35; lectures on "The Selection of the Time," 35; "The Philosophy of Life," 308; poem by, 32, 40; presidency of, 35; Shin'ichi Yamamoto on, 86; Shin'ichi Yamamoto's internal conversation with, 123, 242

Tohoku No. 1 Headquarters District Leaders Meeting, 25

Toki Jonin, 316

Tokyo Metropolitan Assembly, Clean Government Party on, 63–69; election results of, 70–71; scandal in, 63–69

Tokyo Metropolitan University, 8

Toscanini, Arturo, 228

Tottori Chapter, establishment of, 17

Tottori Prefecture, visit to, 13–16
Towada, Koichi, 50
true happiness, 20. *See also* absolute happiness
Tsunesaburo, Makiguchi, 20
Twenty-eighth Headquarters General Meeting, members' reaction at, 30; progress report at, 28–31
twenty-first century, Shin'ichi Yamamoto's vision for, 239

unhappiness, causes of, 252, 263
United Kingdom, Eiko Rich's kosen-rufu work in, 187
unity, 99–100; true, 135
university, Toda's desire for establishing a, 242

value, creating, 129
Verdi, Giuseppe, *Otello and Falstaff*, 228
victory, 127, 216; achieving, 234
violence, 88

Watari, Goro, 314; appointment of, 307
Watari, Michiyo, 307
Watts Riots, 80–81, 87, 108
Weber, Max, 71
West Germany, plans by members for kosen-rufu in, 195, 197–98; members trip to, 205–06; Eiji Onoda's kosen-rufu plans for, 196–97; Koichiro Sada's kosen-rufu plans for, 190–92, 194; Shin'ichi Yamamoto's proposed visit to, 212; visit to, 189–90
wisdom, 127
Wise, Terry, 276
women, overseas propagation and, 187–88
women's division, importance of, 124
women's group leaders, Shin'ichi Yamamoto's session with, 151–53
words, power of, 36
work, 112
world peace, 291; actualizing, 92
World Tribune, birth of, 59; publishing difficulties of, 60–61

Yamagiwa, Hiroshi, 8–10, 120
Yamamoto, Shin'ichi, 80; and *Boys' Adventure*, 5; and *The Daibyakurenge*, 36, 124; and "Desert Moonlight," 15; and *The Daibyakurenge* article titled "Valiant Champions of the Mystic Law," 323; "Excerpts from the Diary

of My Youth," 3–6; health problems of, 150, 152, 253; and *The Human Revolution*, 36, 52, 124; lectures "On Repaying Debts of Gratitude," 35–36; lectures "The Selection of the Time," 36; Nittatsu on, 170; Kosaka Osanai on, 226; photo sessions with, 27–28; and *Politics and Religion*, 36; and *Science and Religion*, 34; Toda on, 116; and "Youth, Become World Leaders!" 125, 194
Yamanishi, Kiyoko, 114–15
Yarmouth Castle (passenger liner), crews mind-set on, 278; disaster of, 275–77
Yashiro, Takafumi, 49
Yomiuri, 56
Yonago, situation in, 13; visit to, 10–11
Yonago Chapter, establishment of, 17
Yonago Community Center, visit to, 17–18
Yonago members, encouragement to, 21–22
young men's division (Brazil), growth of, 113
young men's division (Germany), song of, 222–24
youth, 269

More on Nichiren Buddhism and Its Application to Daily Life

The following five titles can be purchased from your local or on-line bookseller, or go to the Middleway Press Web site (www.middlewaypress.org).

The Buddha in Your Mirror: Practical Buddhism and the Search for Self, by Woody Hochswender, Greg Martin and Ted Morino
A bestselling Buddhist primer that reveals the most modern, effective and practical way to achieve what is called enlightenment or Buddhahood. Based on the centuries-old teaching of the Japanese Buddhist master Nichiren, this method has been called the "direct path" to enlightenment.

"Like the Buddha, this book offers practical guidelines to overcome difficulties in everyday life and to be helpful to others. Readers will find these pages are like a helpful and supportive friend. I enthusiastically recommend it."
—Dr. David Chappell, editor of *Buddhist Peacework: Creating Cultures of Peace*
(Paperback: ISBN 0-9674697-8-3; $14.00;
Hardcover: ISBN 0-9674697-1-6; $23.95)

Choose Hope: Your Role in Waging Peace in the Nuclear Age, by David Krieger and Daisaku Ikeda
"In this nuclear age, when the future of humankind is imperiled by irrational strategies, it is imperative to restore sanity to our policies and hope to our destiny. Only a rational analysis of our problems can lead to their solution. This book is an example par excellence of a rational approach."
—Joseph Rotblat, Nobel Peace Prize laureate
(ISBN 0-9674697-6-7; $23.95)

Planetary Citizenship: *Your* Values, Beliefs and Actions *Can* Shape a Sustainable World by Hazel Henderson and Daisaku Ikeda
"*Planetary Citizenship* is a delightful introduction to some of the most important ideas and facts concerning stewardship of the planet. I cannot think of any book that deals with more important issues."
—Mihaly Csikszentmihalyi, author of *Flow: The Psychology of Optimal Experience,* California
(ISBN 0-9723267-2-3; $23.95)

Unlocking the Mysteries of Birth & Death . . . and Everything in Between, A Buddhist View of Life (second edition) by Daisaku Ikeda
"In this slender volume, Ikeda presents a wealth of profound information in a clear and straightforward style that can be easily absorbed by the interested lay reader. His life's work, and the underlying purpose of his book,

is simply to help human beings derive maximum meaning from their lives through the study of Buddhism."
—ForeWord Magazine
(ISBN 0-9723267-0-7; $15.00)

The Way of Youth: Buddhist Common Sense for Handling Life's Questions, by Daisaku Ikeda
"[This book] shows the reader how to flourish as a young person in the world today; how to build confidence and character in modern society; learn to live with respect for oneself and others; how to contribute to a positive, free and peaceful society; and find true personal happiness."
—Midwest Book Review
(ISBN 0-9674697-0-8; $14.95)

The following titles can be purchased at SGI-USA bookstores nationwide or through the mail order center: call 800-626-1313 or e-mail mailorder@sgi-usa.org.

The Human Revolution, boxed set by Daisaku Ikeda
"A great human revolution in just a single individual will help achieve a change in the destiny of a nation, and further, can even enable a change in the destiny of all humankind." With this as his main theme, the author wrote his twelve-volume account of Josei Toda's life and the phenomenal growth of the Soka Gakkai in postwar Japan. Published in a slightly abridged two-book set, this work paints a fascinating and empowering story of the

far-reaching effects of one person's inner determination. Josei Toda's awakening and transformation, his efforts to teach others the unlimited power of faith, his dedication in leading thousands out of misery and poverty, the efforts of his devoted disciple Shin'ichi Yamamoto—within these stories we find the keys for building lives of genuine happiness.
(World Tribune Press, mail order #4182; $45.00)

The Journey Begins:
First Steps in Buddhist Practice

A new pamphlet on the basics of Nichiren Daishonin's Buddhism. Each step is discussed in very basic terms, but each plays an important role in your practice. For the new member, the points will help you build a foundation in your practice. Return to them again and again throughout your practice to help keep yourself on track and get the maximum benefit from your Buddhist practice.
(World Tribune Press, mail order #4138; $1.00)

My Dear Friends in America,
by Daisaku Ikeda

This volume brings together for the first time all of the SGI president's speeches to U.S. members in the 1990s.
(World Tribune Press, mail order #4104; $19.95)

The Wisdom of the Lotus Sutra, vols. 1–6,
by Daisaku Ikeda, Katsuji Saito, Takanori Endo
and Haruo Suda

A captivating dialogue on the 28-chapter Lotus Sutra that brings this ancient writing's important messages into practical application for daily life and for realizing a peaceful world.

Volume 1 (World Tribune Press, mail order #4281; $10.95)
Volume 2 (World Tribune Press, mail order #4282; $10.95)
Volume 3 (World Tribune Press, mail order #4283; $10.95)
Volume 4 (World Tribune Press, mail order #4284; $10.95)
Volume 5 (World Tribune Press, mail order #4285; $10.95)
Volume 6 (World Tribune Press, mail order #4286; $10.95)

The Winning Life:
An Introduction to Buddhist Practice

Using plain language, this booklet gives a quick-yet-detailed introduction to a winning way of life based on Nichiren Daishonin's teachings. A perfect tool for introducing other to the benefits of practice.
(World Tribune Press, mail order #4105 [English], 4106 [Spanish], 4107 [Chinese], 4113 [Korean]; $1.00)

Faith into Action: Thoughts on Selected Topics,
by Daisaku Ikeda

A collection of inspirational excerpts arranged by subject. Perfect for finding just the right quote to encourage yourself or a friend or when preparing for a meeting.
(World Tribune Press, mail order #4135; $12.95)

For Today and Tomorrow: Daily Encouragement, by Daisaku Ikeda
Daily words of encouragement that are sure to inspire, comfort and even challenge you in your practice of faith. Great for the newest member and seasoned practitioners.
(World Tribune Press, mail order #4100; $16.95)

A Youthful Diary: One Man's Journey From the Beginning of Faith to Worldwide Leadership for Peace, by Daisaku Ikeda
Youthful inspiration for people of all ages. Through the tale of the ever-deepening relationship between the young Daisaku Ikeda and his mentor-in-life, Josei Toda, *A Youthful Diary* is a compelling account of both triumphs and setbacks on the road to establishing the foundation of today's Soka Gakkai.
(World Tribune Press, mail order #4101; $23.95)